Bridge Master

The Best of

Edgar Kaplan

A TRIBUTE TO ONE OF THE GAME'S
LEADING PERSONALITIES AND INVENTORS

Bridge Master

The Best of

Edgar Kaplan

A tribute to one of the game's leading
personalities and inventors

from The Bridge World

BRIDGE WORLD BOOKS • NEW YORK

Printed on recycled paper.

www.bridgeworld.com

Design by Michael K. Mills

ISBN 0-9753419-0-1

First edition, June 2004

10 9 8 7 6 5 4 3 2 1

Table of Contents

Introduction   7

Edgar Kaplan 1925 — 1997   9

Edgar Kaplan Remembered   11

The Bridge World . . .
    R * A * T * S   29
    Authors Anonymous   37
    Clubs   42

. . . and *The Bridge World*
    Continuous Performance   47
    Sophisticated Sequence   50

International Events
    World Championship Quiz   61
    Analysis of The 1958 World Championship 68

System Building
    The Weak Notrump   125
    Responding to the Weak Notrump   131
    Further Thoughts on the Weak Notrump 137

Double Raises in the Minors 144

The Kaplan-Sheinwold Philosophy 148

Short-Suit Tries for Game 153

A New Approach to Slam Bidding 161

National Championships

Life Masters Individual 173

Trials Quiz 180

Trials Diary 185

How the Game is Played

New Science 219

Ethics, Huddles and Protests 226

Opinion: An Interview with Edgar Kaplan 232

At the Table 239

Introduction

This book is a tribute to the late Edgar Kaplan, one of the most remarkable and influential personalities in the history of contract bridge, and a remembrance for his many fans. We hope to provide an opportunity for players to meet him—through his writings, as a student of his teachings, and by developing a better understanding of how he enhanced playing and enjoying the game for everyone.

The material presented here was organized by the editors of *The Bridge World*, the magazine that Edgar led, as publisher and editor, for over 30 years. It consists mostly of what he wrote or said, placed in context by an obituary and an appreciation written by Jeff Rubens, his long-time co-editor. The articles are presented as close to their original form as possible; some terminology has been updated, and modern notation (such as 3=3=4=3 for three spades, three hearts, four diamonds and three clubs) has been used. Informal nuggets, based on casual conversation, interviews, letters, and remarks made as a Vu-Graph commentator, appear throughout under the heading Wit and Wisdom.

A part of Edgar's legacy that we cannot capture adequately in a book is the effect he had on others. Some additional material and links can be found at *The Bridge World*'s Web site at www.bridgeworld.com.

Edgar wrote so much that is worthy of reproduction that it was a difficult, though pleasant, job to decide which pieces to give priority. Indeed (as he was wont to say), the studies and outpourings cover such a wide spectrum that even organization into helpful categories was a challenge. After much consideration, this list evolved: The Bridge World and *The Bridge World* (how Edgar interacted with his personal environment), International Events (reports of world championships), System Building (contributions to the theory of bidding and the construction of one of the most popular systems), National Championships (the events that formed the framework of Edgar's adult life), How the Game is Played (matters of behavior and the Laws), At the Table (deals in which Edgar was involved—usually, but not always, as a player), and, sprinkled throughout, Wit and Wisdom.

Enjoy.

The Bridge World

Edgar Kaplan

1925 — 1997

Edgar Kaplan, one of the major figures in the history of bridge, and editor and publisher of *The Bridge World* for more than 30 years, died of cancer on September 7, 1997. For several years, he had battled against the disease with remarkable optimism, resolution, intelligence and courage. Edgar never surrendered to this fearsome enemy and maintained his usual schedule of tournament attendance and participation until the end. He won a national championship (his twenty-eighth) earlier in the year, and competed in the Spingold and other events at the Summer Nationals a few weeks before his death.

Edgar was born in Manhattan and, with the exception of attendance at college and military service during World War II, lived there throughout his life. From 1962 on, he and his beloved wife, Betty, who died in 1985, resided in the brownstone house on West 94th Street that also housed *The Bridge World*. He is survived by his sister-in-law, Sylvia Kaplan; a niece, Beth; and a nephew, Michael.

*

Edgar Kaplan participated in organized bridge in virtually every possible way, filled a wide variety of roles, made major contributions in important areas, and inspired several generations of participants through his standards of behavior and achievement. He was one of the most successful American players, representing the United States eight times in world championships (twice finishing second in world team events), winning 16 major national team championships, and garnering innumerable lesser titles including, in the one year that he set out to win it, the then-called McKenney Trophy for the most masterpoints in one year. His partnership with Norman Kay was one of the strongest and longest-lasting expert pairings ever. For more than 30 years, Edgar regularly held official and unofficial positions as captain, assistant captain, coach or advisor to American international teams. Most recently, he was captain of the 1995 Bermuda Bowl champion team.

A highly effective teacher and lecturer, Edgar was a co-founder of The Card School in New York. The combination of his teaching style and outstanding writing skills led to a series of successful books: "Winning Contract Bridge Complete," and "Competitive Bidding in Modern Bridge" have been in print for more than 30 years. Also still available, "Kaplan-Sheinwold Updated" is the most recent book on the system that gained many adherents and left its mark on standard bidding techniques, a method originally developed with the late Alfred Sheinwold; it represents the agreements he used with Norman Kay. His other books were "How to Play Winning Bridge" (the original K-S book), "The Complete Italian System of Winning Bridge," and "Duplicate Bridge: How to Play, How to Win."

Edgar Kaplan was the prime mover behind most of the major changes in the Laws during the past few decades; he served on and chaired both national and international Laws commissions, and was widely regarded as the leading authority on bridge law. Often an American delegate to the World Bridge Federation, he was influential on several committees of the world body (frequently Appeals chairman) and for a long time its witty chief commentator. He served as a director of the American Contract Bridge League and, for many years, of the Greater New York Bridge Association.

Most *Bridge World* readers will remember Edgar Kaplan best as an authoritative and entertaining author and a clever editor. By example, he established a high tone, not only in his writing but in all his activities. At the table, Edgar was a quintessential civil player who demonstrated how to compete fiercely at the highest levels while showing respect for partner, the opponents, and the game of bridge.

Edgar Kaplan Remembered

D id you ever read a book that stimulated you to think long and often about something else? I was once intrigued by a volume titled *The 100 Most Influential People in History*. The author established criteria for determining what "influential" meant, then used them to evaluate historical personalities whose mini-biographies he presented. As both the criteria and the evaluations were subjective, the reader could have great fun disagreeing with the author. It interested me little who made the world's top ten, but I was impressed by the demonstrations that showed the great impact a fundamental achievement could have when magnified through the years.

Motivated by that book, I have often wondered whose contributions to bridge have had the most influence in the sense of impact on the way we play the game today. Again, my interest is not so much in rankings as in understanding the influence of history on our current situation. According to knowledgeable bridge people I have presented with this question, the top influencers are (in historical order) Vanderbilt, Culbertson and Goren. Interestingly, all three were, at least to some extent, both popularizers and system builders. Vanderbilt brought together diverse elements and first described the game we now call contract bridge; he decided some of the key features of the new game, but other aspects were produced by his collaborators. Culbertson increased the popularity of bridge so dramatically and permanently that a scorekeeper might make him number one on that basis alone. When you add his development of what remain standard methods; the classification of techniques; the influence on the game's literature; and the creation of *The Bridge World,* which evolved from a Culbertson soapbox to an effective forum for the exchange of ideas, you can see why most people put him at the head of the list. Still, Goren, although he added nothing that seems fundamental, rejuvenated the game to such an extent that, but for his activities, few might play today.

As a popularizer, Edgar Kaplan was not in the same league as those just mentioned. Nonetheless, he belongs on any short list of the most influential people in bridge history. In reviewing his career, I was astonished as I tallied the many different ways his actions and inventions strongly affect how bridge is played today. And even though he was born too late to have had the developmental opportunities of someone like Culbertson, in some areas his contributions are more important than those of the major developers who preceded him. The strength and variety of these influences on bridge form the focus of this highly selective biographical sketch.

Edgar was born in 1925, just about the same time as contract bridge. His parents played cards, and for his father bridge was a lifelong activity. Both Edgar and his brother, Gordin, were intellectually gifted, and both were exposed to games at home. But where Edgar became fascinated by bridge, Gordin considered card playing too frivolous an activity to be worthy of serious attention. Edgar graduated from elite primary and secondary schools, but, perhaps because he was more interested in card playing than in studying, attended college only briefly. Curiously, although I know few people with such weak academic credentials, Edgar remains the best-educated person I have ever met.

After surviving World War II (he was in combat, but he told me that it was basic training, conducted under extreme weather conditions, not the enemy, that threatened his life), he set out to conquer the bridge world. He played rubber and tournament bridge incessantly; co-founded The Card School, on Park Avenue, which successfully offered high-tone instruction for many years; formulated his personal approach to the game that would eventually become the Kaplan-Sheinwold system; and rubbed shoulders with stronger and stronger opponents and partners.

New Science and "New Science"

By 1956, Edgar was established as one of the leading players in the country. A consistently strong tournament performer, high on the masterpoint lists, he had won the Vanderbilt in 1953 and the National Men's Teams in 1955. He had already made a few contributions to *The Bridge World* on bidding methods (featuring weak notrumps and minor-suit raises) and interesting deals when, in the December 1956 issue, his article, "New Science," appeared. My disdain for detailed ranking systems notwithstanding, I assert with total assurance that this is the single most influential article in the history of bridge.

A little background about *The Bridge World* of the fifties may be helpful. The editor, Sonny Moyse, regularly got everyone's juices flowing by stimulating discussion about bidding theories. One year the topic might be four-three fits, another year it might be which suit to open with a particular distribution, and so forth. Moyse never pulled any punches, others replied in kind, and a grand (and usually educational) time was had by all. In the middle fifties, Sonny expended a lot of energy attacking "new scientists," bidders he felt were trying to achieve an impossible exactitude and who, he claimed, would lose substantially on balance by confusing themselves or by giving away information helpful to the opponents. These broadsides, while general, were most often directed at practitioners of early versions of what we now call the Roth-Stone system—methods that had burst onto the scene amid much controversy—and the Kaplan-Sheinwold system. Sonny's attacks had escaped strong reply until "New Science" appeared. [*See page 219.*]

Can you see why this is the most influential bridge article ever? No, it is not just because it expounded on the need for and the benefits of a scientific approach to bidding. Yes, it is one of the best and earliest such expositions, but there are other competent presentations of the subject; anyway, scientific bidding was a development that was bound to arrive in due course. A far more significant impact of "New Science" was to redirect admiration for bridge achievement, away from a generation of experts who depended on table action and inflection, towards players whose ideal was scrupulously to follow the rules about intrapartnership communication.

"New Science" marked the first time anyone had had the nerve to say, publicly and forcefully, that players whose table behavior was marked by huddles and variations in tone were not playing the game as it was supposed to be played. The article implied, correctly, that the effect of this "system" on opponents was comparable to having prearranged signals. (However, Edgar believed that most practitioners of That Old Black Magic were not, by their own lights, cheating. Indeed, that was probably the main reason it required a bombshell in the form of a cleverly worded accusation to have any significant effect.)

I mentioned earlier that the key inventions and combinations distinguishing contract bridge from its predecessors, usually attributed to Harold Vanderbilt, were in fact based on contributions from several people—people credited, ironically, by Vanderbilt, but rarely by anyone else. In a similar vein, it should be mentioned here that, by printing "New Science" in *The Bridge World*, editor Moyse was not merely giving the opposition equal time. A passionate believer in the general-direction approach and in the impossibility of achieving superior results through more precise definition, he was giving air to thoughts about standard bidding that questioned not merely its efficacy but the source of its strength as well. Moyse's recognition of the aptness of Kaplan's Black Magic analogy was comparable to a hyper-orthodox parent's acceptance of a child's marriage outside the faith.

Prior to the publication of "New Science," the bridge-playing public, including most tournament participants, respected and attempted to emulate the sorcerers. A good player was one who helped partner solve problems, but not, alas, only through choice of calls and plays. In contrast, the next wave of upcoming players adopted not only a more scientific bent than their predecessors but also an attitude that scorned transmitting or using extralegal information. I was a member of this "young scientist" group. Typically, when players of my age met knowledgeable opponents of the older generation at the table, the appearance of tactics such as forcing passes in nonforcing auctions, Hesitation Blackwood, and lack of spontaneity from a remaining doubleton produced stares, scornful sneers, and occasionally even derision.

Fortunately, succeeding waves of new players mostly followed the behavioral path of the New Scientists. They found it worthwhile to preserve the integrity of the delicate information structure required for four players to enjoy bridge at the same table. Had witchcraft prevailed instead, our game would undoubtedly be unrecognizably different today. We would have unauthorized partnership communication (as in, say, briscola), and it is not too much of a stretch of the imagination to visualize such activities being systematized, or even extended (as in poker) to coffeehousing, actions taken with a mind to misleading the opponents.

There is, of course, no such thing as a free lunch. Beneficial though the turn away from Black Magic was, it came with a price. In earlier times, when somebody was done the dirty by a little huddle-fumble or an overeager "optional" double, the aggrieved party (perhaps thinking about glass houses, or that it was part of the game) usually said nothing. Those few who complained found the authorities with deaf ears; it was the reigning power structure that, in effect, had licensed the sorcerers. But as the years passed following "New Science," more and more players adopted higher behavioral standards, and many came to realize that they were at a significant disadvantage if only their opponents could profit from unauthorized information. Gradually, an unpleasant situation developed: Old-timers were playing bridge guided by habits developed over decades while contestants from newer generations thought those habits constituted cheating. Worse yet, the high-minded crowd sometimes made unreasonable behavioral demands on novices, whose huddles were usually caused by uncertainty rather than underhandedness. Conflicts arose, and their number increased when some players demanded score adjustments to compensate for having been forced to swallow a witches' brew. By the mid-sixties, organized bridge was breaking apart in a new direction. There was a need for someone to step in and reorganize the procedures relating to unauthorized information, to help everyone distinguish between possibly inadvertent variations in tempo and volume on the one side and prearranged cheating on the other, and to offer reasonable indemnification to players who suffered as a result of "informational infractions." Who could that someone be?

The Tournament Scene

While the behavioral pot simmered through the late '50's and early '60's, in other dimensions tournaments kept cooking in more or less the usual way. To be sure, "usual" then was a bit different from "usual" now. For example, in the age before fixed partnerships became the norm in serious events, there was some respect for individual contests. Indeed, the Masters Individual was regarded as a premier event. And the contest for winning the most master points in a year (then called the McKenney, now named after Barry Crane) was regarded as significant, both by the general public and by the tournament crowd. Nowadays, each of these areas enjoys only a small fraction of its former status.

Among the top players, Edgar Kaplan was one of the least capable in individual events. (By far the most successful stars in this universe were the ones with the most placid personalities, such as B. Jay Becker and Norman Kay.) However, in 1957, when Edgar won the McKenney trophy with what was then considered an astronomical masterpoint total (chicken feed in today's inflation-wracked economy), he somehow won the Masters Individual—oops, I mean the *Life* Masters Individual; even then, events had to be reclassified to reduce the number of inappropriate entries; in the ranking system of the American Contract Bridge League (ACBL), almost every tournament player was a "Master" of some sort or other.

Variations notwithstanding, there are basically two kinds of tournament reports. One aims mainly at presenting interesting or instructive deals, the other at reporting and accounting for the results. Although he was not the sole inventor of any techniques, Edgar brought new dimensions to both varieties. To the "good deals" type, he added the common-theme approach nowadays typically applied in non-reportorial articles. For an illustration, look at his report of his atypical triumph in the Individual. [*See page 173.*]

To the "what happened and why" type of tournament report, Edgar brought fearless journalism. Prior to his entry into this realm, even the pungent criticisms of a Moyse were not directed at players. Bidding philosophies, systems, approaches and myths were blamed for failures during the auction; partnership defense was treated similarly when possible. Other writers were even more restrained. For the less disguisable individual errors in play and defense, authors (even Moyse) sometimes retreated behind not naming the player involved.

Every now and then, someone dared to say who had committed a howler during the play. On these occasions, the blow was usually softened by a not-so-gentle reminder that the perpetrator was well known as the best player in 40 counties in three different states, and had enjoyed that status ever since a tot. True, Player X might have fluffed once before, many years ago, during a back-room game for score caddies . . . Of course, all readers already knew that Player X was a leading expert because, even if they had not previously heard of X's exploits (and mostly they had), they could easily work out that X had not sat down in the Spingold final or the Bermuda Bowl merely as a result of taking a wrong turn in the hotel lobby.

In contrast, Edgar assumed that the reader began with an appropriate respect for the world's top players and moved on from there. If he thought someone had messed up, he said so and explained why. This novel approach brought tournament descriptions up from the old boy network to the level of at least semi-responsible reporting; once Edgar had done it, others did also. The upheaval in bridge journalism began less than two years after "New Science" had begun to revolutionize table behavior. It was less dramatic, but its effects were equally long lasting.

In his first big-time tournament report, arguably the best ever, Edgar used a box-score approach, daring to record his view of the *exact* effectiveness of each of the participants in the match between Italy and the United States that decided the 1958 Bermuda Bowl. Every educated person should be familiar with this document. [*See pages 61 and 68.*]

Even though this report revolutionized bridge journalism, Edgar never again wrote one in this style—for a very good reason. In later years, he gave up the painstaking evaluation of individual performances in his tournament reports, not because he thought it was inappropriate or unrewarding, but because it took too much time. When I was an active player, I tried to analyze my own results in detail, to the level of precision of Edgar's 1958 report but scoring much more critically—to me, a call or play was no better because it lost less than it might have. Even that limited effort devoured enormous blocks of time, and I persisted only because I was (and still am) convinced that being my own severest critic improved my game significantly. I wonder how many other serious competitors were influenced by Kaplan standards. The only other person I knew who regularly studied match records in that style was the late Monroe Ingberman. He and I often discussed rehashing techniques and the evaluation of numerical results. Monroe analyzed other people's matches mostly as a hobby, only partly as a route to improving his own table performance. He was occasionally paid for his labors, by The Aces for example, and he told me that creating the reports was so time consuming that although he thought he was being paid fairly he nonetheless earned less than the minimum wage. Clearly, all the evidence suggests that Edgar's decision to reduce the level of detailed calculation in his reports, however unfortunate for his readers, was sensible.

So, Edgar's latter-day tournament reports, which have appeared regularly in *The Bridge World* for the past 30-plus years, never again reached the spectacular height scaled in 1958. They have been merely excellent. For a fair comparison, consider the historic 1958 analysis side by side with the first report Edgar wrote as a *Bridge World* editor, a first-person account of the International Team Trials (which then followed a pairs format) to determine the 1967 international team. Observe in particular the adjustment in emphasis from analytic dissection to reportorial entertainment. [*See pages 180 and 185.*]

Although the revolution in reporting had positive effects on articles in magazines (and, to a much lesser extent, on those in newspapers), it had mixed effects on official reports. For example, at one time the editors of the world championship books tried to enliven their product with critical analysis, and the series degenerated into descriptions that failed to distinguish between fact and opinion, punctuated with unauthoritative attacks on the players. A letter to *The Bridge World*'s Bits and Pieces column exposed the scandal. Although you will not recognize the letter-writer's name from lists of tournament winners, you may know more about him than you think. Elizabeth and Edgar S. Kaplan used to call each other "bear" as a term of endearment. (Do you think it was stooping to the opponent's level, or appropriate turnabout, to respond to anonymous criticism pseudonymously?) [*See page 37.*]

The Bridge World

To maintain the continuity of the tournament-report saga, I have skipped over the time that Edgar, late in 1966, purchased *The Bridge World* from the McCall Corporation. He took over as publisher and editor, and hired me to act as co-editor; the first issue we produced was for January 1967. Later, when the arrangement proved successful, he converted our relationship to equal owners of the company. My experiences as Edgar's business partner can be described briefly. Over the 30-plus-year stretch that we careened through ups and downs with the magazine we never had a serious conflict; indeed, I would be hard-pressed to name any significant difference of opinion we had (excluding bridge theories and actions, of course—we rarely agreed in the Master Solvers' Club).

Following in the footsteps of Culbertson, Edgar was not a practical publisher. He believed that the show must go on but that deadlines were for people who let external forces exercise too much control over their lives. Furthermore, even after we had produced hundreds of issues, a few dozen on time, he still failed to grasp (or perhaps so pretended) the concept of "critical path," the idea that activities requiring a certain period to complete had to be started suitably early and kept on schedule in order to be finished when needed. Edgar was guided more by the appearances of the muse than by the requirements of the calendar. Undoubtedly, this behavior pattern improved the quality of his work, but it also grayed the hair of his colleagues. The literature has it that when Culbertson put the historic first issue of *The Bridge World* (October 1929) to bed, he only then began to consider what might be in the second issue; Edgar was in this mold. [For a playful but not necessarily fictional view of the Kaplan Regime on 94th Street, *see pages 47 and 50.*]

Things were quite different when Edgar put on his other hat. As an editor, he was superb. It wasn't just that his love for bridge shone through everything he touched. He had a marvelous gift for language, for finding exactly the right word, for creating the appropriate tone, for giving just the correct impression. His precision in diction was matched by a pedantic interest in grammar. In another direction, Edgar had a knack for writing sentences that would mean quite different things to different people. It is not easy for me to conceal my collection of favorites among his *double* (sometimes triple!) *entendres*, but a promise is a promise.

As co-editors, we acted more or less symmetrically at first. We shared all activities except our own writing. In that sphere, I wrote and he edited or he wrote and I edited. This turned out not to be our most efficient collective mode. He thought the things I had to say were of interest to readers; I thought his manner of expression was outstanding, and, in the area of bridge, nonpareil. Gradually, we gravitated to a highly asymmetric system. He would painstakingly hand-write his material directly into final form, someone would type it, and I would check it. In contrast, I would type what might on a good day be called a first draft; then, doing no revising whatever, I would pass it over to Edgar for processing into prose. Of course, I learned a great deal from this experience, as can easily be seen by comparing things not edited by Edgar that I wrote during the '60's and during the '90's. As against that, because so much of what I wrote was headed directly for filtering by Edgar, I fell into the habit of concentrating on getting the ideas right to the exclusion of just about everything else. My revising skills have no doubt atrophied by this time. And, sad to say, without Edgar's genius for exactly the right way to express things, *The Bridge World* will never be the same again.

Huddle Muddle

One reason that "New Science" had such an enormous impact on bridge behavior was that no one could publicly disagree with its thesis. If you believed that extracurricular actions excluded by the Laws should be excluded from the table, you applauded and meant it; if not, you just applauded—one could hardly come out in favor of underhandedness. However, in succeeding years, when Edgar designed procedures to cope with the rash of protests against witchcraft, intentional or innocent, his proposed solutions met with much resistance. They were, so to speak, beset from both the right and the left. On one side, some traditionalists believed that in a game played by ladies and gentlemen it was inappropriate to raise any question of another competitor's behavior. (For many years, the same attitude pervaded officialdom's approach to accusations of cheating. Some things, it was believed, are better swept under the rug; the trick is to find a large enough rug.) On the other side, zealots who wanted to keep bridge pure demanded that inappropriate behavior, if not actually penalized, at least be recorded and perhaps publicized.

Edgar tried to steer between extreme views. His theory was that matters of unauthorized information should be treated similarly to revokes, not as though they were akin to having prearranged signals. And he believed that merely disallowing gains from actions with a questionable basis would eventually reduce the occurrence of such actions. This collection includes both the seminal article from *The Bridge World* on what was then a new approach to the problem [*see page 226*] and excerpts from an interview on the subject in *The Bridge Journal* [*see page 232*]. Notice especially, first, the disparate points of view that Edgar had to contend with in trying to form a consensus; and, second, the outrageous table actions that were discussed in the headline cases of that day.

Did Edgar's approach succeed? Yes and no. The central idea of likening a dispute about unauthorized information to a civil, rather than to a criminal, complaint was a positive step, both in theory and in practice. Partly as a result of the inculcation of this principle, sorcerers gradually went out of business and players were able to protect their rights without generating hard feelings. That was the good news. Unfortunately, as the years rolled along fewer tournament players maintained the altruistic attitude towards behavior of the sixties and more substituted the litigious approach of later decades. In self-defense, readers demanded, and *The Bridge World* published, several long series of articles on the implementation of the Laws in this area and on how to protect one's rights. Alas, the availability of remedies led to their overuse, often to their misuse. If you can't beat them, sue them. Despite the virtual disappearance of the more blatant offenses of the Black Magic era and despite much more player education, there were more actions called into question, more calls for the Director, more meetings of the Appeals Committee, more lawyering. This is certainly not what Edgar had in mind. He had improved things but at the same time had underestimated the difficulty of the problem.

Legal Eagle

In order to formulate his solutions to the problem of announcing agreements (such as the Alert procedure) and that of receiving unauthorized information, Edgar had needed to determine the possible forms such solutions could take. This led him to a serious study of the Laws of bridge; which in turn led to the discovery that those Laws included hundreds of flaws, in various sizes and flavors; which in turn led him to try to correct those deficiencies; which in turn led to the realization that the mechanism for adjusting the Laws was awkward; which in turn led to hundreds of hours of analysis (taking away time that should have been spent on *The Bridge World*—guess who did that work instead) and correspondence (which, since Edgar conveniently was unable to type, had to be handled by *The Bridge World*'s typists—guess who filled in for them to get the magazine out); which in turn led to endless discussions and arguments; which in turn led to more analysis, correspondence, typing, discussions, rewritings, arguments, analysis, correspondence, typing, discussions, rewritings, arguments, typing, and so on, endlessly.

You can see that typists' contributions to the Laws have been enormous. If we hadn't been there to pitch in while the Laws were being reconstructed, *The Bridge World* would have gone bankrupt, Edgar's activities would have been curtailed, and the very fabric of our game would have disintegrated. As it was, at various places along this very long line Edgar became an expert on the Laws; then the world's leading expert on the Laws; then, astonishingly, someone who knew everything there was to know about the Laws, including, in most cases, the personal view on each controversial provision held by each member of the National Laws Commission and the World Bridge Federation's Laws Commission. (It would not have surprised me to learn that he had had informants inside the Portland Club.) Sooner or later, he became chairman, or co-chairman, or *éminence grise*, or whatever, of those commissions. (I was too busy filling in as typist to follow the details.) Anyone who has even the remotest familiarity with the history of the Laws knows the result of all this: We now have Laws purged of obvious flaws and a decent method for amending them.

The First Hurrah

Once upon a time, Edgar decided he could better further the bridge causes he was championing as a member of the American Contract Bridge League's Board of Directors. Accordingly, he appointed a campaign manager (guess who) and set out to convince the local electors that he was the right man for the job. His elevation owed less to the talents of his staff than to the makeup of the Greater New York Bridge Association's directorate: There were more people interested in improving bridge than in preserving the traditional political structure.

Measured by the usual yardsticks, Edgar's tenure on the ACBL Board was successful. Much constructive legislation emerged that would probably have been at best delayed had he not been a Director. However, there were at least two negative aspects to his political career. One: Dealing with League business, and especially handling the personal politicking that was necessary to achieve legislative results, was a drain on Edgar's very valuable time. And Two: The reforms he achieved and the superior tone attained by the League during this period were only temporary. You see, Edgar did not really change the ACBL Board. What he did was to use personal persuasion to show individuals then on the Board the superior way. Of course, it helped that his cases were strong, just as Perry Mason is aided by his clients' really being innocent. But without Perry defending, innocent people might be convicted. Edgar's appearance on the ACBL Board did not change the power structure, the indirect method of electing Directors, or the type of person who was chosen. When Edgar was no longer on the Board, no longer there to provide personal guidance, the Directors reverted to form. Gradually, some of the things he had accomplished were dismantled, and the ACBL sank back to its former mediocrity.

Coach and Captain

As a winner of many national team championships and international trials, Edgar was often a member of a United States team fighting for a world championship. When he wasn't playing, he was frequently a team captain, assistant captain, or coach. In all these latter capacities, whatever his title, his primary function was to provide the team, both before the event and just before each individual match or session, with information about the opponents' methods. Edgar had an amazing facility for absorbing other people's systems. He could read a book about a system and remember the system, including, in some cases, the coded responses to specialized asking-bids. No wonder he never felt the need for a computer! Wait; it gets better. He could read a system book *written in any of a wide variety of languages, most of which he could not speak,* and know the system.

Edgar had been intrigued by the early relay systems; in fact, there was a time when he and I regularly bid hands in Pierre Collet's Beta system. (How he got me to learn the system I don't recall. I was—and still am—keenly interested in relay systems and studied them extensively. But unless there was a special reason, I had no interest in *remembering* any of them. Edgar absorbed all systems regardless.) But everyone has limits. Edgar balked at learning the detailed codes of the more modern relay systems. There were many such methods, they were more complicated (in the sense of nonuniformity) than the earlier ones, and (as a careful student of Challenge the Champs, the series of bidding matches in *The Bridge World*, could have observed) they kept changing, year to year or even month to month, as the authors continually reoptimized.

Still, if you wanted someone who knew the other guy's methods and had sensible suggestions for what to do against them, Edgar was your man. This was another field in which he pioneered. Prior to his first appearance as system mentor, American international players had mostly ignored their opponents' methods, hoping that they would go away, an approach that proved spectacularly ineffective.

Top and Bottom Kibitzers

Edgar Kaplan was so enamored of bridge that if he couldn't be playing, he wanted to be watching. In this he was much unlike most of the Bridge Players (upper case) I have known. Seeing him in his spectator's role might have caused someone who didn't know the truth to wonder whether he was a Player at all. My reaction to losing a match was to go off somewhere, preferably on Mars, and sulk. I certainly didn't want to watch the next round of the tournament. But Edgar was such a fan of bridge that after a losing encounter he'd show up on time for the next round with his pencil and pad. He was a fine kibitzer, both in behavior and level of interest. (In contrast, his wife, Betty, was too impatient to be a decorous observer. She belonged at North, South, East or West; Edgar was also comfortable at Northeast, Southeast, Southwest or Northwest.)

No, Edgar doesn't get into the Kibitzers' Hall of Fame; that's populated mostly by ardent fans who are not themselves world-class performers. But I suspect that Edgar is the top-rated spectator among the great players of history. The bridge world has profited amply from this. Combining his playing expertise, kibitzing talent, analytical skills, and witty conversation, Edgar was far and away the best bridge broadcaster ever. He was the chief commentator at World Bridge Federation championships (usually functioning in conjunction with a Vu-Graph exhibition) for so long that no one seems able to remember just how long it was. He improved on-site presentations by setting performance standards, and he trained and encouraged those who showed aptitude for the job.

Edgar and Betty

Betty Kaplan may not have been up to snuff as a kibitzer, but she made up for that in so many ways that it would take another entire article to recount them. No one appreciated these qualities more than Edgar, who adored her. I did not know the Kaplans when they married, after Betty and Freddy Sheinwold divorced; my perspective of their elopement was that of a newspaper reader. That event seems a tame occurrence compared to the high tragedy and spectacular activities that appear regularly in today's headlines, but the media of that day went wild: Bridge Expert Runs Off with Partner's Wife. The sequence of events fractured the eponymous Kaplan-Sheinwold partnership, but the story had a civilized ending that ought to be newsworthy. It wasn't too many years after the Kaplans' marriage that Freddy and Edgar were back on speaking terms. Later, they were good friends again for many years and drew especially close, I thought, after Betty's death.

Betty was an essential part of Edgar's life; he was devastated by her death and never fully recovered. As general manager, she was also a central part of *The Bridge World*. When she left us it was as though something had broken that you knew couldn't be repaired.

Life Beyond Bridge

Betty Kaplan shared all of Edgar's major life interests. Since he spent so much time playing, studying and writing about bridge, you might imagine that his other interests would be limited. Not so. It's hard to determine the source of all the extra hours that populated his days, but he was a gourmet cook (except when away at a tournament, the Kaplans almost always ate food they themselves had prepared), an ardent tennis fan (even *The Bridge World* came to a grinding halt when the U.S. Open dominated the New York sports scene, and Edgar could more easily have named the 9th through 16th seeded entries in a Grand Slam event than in the Vanderbilt or Spingold—the top eight, of course, would have been no challenge in either case), and a medium-level follower of all the major professional team sports (a clue to his added hours: he sometimes watched games on tape, television remote control in hand to excise irrelevant periods of time; when he watched a game "live" he worked on *Bridge World* activities during gaps in the action). Where he found time to read so many books I have no idea. I can give a partial explanation of how he pursued his strong interest in music. He would often listen while doing something else. Through middle age, Edgar also *played* music, a pastime that gets special mention here because it was something he did regularly at which he did *not* become expert. Betty was the star musician in the family. She played with professional quality and was for many years a principal of the music school down the block on West 94th Street.

A Man for All Seasons

If any one thing can be said to characterize Edgar's performance in the variety of bridge activities at which he excelled, it was his versatility. As a teacher at The Card School, a lecturer at tournaments, and an author of several outstanding instructional books, he was able to communicate effectively with players at all levels of skill and experience, not just those who read *The Bridge World*. It takes no great talent to form a compatible (and winning) partnership with Norman Kay, but Edgar played effectively opposite practitioners of a wide variety of systems and styles. He was flexible in system building as well. The foundation of Kaplan-Sheinwold is more a blending of ostensibly eclectic elements into a coherent whole than a sparkling new concept, but Edgar combined the ingredients cleverly and added some finishing touches of his own. Later, when circumstances required splitting the underlying method into two subsystems, traditional K-S nonvulnerable and "timid K-S" vulnerable, he demonstrated that the original system had stemmed from a complete understanding of the interactions of different techniques. His monograph on the updated version of K-S, code named M5 because it was the fifth system monograph he wrote, has remained in print for ages. Chances are you could read M5 once or twice, sit down at a table, and be able to use the system well.

In writing, Edgar was more flexible yet. Much the way an attorney or a debater must promote or defend different positions on different days, Edgar glided effortlessly from one perspective to another, and from one opinion to another. As a demonstration of this, we bring forward a *Bridge World* piece of self-indulgent egomania by nobody's favorite hero. [*See page 42.*]

Last Round

Of all Edgar Kaplan's many accomplishments, the one I admire most is the conduct of his battle against cancer. I can find no word short of "incredible" to describe satisfactorily his behavior during the horrible period of his illness. Simply put, Edgar would not let the disease and its concomitant treatment (often the worse of the two) degrade his dignity, nor disrupt the routines of his life, nor reduce his eternal optimism. Edgar divided time not by years or months but by national and international championships. Since his formative years, his life had always been looking forward toward the next tournament. He never lost that outlook.

The Summing Up

Edgar Kaplan succeeded spectacularly at bridge in almost every realm, even in fields whose existence no one could have anticipated at the time he learned the game. He managed to organize his achievements so that they had a significant positive effect on virtually everyone who now plays or ever will play the game, every bridge activity, every publication, every tournament. Only he knew if these multi-dimensional triumphs overshadowed the disappointment of failing to fulfill the dream of his youth, winning a world team championship.

Early in their lives, Edgar and his brother Gordin went their separate intellectual ways. Gordin, who became one of the world's leading cancer researchers, sometimes chided Edgar for failing to direct his considerable abilities in a more "useful" direction; Edgar would reply

27

that increasing people's enjoyment was a rewarding activity. Let's see if we can settle the family argument. It would be unsatisfactory if all talented and creative human beings pursued careers in recreational areas. But would it be any better if everyone in that group were instead totally dedicated to improving the human condition by conquering disease, famine, weather and other ills of the planet? Then, the sole objective of improving human health and safety would be to enable further improvements in human health and safety. No, the world needs both its Edgars and its Gordins. If it fails to accommodate either group, it will be the poorer.

THE BRIDGE WORLD . . .

Edgar wrote charmingly about the peculiarities of the subspecies of homo sapiens known as bridge players. With a professional touch, he combined the human comedy with interesting deals. A high point in this area was this enormously popular piece, published under the byline of his wife, Betty.

R ★ A ★ T ★ S

This is really three articles in one. The first part is a sort of matrimonial quiz, on how to defend with your husband. The second part is devoted to a marvellous new System I have devised—not one of your modern methods for getting to the perfect contract every time in only eight easy rounds of bidding, but a System with a truly important objective: defending yourself against your husband. The third part shows you the quiz answers, the System in action, and some interesting deals from the Bermuda Regional. First, the quiz.

In the four deals below you are East, behind the dummy. West, your husband, leads; you win with the ace. What is your play to trick two?

(1)

NORTH (*dummy*)
♠ 10 7 6 4
♡ K 6 5
◇ A K J 8
♣ Q J

EAST (*you*)
♠ A Q 8
♡ 4 3
◇ 9 6 5 4 3
♣ A 7 2

SOUTH	WEST	NORTH	EAST
—	—	1 ◇	Pass
1 ♡	Pass	1 ♠	Pass
3 ◇	Pass	3 ♡	Pass
4 ♡	Pass	Pass	Pass

Edgar's lead: the three of spades. Declarer plays the spade five.

(2)

NORTH (*dummy*)
♠ 5 4
♡ K J 3
◇ 10 7 4
♣ A J 9 8 6

EAST (*you*)
♠ A 8 7
♡ 9 8 7
◇ K J 9 8
♣ 7 3 2

SOUTH	WEST	NORTH	EAST
—	—	Pass	Pass
1 NT*	Pass	3 NT	(All Pass)

*15-17

Edgar's lead: the queen of spades. Declarer plays the spade six.

(3)

NORTH (*dummy*)
♠ A 10 9 5
♡ 7 6 5
◇ K
♣ K Q J 10 3

EAST (*you*)
♠ 4
♡ J 4 2
◇ Q 10 8 4 3
♣ A 9 6 4

SOUTH	WEST	NORTH	EAST
1 ♠	Pass	4 ◇*	Pass
4 ♠	Pass	Pass	Pass

*spade raise with short diamonds

Edgar's lead: the five of clubs. Declarer plays the club seven.

(4)

NORTH (*dummy*)
♠ 10 3
♡ 9 7 5
◇ A Q J 10 5 4
♣ A 2

EAST (*you*)
♠ A 9 2
♡ A 6 3 2
◇ 8 7 2
♣ 10 9 5

SOUTH	WEST	NORTH	EAST
—	—	—	Pass
1 ♣	Pass	1 ◇	Pass
1 ♠	Pass	3 ◇	Pass
3 NT	Pass	Pass	Pass

Edgar's lead: the queen of hearts. Declarer plays the heart four.

Let me explain why I specify that you are playing with your husband—that is, I'll explain to the boys; the girls already know. You see, these are particularly dangerous positions for a wife. If you return the suit he led when a shift would work better, that's dumb—and you'll get bawled out. But if you switch and *that's* wrong, you'll get flayed alive. This isn't male chauvinist piggery—it's not men who are beastly, just husbands. When someone else makes a mistake with them, their sweetness can be cloying: "That was such a tough decision; how could you tell?" But with you, it's "What makes you think you're a genius? Can't you just . . . " Or, the sarcastic approach: "Sorry, dear, my fault. I know how you hate to return my suits, so I should have led a diamond, and then you'd have . . . " A great expert, normally the gentlest of men, once roared at his wife (and at the hundreds within earshot), "To think that this is the mother of my child!"

How wives hate it! It's not only that you are being publicly humiliated; it's almost as bad that he is making a public spectacle of himself. Worse still, it's a vicious cycle. You got screamed at on one board, so you're all in turmoil on the next, and you make a mistake, so the vitriol flows again, and . . .

Now, that brings me to our trip to the Bermuda Regional. Bermuda is one of the most beautiful islands on earth. The hotel is magnificent, the weather is idyllic, and the tournament is marvelously scheduled, with most of the championships in the evenings so that the afternoons are free for sunning or swimming or shopping or sight-seeing. But how can you enjoy the afternoons if you spend the evenings being ridiculed in front of the opponents? I had a plan, my System for taming Edgar.

My method was not a total ban on post-mortem conversation—that just doesn't work. In the first place, it's almost as bad to sit there and watch him rolling his eyes and making faces—then to have to listen to him later, oozing virtue, claiming that he "never said a word." In the second place, he'll get an ulcer if he has to hold it all in. No, he is entitled to vent his spleen—but only systemically, by using the code-words the System allows. If I commit an ordinary misdemeanor, he may style it Reasonable. If it is a felony, he may refer to my action as Attractive. If it is a heinous crime, he may call it Thoughtful.

Edgar gave his solemn promise, but raised one objection. Yes, those code-words would suffice for most occasions; however, for truly traumatic ones—not, dear, that he dreamed there would be any, but just in case—he wanted a word he could hiss. So, I gave him Scintillating. Four words, that was all: Reasonable, Attractive, Thoughtful, Scintillating. The mnemonic was RATS. To show you the System in action, I return to my four deals from Bermuda.

(1)

NORTH
♠ 10 7 6 4
♡ K 6 5
♢ A K J 8
♣ Q J

WEST
♠ K J 9 3 2
♡ 9 8 7 2
♢ —
♣ 10 8 6 4

EAST
♠ A Q 8
♡ 4 3
♢ 9 6 5 4 3
♣ A 7 2

SOUTH
♠ 5
♡ A Q J 10
♢ Q 10 7 2
♣ K 9 5 3

This was early in the maiden voyage for RATS. Edgar led a spade against four hearts. I won and figured out from the auction that he was probably void in diamonds. So, I returned the diamond three; he ruffed, put me in with the club ace, and ruffed again. Down one—I was tickled pink. But he wasn't—he looked like Mount Vesuvius glowering at Pompeii. Come to think of it, if I had continued spades.

"Am I an idiot? If I wanted a ruff, would I have led a low . . . " I glared my fiercest glare, and he subsided. "I guess the diamond return was reasonable," he said with a grin.

(2)

NORTH
♠ 5 4
♡ K J 3
◇ 10 7 4
♣ A J 9 8 6

WEST
♠ K Q 10 9 3 2
♡ 10 2
◇ 6 5 2
♣ Q 4

EAST
♠ A 8 7
♡ 9 8 7
◇ K J 9 8
♣ 7 3 2

SOUTH
♠ J 6
♡ A Q 6 5 4
◇ A Q 3
♣ K 10 5

RATS was purring along happily when we picked up these cards against a pair of young marrieds who, incidentally, sounded as though they needed our System. Against three notrump (why will people open such hands with one notrump?), Edgar led the spade queen, which would ask me to drop the jack if I had it. Unfortunately, I didn't have it, so I presumed that he had led from queen-jack. There were just enough points missing for him to hold the diamond ace; therefore, I shifted hopefully to the jack of diamonds—not exactly double-dummy defense, as you will observe.

Luckily, declarer (the young wife) went up with her ace, ran hearts, and then finessed me for the club queen, correctly divining that the mercifully uncashed spade length was on her left. Down two anyway! Now, of course, the young husband lashed out with kind and helpful remarks about "12 top tricks." And Edgar smiled sweetly at me and said, "It was very attractive to switch to diamonds, dear."

"See!" said the wife to her husband, "She makes the wrong play, and listen to what he says to her!"

"I wonder," snarled her husband, "what he would be saying if you had had the brains to take your tricks." He didn't know the System, you see. But—I wonder too.

(3)

```
                    NORTH
                    ♠ A 10 9 5
                    ♡ 7 6 5
                    ◇ K
                    ♣ K Q J 10 3
    WEST                              EAST
    ♠ 8 6 3 2                         ♠ 4
    ♡ Q 10                            ♡ J 4 2
    ◇ A 9 7 6 5 2                     ◇ Q 10 8 4 3
    ♣ 5                              ♣ A 9 6 4
                    SOUTH
                    ♠ K Q J 7
                    ♡ A K 9 8 3
                    ◇ J
                    ♣ 8 7 2
```

Edgar led his singleton club against four spades; we could have taken a club and a ruff, cashed the diamond ace, and waited for our heart trick—down one. But how was I to know the five was a singleton? If clubs were two-two, we had to take a lot of tricks in an awful hurry. So, I switched to hearts, and made the expert lead of the jack—I am an International Master, after all.

This time, declarer could have taken 13 of the last 12 tricks. However, he was under a tiny misapprehension about the hearts—Edgar had dropped the queen under South's king (a play that led me to suspect that this would be a perfect deal for our System), so declarer thought I had started with jack-ten-fourth. He drew all the trumps (I pitched diamonds), and started cashing dummy's clubs. This was the position after nine tricks (eight to declarer, one to us), with dummy on lead:

34

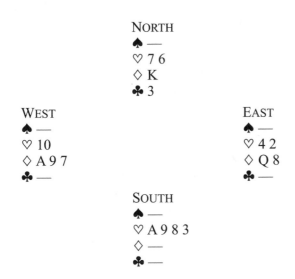

NORTH
♠ —
♡ 7 6
♢ K
♣ 3

WEST
♠ —
♡ 10
♢ A 9 7
♣ —

EAST
♠ —
♡ 4 2
♢ Q 8
♣ —

SOUTH
♠ —
♡ A 9 8 3
♢ —
♣ —

Declarer, remember, thought I had the ten-four-two of hearts left. So, he didn't want to cash dummy's last club, since it would squeeze his own hearts: if he pitched the three, he could take only one finesse; if he pitched the eight, I could cover dummy's spot with "my" ten, blocking the suit. The solution was obvious—he led the heart seven and passed it. I unblocked my diamond queen on Edgar's ace (I told you, I'm an International Master)—down two!

"A thoughtful jack of hearts, my sweet."

Wit and Wisdom

An appellant at a score-adjustment hearing explained that she often led singletons against notrump contracts (not only when partner had delayed before passing). As Appeals Committee Chairman charged with pacifying the losing parties, Edgar effectively replied: "We have no doubt that you do, but your partner's hesitation no longer makes it possible for you to be so brilliant on this deal."

(4)

NORTH
♠ 10 3
♡ 9 7 5
◇ A Q J 10 5 4
♣ A 2

WEST
♠ K J 8 4
♡ Q J 10 8
◇ 6
♣ J 7 6 3

EAST
♠ A 9 2
♡ A 6 3 2
◇ 8 7 2
♣ 10 9 5

SOUTH
♠ Q 7 6 5
♡ K 4
◇ K 9 3
♣ K Q 8 4

Edgar led the queen of hearts against three notrump; I took my ace and huddled. (And he scowrmgled at me—oh, he didn't exactly scowl or squirm or wiggle, but I knew, I just knew, he was saying to himself, "What in blazes can the woman be thinking about?") Still, a heart return looked wrong—declarer certainly had to have the king this time, and diamonds were running. I made up my mind to switch to spades, and, as I was about to lead the deuce, it occurred to me that if I caught Edgar with two top honors, my nine would block the suit. So, I led the nine. How about that for clear thinking? Late in the session, too. What a triumph for RATS that my mind was on my bridge instead of on my miseries!

Edgar won with his jack of spades, considered for a bit (he never pays any attention when I scowrmgle)—and placed his jack of hearts firmly on the table. Declarer took the balance, since the sixth diamond squeezed my dear love in hearts and clubs. Making five. Five!

There was electricity in the air; the storm was about to burst. "The nine of spades," Edgar began. "You had to lead. . . " And then he stopped short, for he realized that indeed I had to lead it—it was the only card in my hand that could defeat the contract. Into the sudden silence, I dropped the last word—

"Sssscintillating."

Authors Anonymous

Edgar often attacked presumptuousness with ridicule, as this pseud-onymous letter to the editor of The Bridge World illustrates.

TO THE EDITOR:
I have recently been studying the book of the 1970 Bermuda Bowl. The ACBL, which published it, is to be congratulated not only on the handsome and efficient format but also on the speed with which it was prepared. But—there's always a "but"—maybe the editor should have taken a little more time and read over the deal analyses furnished by his anonymous contributors.

My objections are not to outright errors in analysis. Sure, I disagreed with the authors occasionally, but I do not have the arrogance to assume that my analysis is right and theirs wrong. The trouble is that just this sort of arrogance is strewn throughout the book. For example, in the Final, Lin, East for China, held:

♠ K 7 ♡ J 10 4 ◇ K 6 5 3 ♣ A J 8 2

His partner, nonvul. vs. vul., opened two clubs (minimum opening, five or more clubs) as dealer; North cue-bid three clubs for majors, and Lin bid three notrump. It went four spades behind him, passed back to him. Now Lin, with 12 balanced points opposite an opening bid, dou-bled his vulnerable opponent. Says the book: "East should without any doubt have bid either five clubs or four notrump over four spades." (As you may have surmised, four spades doubled made, while five clubs would be a cheap save.) Well, maybe it's wrong to double and maybe it isn't, but doesn't that egomaniacal "without any doubt" get you?

They went after Lin again when, as dealer with no one vul., he held:

♠ K ♡ A K J 10 7 6 4 ◇ 10 6 4 3 ♣ Q

He opened one heart. "In view of the one-suited nature of his hand—and the weakness of his spades—South might have judged to open with a bid of four hearts. . . . Lawrence's bid of four hearts appeals as the correct way to initiate his one-suited hand." Over one heart, LHO overcalled two clubs, passed back to Lin, who rebid two hearts, of course. Says the book: " . . . he could have scored a great success simply by passing, which indeed would appear to be the marked move on the hand." Indeed—because the opponents then bid up to four spades and made it.

South dealer
Neither side vulnerable

NORTH
♠ J 6 2
♡ 9 8
◇ A Q J 5 2
♣ 7 5 2

WEST
♠ Q 10 8 5 4
♡ 2
◇ K 8
♣ A K 10 9 4

EAST
♠ A 9 7 3
♡ Q 5 3
◇ 9 7
♣ J 8 6 3

SOUTH
♠ K
♡ A K J 10 7 6 4
◇ 10 6 4 3
♣ Q

OPEN ROOM

SOUTH	WEST	NORTH	EAST
Lin	Eisenberg	Cheng	Goldman
1 ♡	2 ♣	Pass	Pass
2 ♡	2 ♠	Pass	3 ♠
Pass	4 ♠	(All Pass)	

CLOSED ROOM

SOUTH	WEST	NORTH	EAST
Lawrence	Huang	Hamman	Tai
4 ♡	4 ♠	(All Pass)	

You may notice that four spades can be beaten by a heart lead and diamond switch (but both Souths continued hearts; now Eisenberg made the game by playing a spade to dummy's ace, while Huang led a spade to the *nine*, got the diamond switch, and went down). You may also notice that even though it is "correct" (in the anonymous author's opinion) to open four hearts, and even though the "marked move" is to pass two clubs, North-South own the deal for five diamonds or hearts; and they'd have been there if North bid three diamonds over two spades, as he well might have. Maybe South's hand isn't so "one-suited" after all, and maybe that's why Lin opened with one, and maybe that's why it was *Lin,* not the anonymous author, who was the finalist in the World Championship.

Lin was not the only one to receive condescending instruction from the Great Unknown. Here are two remarks culled from one pair of facing pages: (1) " . . . they displayed an unaccountable lack of judgment in failing to double . . . "; and, (2) " . . . he should definitely have either respected South's penalty double or should have removed to six clubs" (this last comment addressed to Hamman). Similar pieces of impertinence are everywhere in the book. Why impertinence? Because it is Hamman, the World Champion, whose judgment is entitled to respect, regardless of the result on one board. The anonymous author may not even understand the bidding system on which the action he criticizes was based.

Wit and Wisdom

"I decided I was a good bridge player when I found out that people whose names I had heard all my life, people I respected, did the same dumb things I did."

•

"One might find truly talented students in beginner classes, but beyond that level, no. The truly talented teach themselves by playing in the best games that can stand them."

Let me illustrate *that* with a few examples. On page 72, we read, "The strong opening artificial bid of one club, in this case the Roman club, moved Brazil toward a slam . . . " The hands were:

NORTH	SOUTH
♠ A 5 4	♠ K 10 9 6 3
♡ K Q 10 7 5	♡ 4
◇ A K 8 7	◇ 10 4 2
♣ 5	♣ A J 7 6

Barros	*Ferreira*
1 ♣	1 ♠
2 ♡	2 ♠
3 ◇	3 NT
4 ♠	5 ♣
5 ♡	5 ♠
Pass	

The book says, "North's club opening was, in this case, based on a strongish two-suited hand, and South's spade response showed that suit in a hand of 8-11 points." Well, this is gibberish to anyone who knows the Roman System. One club is not a "strong" artificial opening in Roman. A "strongish two-suited hand" in hearts and diamonds is opened in the shorter or lower suit.

The explanation is simple. Barros-Ferreira play not Roman but *Blue Team*, as reference to the front of the book would show, so the opening showed strength, and the response showed not spades but three control points (counting aces as 2, kings as 1). (Incidentally, five spades made, while our team played in two diamonds.)

WEST	EAST
♠ A Q 4	♠ 10 7 3
♡ A J 8	♡ K 9 7 5 2
◇ K 10 7 3	◇ 9 2
♣ A K 2	♣ Q 10 5

Faria	*Bastos*
1 NT	2 ♣
2 NT	3 ♣
3 ◇	3 ♡
3 NT	Pass

"The Roman notrump showed 17-21 points and the two club request elicited the information that the opening bid was maximum . . . ," the book tells us on page 82. How fortunate that we have an all-knowing author to explain the mysterious sequence! Only, the Roman notrump is 17 to 20, not 21, and in Roman there is no such rebid as two notrump to two clubs (since two clubs forces two diamonds, preparing a signoff).

The explanation? Faria-Bastos play *Arno,* not Roman. The opening was an artificial force (the equivalent of a standard two clubs); the response was not a "request"—the fact is, it showed no aces on the same scale as Blackwood. Two notrump indicated a balanced hand, and the rest was a normal Stayman auction.

So where did that fantasy in the book come from? It came from the ego of the anonymous author, who knows so much more about bridge than the champions that he patronizes them, and who is so afraid to admit that there might be something he doesn't know that he feeds us malarkey and hopes that we won't notice.

E. S. BAER
Newark, NJ

People who took themselves too seriously or belittled the achieve-
ments of others were fair game for Edgar's pen. Here, writing under the
pseudonym Moneybags, he manages to bring the spotlight's glare on
two categories of bridge narrowmindedness. Adept at presenting any
viewpoint, Edgar frequently helped those who disagreed with his posi-
tions to frame their objections effectively.

Clubs

Every once in a while, a visiting Life Master from out of town,
bulging with masterpoints, wanders into my club looking for a
duplicate game. The Secretary informs him that we do have a Thursday
morning duplicate for members' wives, but nothing but rubber bridge
at the moment. So he cuts into the big game, my game, with the air of
Mickey Mantle playing with the Little Leaguers.

Not that I object, so long as his check is good. For years I have gone
to the Caribbean for a month every winter, and financed the trip from
my bridge winnings. I'm grateful, believe me. But I would be able to
travel on my own yacht if these characters didn't cut me as a partner so
often.

Now, I am not so stupid as to take offense when one of these visiting
firemen blows a cold game contract trying to make an overtrick on a
dummy-reversal squeeze cum throw-in; nor when he balances against a
partial and goes for 500; nor when he revels in sacrifice bidding nonvul.
against vul., throwing good money after bad—that's the nature of the
beast. What I will never understand, though, is why these duplicate
wizards are always bidding clubs. Clubs! A disgusting suit, fit only for
women and children. Yet every last one of these Life Masters is a club-
lover.

Last month, for example, one of these dignitaries was honoring us
with his presence. On the first deal of the rubber (he cut against me,
thank the Lord), his partner was in three notrump and claimed nine
tricks after the lead. The Master was busily lecturing partner on how he
could have developed a squeeze for a tenth trick when I interrupted to
remind him that it was his deal.

So he dealt:

South dealer
North-South vulnerable

NORTH
♠ —
♡ K 10 9 7
♦ A 7 6 5 2
♣ K 7 4 3

WEST
♠ A K J 8 7 6 5 2
♡ 8 6 2
♦ Q 4
♣ —

EAST
♠ 3
♡ 4 3
♦ K J 10 9
♣ J 10 9 8 6 5

SOUTH
♠ Q 10 9 4
♡ A Q J 5
♦ 8 3
♣ A Q 2

He opened the South hand with one club, of course. I was West, and jumped to four spades. Even I wouldn't have made this one, but North, naturally enough, went to five clubs, doubled by my partner. Now old Masterpoints squirmed and huddled and finally passed, so I glared at North—who had sense enough not to try any nonsense with me at the table and passed also.

Declarer ruffed the spade lead, came back to his hand with a heart, and tried to ruff another spade. Partner overruffed and returned the jack of trumps. Belatedly, declarer conceded a diamond, and East returned another trump. So South made only seven tricks, down 1100.

Obviously, he mangled the play, but these duplicate players often do when in a hopeless contract—what are another 600 points when they're in for a "zero" anyway? What I am getting at, though, is that hideous opening bid. If the Master lacked the courage for one spade (which would lead to a three-notrump contract that even he could not blow) what is wrong with one heart? I would undoubtedly make five hearts with the South cards, so he could hardly lose 1100 there. What suicidal impulse compelled him to bid clubs?

A little while later, he tried his little tricks as my partner, but I was too much for him:

```
                    NORTH
                    ♠ K 10 9 6 4
                    ♡ 3
                    ◇ Q 10
                    ♣ A K 9 5 3
WEST                                    EAST
♠ A 5                                   ♠ 8 3 2
♡ J 10 7 4                              ♡ A K 9 6 2
◇ K 9 8 6 4 2                           ◇ A 7 5 3
♣ J                                     ♣ 2
                    SOUTH
                    ♠ Q J 7
                    ♡ Q 8 5
                    ◇ J
                    ♣ Q 10 8 7 6 4
```

West passed, and my hero, North, surprised no one when he opened one club. East overcalled one heart, and I, of course, bid one spade. West bid four hearts, and North four spades. This was passed around, and West went to five hearts, North to five spades. East doubled, and there I was. West led his singleton club.

You would doubtless win the club, lead a trump, and go down gracefully, but that is not the way I get my winter suntans. East was beaming approval at the club lead and preparing his little post-mortem speech about how his clever double had directed the lead. So I won in dummy and played the heart. East was equal to the occasion: he thumbed his deuce of hearts onto the table and awaited his ruff. I gave myself the pleasure of speaking sharply to him about his unethical conduct as I totaled up the rubber.

My point here is not my clever play—I am accustomed to making what I bid. It is the idiotic one-club opening that sticks in my throat. Had my Master opened one spade like a man, East would have passed; I would have closed the auction with four spades—and this contract is foolproof. After all, I might have gone down in five spades; opponents do occasionally pull the right card by accident.

Lately, I have been exposed to droves of our local duplicate stars. As a rule they wisely shun money games, but we have started IMP games once a week, and this brings them out. The sight of a duplicate board on the table soothes them, and they can forget that green points are at stake.

Of course, this means an orgy of club bids every Thursday night. Landy clubs and Short clubs and Drury clubs and Big clubs and just plain stupid clubs. Here is a deal from last week's game:

NORTH
♠ A Q 7 4 3
♡ Q 9 2
◇ A 5
♣ Q 7 2

WEST
♠ J 9 2
♡ J 8 7 3
◇ 10 8 4 2
♣ K 8

EAST
♠ K 10 6 5
♡ 6 5
◇ Q J 9
♣ A 10 9 3

SOUTH
♠ 8
♡ A K 10 4
◇ K 7 6 3
♣ J 6 5 4

My partner, North, opened one spade, I responded two hearts with the South hand, and he sensibly jumped to four hearts—adding a point or two for my declarer play. West led a diamond, which I won in my hand. Now a spade to the ace and ruff a spade, a diamond to the ace, ruff a spade. A diamond let me make dummy's deuce of trumps, a spade ruff with my heart king; a diamond to dummy's heart nine and the last spade ruffed with my ace. And the heart queen was still in dummy for my tenth trick. Plus 620.

Not a very difficult contract; even the Life Master at the other table shouldn't be down more than one. But, naturally, they never bid hearts over there:

NORTH	SOUTH
1 ♠	2 ♣(!)
2 NT	3 NT
Pass	

(*Repeated for convenience*)

```
                    NORTH
                    ♠ A Q 7 4 3
                    ♡ Q 9 2
                    ◇ A 5
                    ♣ Q 7 2
WEST                                      EAST
♠ J 9 2                                   ♠ K 10 6 5
♡ J 8 7 3                                 ♡ 6 5
◇ 10 8 4 2                                ◇ Q J 9
♣ K 8                                     ♣ A 10 9 3
                    SOUTH
                    ♠ 8
                    ♡ A K 10 4
                    ◇ K 7 6 3
                    ♣ J 6 5 4
```

NORTH	SOUTH
1 ♠	2 ♣(!)
2 NT	3 NT
Pass	

Note the elegance, the sheer, exquisite delicacy, of that two-club response. My teammate, East, would no doubt have led the ten of clubs and given away the contract if left to his own devices, but the auction trapped him into leading the diamond queen. Declarer considered himself most unlucky to go down 300. He has my sympathy, and I have his cash; those 14 imps were convertible, at our stakes, into one sunny day on the beach. So why should I complain if the Masters can't learn to leave their duplicate club bids at the duplicate club?

. . . AND *THE BRIDGE WORLD*

The magazine founded by Ely Culbertson in 1929 never matched anyone's idea of a business organization (and never so pretended). Under Edgar's leadership, it reached a new level of emphasizing what was really important: bridge. Edgar wrote the first of these two pieces to give the readership some idea of how the magazine functioned. It was so well received that it spawned the second, more extensive look at what went on behind the scenes, to which others contributed as well.

Continuous Performance

You might think that if you dropped in at the *Bridge World* office you would find a hive of activity—manuscripts being read, proofs being corrected, busy knots of editors discussing how to increase circulation or how to get some advertising. Not at all. The odds are that you would step right into the middle of a staff discussion of a bridge deal. And an interminable discussion at that, lasting for hours (it's a recurring miracle and a credit to the iron will of the Publisher that the magazine ever gets out on time); a vast circular discussion, which resembles a continuous performance at the movies, in that you can enter at any point secure in the knowledge that the whole show will eventually be repeated for your benefit.

The other morning, I got up rather late, had my breakfast, read my mail, and ambled over to the office to find the whole staff already hard at work. "It's just a guess," Judy was saying as I walked in. This was the deal they were slaving over:

WEST (*declarer*)	EAST (*dummy*)
♠ A 3	♠ Q 10 8 5 4
♡ A K 6 2	♡ 8 3
◇ A K J	◇ Q 4 3
♣ J 10 8 6	♣ 7 5 3

Your contract, doubtless owing to some overbid by partner, is three notrump, and the queen of hearts is led. Obviously, your only hope is to get four spade tricks; so you cash the ace of spades (the six is played on your left, the deuce on your right) and lead your three (the seven is played on your left). Do you play the ten or the queen from dummy?

"It's just a guess. Jack-third on your left is exactly as likely as king-third, and nothing else matters. So it's just a guess."

"Not at all," said subtle Jeff. "Consider this—what would you play from dummy if the nine had dropped on your right?"

The queen, everyone agreed. The K-9 doubleton would do you no good, so you have to play for J-9 doubleton.

"Sure. So if your right-hand opponent had K-9-2 originally, he would automatically have falsecarded with the nine, to get you to put up the queen on the next round. Thus, if you put in the ten here you are playing your RHO for K-9-2, the impossible holding. So you must go up with the queen."

We digested this in silence for a few seconds, but no one was happy with it. Betty Jr. (we have two Bettys in the office, which might cause confusion if anything went on here except bridge arguments) observed that she would know what to play intuitively; she would rather depend on her table feel than on Jeff's logic. And William, an aspiring young expert with over 100 master points (each one representing a triumph of guile over technique), had a more serious objection.

"If I were playing against you, Jeff," he said, "I would expect you to play the nine from K-9-2, so I would put in dummy's ten when you falsecarded. And if I were defending against you, I'd drop the nine from J-9-2."

It was time for me to put in my oar. "There's something else you all haven't considered. What would you do if the jack had dropped from your right on the ace? Clearly, you would have played RHO for K-J blank and put in dummy's eight on the next round. So if RHO has J-9 doubleton, he must make the standard falsecard of the jack. The nine can't be from J-9 if you have a good player on your right."

"You mean," said Betty Jr., "that the nine has to be a falsecard, unless it's from K-9, which does you no good?"

"Of course," said William. "It has to be Jeff's automatic falsecard from K-9-2, or my double-cross from J-9-2, or a triple-cross from K-9-2, or even," and he looked at me, slyly, "a quadruple-cross from J-9 doubleton if you're playing against certain people."

"Maybe," Jeff observed, "the optimum strategy for declarer is just not to look at the card played on his right, but to go up with the queen every time. Then he'll be right on half the three-three breaks and gain whenever RHO has J-9 doubleton. This would put you over 50%."

"But what about K-J doubleton?" I asked. "Isn't that as likely as J-9?"

"It's just a guess," said Judy. And that's where we came in.

Sophisticated Sequence

A one-act play

The Characters

(in order of appearance . . . on the masthead)

EDGAR, a quixotic magazine publisher.

JEFF, a harassed editor.

BETTY, a peripatetic but highly efficient editorial assistant.

ELIZABETH, a weary complaint-answerer.

WILLIAM, a circulation manager aspiring to expert status.

The Time: Late afternoon of the last possible day.

The Place: The second floor of a brownstone

on the Upper West Side of Manhattan.

The curtain opens to reveal the luxurious editorial office of The Bridge World. Every available inch of wall space is filled with shelves of books, magazines and papers. There is a large table and several file cabinets. A door, center, leads to a stairway. Another door, right, reveals the cramped quarters of the subscription department. There are three desks. At the left-most desk, which is equipped with normal accoutrements, sits BETTY, reading galleys. At the middle desk, which is completely bare except for a typewriter, is JEFF, simulating intense thought. The desk on the right, which is in a complete state of disarray and piled two feet high with books and papers of assorted sizes and colors, is unoccupied. The left and right desks have telephones.

A large steampipe, the house intercom, occupies a prominent position front left. A series of loud clanks emanates from the steam pipe. Dash-dot-dot-dot. Dash-dot-dot-dot.

BETTY *picks up her telephone.*

BETTY (*to telephone*): Hello. Yes. . . . Almost. . . . Everything is finished except Bits and Pieces; we need 46 more picas. . . . Jeff says he's working on it. . . . Yes. . . . Ronnie said he'd call later. . . . O.K.

BETTY *replaces the receiver.*

BETTY (*to* JEFF): Well?

JEFF (*looking up, waving a sheet of paper*): I want to use this letter. Woman and her husband's sister had an argument about the play of honor sequences on defense. Sister, who alleges she has 12 master points, claims you always play the top card to tell partner what you have. Our correspondent feels otherwise and appeals to us to help her tell her sister-in-law where to go.

BETTY (*taking the letter*): Very good. You write the answer, and I'll type the letter. (*She looks at the letter.*) Say, where is this letter from?

JEFF: I don't know. I lost the envelope.

BETTY: Oh no, not again! Where do you want this time? Shangri-La? How about the North Pole for a change?

WILLIAM *enters from the subscription department with a jiffy bag.*

WILLIAM: The book we sent to Kennedy Airport for the man who wanted to read it on his trip has come back. I guess they couldn't find him. We don't have his home address.

JEFF: I guess we hold it for him. Tell me, William, how do you handle your honor sequences on defense?

WILLIAM: You mean what card should you play from Q-J-10-x, and like that?

JEFF: Like that.

WILLIAM: I guess it depends on the situation. If you lead the suit, it's the queen. Some people lead the jack on opening lead, but that's not standard.

BETTY: But if you are playing on your partner's lead, the normal play is the ten—the lowest of equals—so the woman is right.

WILLIAM: What woman is right?

JEFF: The woman who wrote this letter. Actually, there are a lot of different situations you can face with that combination. . . .

WILLIAM: Sure. Suppose partner leads the king, and you want to get the lead. You play the queen to say it's safe to underlead the ace.

BETTY: Or you might drop the low one to tell him to lead something else . . . so you wouldn't play any of the honors.

JEFF: And if you were trying to make an informative discard from this holding you would play the queen.

EDGAR *enters through the center door.*

EDGAR: What's going on here?

BETTY: We're helping Jeff answer a letter about how a defender should

51

play from Q-J-10-x . . .

WILLIAM: . . . and it's time for you to put your oar in.

JEFF: It wasn't restricted to Q-J-10-x . . .

EDGAR: You know, in the Olympiad, I made a terrible play from just that combination.

EDGAR *goes to the rightmost desk and unerringly reaches seven inches into a pile of papers. Out comes a set of World Championship records.*

EDGAR: Here it is. Deal 43 of the final.

South dealer
Neither side vulnerable

NORTH
♠ Q J 5 4
♡ 9 6
◇ A 8 4
♣ A J 10 2

WEST
♠ 10 9 3
♡ K 8 5 3 2
◇ J 10
♣ Q 8 5

EAST
♠ 6 2
♡ Q J 10 4
◇ K 6
♣ K 7 6 4 3

SOUTH
♠ A K 8 7
♡ A 7
◇ Q 9 7 5 3 2
♣ 9

SOUTH	WEST	NORTH	EAST
D'Alelio	*Kay*	*Pabis Ticci*	*Kaplan*
1 ♠	Pass	2 ♣	Pass
2 ◇	Pass	3 ♠	Pass
4 ♣	Pass	4 ◇	Pass
4 ♡	Pass	4 NT	Pass
5 ♡	Pass	6 ♠	Pass
Pass	Pass		

JEFF: Not a very good slam. No play with a heart lead, and with a club lead you're still in trouble if the diamonds lie badly or if the trumps break four-one.

EDGAR: In fact, after a club lead, you should cash the ace-king of spades, and if the suit splits four-one you must duck a diamond and rely on a two-two diamond split.

JEFF: Or the singleton king of diamonds in the hand with the singleton spade, which isn't very likely.

EDGAR: The slam was bid in the other room also, but the bidding there clearly indicated a heart lead; and anyway, North was the declarer, and East had no trouble leading a heart. To avoid a huge adverse swing, Norman had to find the heart lead from the West hand, which he did. This was by no means obvious, for North's two-club response, a prelude to a forcing spade raise, need not show a club suit, and South had control-bid both clubs and hearts.

JEFF: Perhaps he figured he needed only a queen from you if he led a heart but a king if he led a club.

EDGAR: Maybe so. Anyway, Norman led the three of hearts, and I made the silly play of the ten.

WILLIAM: What difference does it make which honor you play? You know from the lead of the three that declarer has at least one more heart with his ace, and you know you will get in with the king of diamonds to cash the setting trick in hearts.

EDGAR: That's just the point. I was very happy about the whole thing. I knew we had the contract down, and I knew that Norman had made the winning lead, because South's club control must be a singleton. But what about poor Norman? He has led away from a king and is anxious to discover how it will come out.

JEFF: And you made him wait an extra second.

EDGAR: When I played the ten, Norman probably had a bad moment, thinking declarer would win with the queen. I owed my partner the courtesy of playing the queen on the first trick, so that he would know at once he had made the best lead.

BETTY: I should make such mistakes!

EDGAR: It's actually quite a serious error, particularly playing with Norman. He is the most thoughtful of partners and would never have done to me what I did to him.

BETTY: That's very interesting, but we can't put all that in Bits and Pieces.

JEFF: Not in 46 picas, anyway.

BETTY: C'mon now, let's get this finished. I have an appointment.

BETTY *and* JEFF *begin typing.*

JEFF (*aloud, as he types*): The defenders play different cards from an honor sequence to achieve various goals. If the suit is being led, for example, . . .

EDGAR (*to* WILLIAM): What's been covered so far on these defensive honor plays?

WILLIAM (*to* EDGAR): Well, there is the lead of the suit, and the different plays by third hand . . .

WILLIAM *and* EDGAR *walk to the left and continue their discussion as* BETTY *and* JEFF *continue to type.* ELIZABETH *enters from the subscription department carrying a pile of papers of assorted sizes. She walks to a large cylindrical packing carton labeled "To Be Filed" and unceremoniously dumps the papers into the carton. Unnoticed by anyone else in the office, she returns to the subscription department.*

EDGAR: Before you finish that—I think we've left out a few important situations. For example, sometimes when you lead from Q-J-10-x you should lead the low one. Didn't Truscott write an article about underleading honor sequences?

JEFF (*looking up*): Yes. Never Say Always, November 1960 issue, gray cover, page five.

BETTY *reaches up to a shelf containing bound volumes and begins flipping pages.*

EDGAR: If the suit has been bid on your right, and you want to lead it against a notrump contract, you should probably lead the x.

BETTY: Hah! Doubly wrong. The article is on page seven, and the cover is tan, not gray.

JEFF *bounces up to look at the issue.* BETTY *walks to a wall chart and makes some mysterious marks with a pencil.*

BETTY: You are now 41 right and 27 wrong.

JEFF: Whaddaya mean tan? I say it's gray. Look, . . .

ELIZABETH *re-enters, carrying a watering can.*

EDGAR (*seeing* ELIZABETH): What ho.

BETTY: It's tan.

JEFF (*to* ELIZABETH): What color is this cover?

JEFF *holds up the issue.*

ELIZABETH: Light brown, I would say.

BETTY: See, that's tan.

JEFF: Gray is close enough.

EDGAR (*to* ELIZABETH): What do you play from Q-J-10-x as a defender?

ELIZABETH: I don't know. How about the jack? Nobody ever seems to play the jack.

WILLIAM: The jack? We have situations in which you should play the queen, the ten, and the x, but you never play the jack.

JEFF: I'm not so sure about that. I can think of at least two situations in which the jack would be correct. Isn't gray close enough for this color?

EDGAR: One of them is probably some devious suit-preference signal.

ELIZABETH: I think gray is close enough.

WILLIAM: Whatever it is, it's a bad color. Let's not use it in the future.

BETTY *scowls and makes an erasure on the wall chart.*

JEFF: Not exactly a suit-preference, but a request to shift. Suppose your partner leads the king, and you are desperate to have him shift to some other suit at once. If you play the jack from Q-J-10-x, announcing that declarer has the queen, partner will probably figure out the play you want him to make.

WILLIAM: But the jack could be from jack-doubleton.

JEFF: Perhaps partner can tell declarer is not long in the suit led. Or the contract might be one notrump.

ELIZABETH (*watering plants on the window sill*): That's a bit farfetched. What's the other case?

JEFF: Sometimes you should play the jack as third hand, instead of the "normal" ten, to help partner when he gets in next. Consider this deal:

NORTH
♠ 2
♡ A Q 5
♢ Q J 10 9 6
♣ J 8 7 5

WEST
♠ A 9 8 5 3
♡ J 9 8 6
♢ K 5
♣ 4 2

EAST
♠ Q J 10 4
♡ 4 3 2
♢ 3 2
♣ K 10 9 3

SOUTH
♠ K 7 6
♡ K 10 7
♢ A 8 7 4
♣ A Q 6

SOUTH	WEST	NORTH	EAST
1 NT*	Pass	3 NT	(All Pass)

*15-17

JEFF: West leads the five of spades, East plays an honor, and South wins with the king. Declarer leads a heart to dummy's ace and loses a diamond finesse. What should West do? If East played the ten of spades on the first trick, West should probably shift to a club, hoping for a position such as this:

EAST
♠ J 10 4
♡ 4 3 2
♢ 3 2
♣ A 10 9 6 3

SOUTH
♠ K Q 7 6
♡ K 10 7
♢ A 8 7 4
♣ K Q

In any event, it would be easy for West to go wrong. But if East plays the *jack* of spades on the first trick, marking declarer with the ten of spades, a club shift has nothing to gain. West might as well lead a low spade, hoping that East has the queen.

BETTY: What issue is that in?

JEFF: I'm not saying. I don't know if the cover is turquoise or aqua.

EDGAR: Let's see what we've got now. As first hand, the conventional lead to give information to partner is the queen (or, as some people play, the jack), although any honor might be led for deceptive purposes. Also, the low card should be led into a bid suit, or up to certain combinations in dummy, as in this case:

NORTH
♠ 9 8 7 6

WEST		EAST
♠ A 5 2		♠ Q J 10 4

SOUTH
♠ K 3

If East is on lead in a notrump contract, and East-West need four spade tricks, East must lead low. As third hand, the normal play is the ten, but sometimes, as we have just seen, you play the jack (to help partner), or the x (to discourage a continuation), or the queen (to suggest an underlead if partner has led from ace-king). And you also discard the queen if you want to tell partner what you have.

ELIZABETH: What about as second hand, when declarer leads the suit and you want to split your honors and also tell your partner what you have?

WILLIAM: That's a matter of partnership understanding. Edgar likes to play the queen—the top of a sequence; Jeff thinks it's better to play the jack—the second highest honor.

BETTY: I think we should finish the issue. It's getting late and . . .

EDGAR: That leaves us with fourth hand. Can anybody think up an unusual play from Q-J-10-x as fourth hand?

JEFF: What about a mandatory falsecard?

EDGAR: You mean under king-nine fifth which declarer is trying to ruff out? But why didn't declarer lead up to the king?

JEFF: Maybe he hasn't got enough entries.

EDGAR: Right. Here's a possible situation:

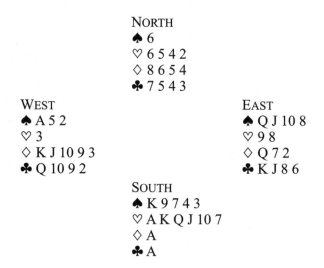

NORTH
♠ 6
♡ 6 5 4 2
◇ 8 6 5 4
♣ 7 5 4 3

WEST
♠ A 5 2
♡ 3
◇ K J 10 9 3
♣ Q 10 9 2

EAST
♠ Q J 10 8
♡ 9 8
◇ Q 7 2
♣ K J 8 6

SOUTH
♠ K 9 7 4 3
♡ A K Q J 10 7
◇ A
♣ A

EDGAR (*continuing*): South is in six hearts and West leads a trump.
Declarer wins and leads a low spade. East must win with an honor
and return a trump. Now declarer ruffs a spade, and East drops
another honor. Declarer must guess whether the ace of spades is
tripleton, so it is right to lead a low spade and ruff, or East started
with queen-jack-ten-tripleton in spades, so it is right to lead the
king. If East wins the first spade trick with the eight, declarer has no
chance to go wrong.

ELIZABETH: So which honor does East play?

WILLIAM: It doesn't matter, as long as he plays one of them.

BETTY: Say listen, we only have 46 picas . . .

EDGAR: Maybe it does matter which one you play. You must play the
way declarer thinks you would play with queen-jack-ten-tripleton.

JEFF: I think the most important thing is to convince declarer that you,
East, do not have the ace-tripleton of spades. If you can do that, he
will have only half the original ace-tripletons to consider against the
queen-jack-ten-blank possibility. Of course, playing for the tripleton
ace will still be the percentage play.

BETTY (*loudly*): It's six o'clock!

WILLIAM: Six already? I have to catch a train to get to the Regional
tonight!

WILLIAM *runs into the subscription department.*

ELIZABETH: And I'm late to give a flute lesson. Last one out remember to unplug the coffee pot!

ELIZABETH *exits, center.*

EDGAR: If you play the queen first, then the ten, declarer won't think you have the ace, and he'll know you have the jack.

JEFF: That's right. Nobody thinks of that play from ace-queen-ten, but it looks like a sneaky sort of play from queen-jack-ten.

WILLIAM *re-enters, running, carrying a box the size of a dishwasher filled with outgoing mail.*

WILLIAM: See you all some time.

WILLIAM *exits, center.*

JEFF *(calling after him)*: Win a lot of red points.

BETTY: Can't we get finished and discuss this deal later? I have an appointment at . . .

The telephone rings. JEFF *answers.*

JEFF *(to the telephone)*: Bridge World. Oh, hi Ron. Yes. . . . No kidding? . . . That's great . . . Yes, I'll tell him. . . . Bye.

EDGAR: Of course, declarer may doubt you would play that way from queen-jack-ten, because it's so obvious. Maybe jack then ten is better against a shrewd declarer.

BETTY: Look, we have to get the issue out today . . .

JEFF: That was Ronnie on the phone. He says we almost broke even last month!

EDGAR: Indeed. That's marvelous. Let's go downstairs for a drink to celebrate.

JEFF: Good idea. I think you should play queen and then ten to convince declarer you haven't got the ace yourself.

EDGAR *and* JEFF *begin to leave through the center door.*

BETTY: Hey. Wait-a-minute!

EDGAR'S VOICE *(from the stairway)*: It depends on the declarer. Suppose Roger were the declarer, what would you do then?

JEFF'S VOICE: That's a tough one. Maybe you should play low the first time, because the chance of beating the slam isn't good enough to make up for the time it would take him to make the decision.

BETTY: The issue! The issue!

CURTAIN

INTERNATIONAL EVENTS

Edgar's analyses of world-championship events were renowned. This is his first such effort, the historic description of the 1958 Bermuda Bowl that revolutionized tournament reporting.

World Championship Quiz

This quiz enables you to face some of the key decisions in the famous 1958 world-championship match between the United States and Italy. Assume rubber-bridge conditions. Page references show where the results can be found in the report that follows.

1. With North-South vulnerable, you, South, hold:

♠ A Q 9 5 4   ♡ 10 9 8 5   ◇ K 6 5   ♣ 8

SOUTH	WEST	NORTH	EAST
You			
Pass	Pass	Pass	1 ◇
Pass	2 ◇	3 ♣	Pass
Pass	3 ◇	Pass	Pass
?			

What call do you make? (*See page 70.*)

2. With North-South vulnerable, you, South, hold:

♠ K Q 4 3   ♡ 5 2   ◇ Q 8 7 6   ♣ J 9 8

SOUTH	WEST	NORTH	EAST
You			
—	—	1 ♡	Pass
1 ♠	Double	Pass	1 NT
Pass	Pass	Double	Pass
Pass	2 ♣	Pass	Pass
?			

What call do you make? (*See page 78.*)

3. You, South, are on defense in this situation:

South dealer
Both sides vulnerable

EAST (*dummy*)
♠ —
♡ A Q J 3
◇ J 10 8 2
♣ K Q 8 5 2

SOUTH
♠ A K 10 9 4
♡ 10 7 5
◇ K 7
♣ A J 6

SOUTH	WEST	NORTH	EAST
You			
1 ♠	Pass	Pass	Double
Pass	2 ♡	2 ♠	3 ♡
Pass	4 ♡	Pass	Pass
Pass			

Declarer ruffs partner's deuce-of-spade lead in dummy and plays the club queen. You win and lead the spade king, forcing dummy to ruff again. Next comes the eight of diamonds from dummy.

Which diamond do you play? (*See page 72.*)

4. As West, you hold:

♠ A 6   ♡ A Q 7 6 3 2   ◇ A 7 3   ♣ Q 7

With the opponents silent, you open one heart, partner responds two clubs, you jump to three hearts, and partner bids three notrump.

Do you quit or move on? (*See page 84.*)

5. You are West, on defense here:

WEST (*you*)
♠ A K J 6 3
♡ —
◊ 6 4 3 2
♣ Q 10 8 3

SOUTH (*dummy*)
♠ Q 9 8 7 4
♡ 10
◊ A K J 10 7
♣ 7 4

SOUTH	WEST	NORTH	EAST
	You		
—	—	—	1 ♡
1 ♠	Double	2 ♡	Double
Pass	Pass	Pass	

Your double of the spade overcall was for penalty. (Nowadays, most experts use such doubles for takeout, but in the 1958 match the only pair using that treatment was sitting North-South on this deal.) Partner leads the club king (four, three, deuce) and shifts to the diamond five. Declarer wins in dummy, following with the eight. The heart ten is led and holds, declarer and partner playing the four and the three. Next comes dummy's remaining club.

Which club do you play? (*See pages 84 and 85.*)

6. With East-West vulnerable, you, North, hold:

♠ 6 2   ♡ A J 10 7 5 2   ◊ —   ♣ A 8 5 4 2

SOUTH	WEST	NORTH	EAST
		You	
—	—	1 ♡	Double
3 ◊*	4 ♠	?	

*weak

What call do you make? (*See page 87.*)

7. As North, you lead the five of clubs against West's four-spade contract:

NORTH (*you*)
♠ K J 5 3
♡ Q 8 2
◇ A 6
♣ Q 10 7 5

EAST (*dummy*)
♠ Q 9 4
♡ J 6 5 4
◇ J 10 9 7 5 2
♣ —

SOUTH	WEST	NORTH	EAST
		You	
—	—	—	Pass
Pass	1 ♠	Pass	2 ♠
Pass	3 ♡	Pass	4 ♡
Pass	4 ♠	(All Pass)	

Declarer ruffs in dummy; partner plays the four, declarer the deuce. The next trick is heart four, seven, ten, queen.

What do you lead now? (*See page 86.*)

8. With East-West vulnerable, you, North, hold:

♠ K 10 9 5 4   ♡ 10 7 4 3   ◇ A   ♣ Q 8 6

SOUTH	WEST	NORTH	EAST
		You	
—	—	Pass	1 ♣
Pass	1 ◇	?	

What call do you make? (*See page 87.*)

9. East-West vulnerable

NORTH (*dummy*)
♠ A K 10 9
♡ A 10 9 3
◇ J 4
♣ K Q 4

SOUTH (*you*)
♠ J 8
♡ Q 8 7 5 4 2
◇ A 10 9 3 2
♣ —

SOUTH	WEST	NORTH	EAST
You			
—	Pass	1 ♣	Pass
1 ♡	Pass	3 ♡	Pass
4 ◇	Pass	4 ♠	Pass
4 NT	Pass	5 ♡	Pass
6 ♡	Pass	Pass	Pass

West leads the deuce of clubs.

Plan your play. (*See page 89.*)

10. With only the opponents vulnerable, partner deals and opens two hearts (weak), second hand leaps to four spades, and you hold:

♠ 7 3 2   ♡ A 9 5   ◇ A K 9   ♣ K 7 5 2

What call do you make? (*See pages 96 and 97.*)

11. Both sides vulnerable

NORTH (*dummy*)
♠ A 9 8
♡ 5
◇ A K 9 8
♣ A Q 9 8 3

SOUTH (*you*)
♠ 7 6 4 2
♡ K Q 9 8 6 3
◇ 3
♣ 6 2

SOUTH	WEST	NORTH	EAST
You			
Pass	Pass	1 ♣	Pass
1 ♡	Pass	2 ◇	Pass
2 ♡	Pass	2 NT	Pass
3 ♡	Pass	Pass	Pass

West leads the spade jack.
Plan your play. (*See pages 90 and 91.*)

12. Both sides vulnerable

NORTH (*you*)
♠ A 5
♡ Q 10 9
◇ A Q J 7 6 5
♣ 10 4

SOUTH (*dummy*)
♠ K 4 2
♡ 8 3
◇ K 9 3 2
♣ A K 8 7

SOUTH	WEST	NORTH	EAST
		You	
—	—	1 ◇	Pass
2 ♣	Pass	2 ◇	Pass
2 ♠	Pass	2 NT	Pass
3 NT	Pass	Pass	Pass

The opening lead is the five of hearts. West wins with the king and returns the heart four.

Which heart do you play? (*See page 100.*)

13. With East-West vulnerable, you, North, hold:

♠ K 4   ♡ A Q J 9 5 3   ◇ K 8 7 5   ♣ Q

SOUTH	WEST	NORTH	EAST
		You	
—	—	—	1 ♠
4 ♣	4 ♠	?	

What call do you make? (*See page 110.*)

14. With North-South vulnerable, you, West, hold:

♠ Q 8   ♡ 10 5 4   ◇ K 4 3   ♣ A 7 6 5 3

SOUTH	WEST	NORTH	EAST
	You		
—	Pass	1 ♣	2 ♠*
Pass	?		

*preemptive.

What call do you make? (*See page 114.*)

Analysis of the
1958 World Championship

In this article, the then-current scoring by "old imps" (called IMP) has been preserved. For a good approximation to current-day imps, double the old-imp numbers.

I have just finished an exhaustive analysis of all 164 deals of the 1958 World Championship match, United States vs. Italy, at Lake Como.

Mainly, my objective has been to assign "charges." How many international matchpoints did each player cost his team? Who were most effective and least effective for each side?

Before presenting conclusions, let me outline my method of charging. Take, for example, Deal 100:

West dealer
Both sides vulnerable

NORTH
♠ J 9 5
♡ J 10 5
◇ A 10 8
♣ K 10 7 5

WEST
♠ Q 2
♡ K 8 7 3
◇ K J 7 5 4
♣ A J

EAST
♠ A 10 7 6 4 3
♡ A 6
◇ Q 9 2
♣ 9 2

SOUTH
♠ K 8
♡ Q 9 4 2
◇ 6 3
♣ Q 8 6 4 3

Silodor and Rapée bid the East-West cards to the normal unbeatable contract of four spades. However, at the other table the bidding went:

SOUTH	WEST	NORTH	EAST
Roth	*Siniscalco*	*Stone*	*Forquet*
—	1 ♡	Pass	1 ♠
Pass	2 ◇	Pass	3 ♠
Pass	3 NT	(All Pass)	

With the normal club lead, three notrump is down two. But Stone led the spade nine! Roth took his king and shifted to a low club, and even now Siniscalco had only eight tricks, but on the run of spades both Stone and Roth discarded enough clubs to let declarer get his ninth trick in diamonds.

The U.S. gained one IMP anyway, but would have gained seven if Roth-Stone had been plus 200. The six IMP difference I charged mostly to Stone but a little to Roth.

What of Siniscalco and Forquet—did I charge them for their terrible three notrump contract? No, for it cost only one IMP, and I had decided that swings this small were beneath notice. But I did put a "black mark" in their column to indicate an unpunished error.

I have two other types of notations on my books, both of which show up on Deal 111:

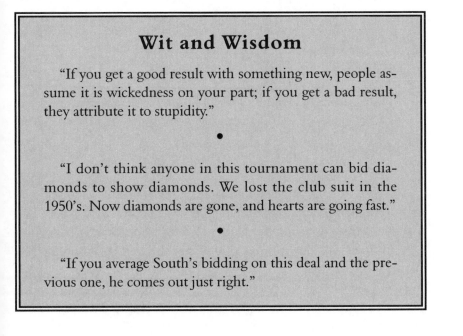

Wit and Wisdom

"If you get a good result with something new, people assume it is wickedness on your part; if you get a bad result, they attribute it to stupidity."

•

"I don't think anyone in this tournament can bid diamonds to show diamonds. We lost the club suit in the 1950's. Now diamonds are gone, and hearts are going fast."

•

"If you average South's bidding on this deal and the previous one, he comes out just right."

South dealer
North-South vulnerable

                          NORTH
                          ♠ 6 3
                          ♡ A 7 4
                          ◇ 9 7
                          ♣ K Q 10 6 5 4
        WEST   EAST
        ♠ J 10 2   ♠ K 8 7
        ♡ Q 6 3   ♡ K J 2
        ◇ J 10 8 4   ◇ A Q 3 2
        ♣ A J 2   ♣ 9 7 3
                          SOUTH
                          ♠ A Q 9 5 4
                          ♡ 10 9 8 5
                          ◇ K 6 5
                          ♣ 8

CLOSED ROOM

SOUTH	WEST	NORTH	EAST
Avarelli	*Rapée*	*Belladonna*	*Silodor*
Pass	Pass	Pass	1 ◇
1 ♠	2 ◇	(All Pass)	

OPEN ROOM

SOUTH	WEST	NORTH	EAST
Roth	*Siniscalco*	*Stone*	*Forquet*
Pass	Pass	Pass	1 ◇
Pass	2 ◇	3 ♣	Pass
Pass	3 ◇	Pass	Pass
Double	Pass	Pass	Pass

The play was the same at both tables. Singleton club lead, ace winning. Diamond finesse lost to the king; heart ten to North's ace. Two high clubs cashed, then two spades and a ruff. Silodor was down two, 100; Forquet was down three, 500. The U.S. gained five IMP. How should it be charged?

I can't see why any of the Italians should be faulted. Avarelli's spade overcall is reasonable; so is Belladonna's pass over two diamonds.

Forquet's opening at the other table is sound, and while Siniscalco's three-diamond bid is questionable, I refuse to charge it, for I probably would have bid three diamonds myself—at IMP scoring, nonvulnerable, with both opponents passed hands.

Really, Roth and Stone created the swing out of thin air—Stone, with his third-hand pass and his courageous vulnerable three-level overcall; Roth, with his pass over one diamond and excellent penalty double.

So I gave Roth and Stone a *credit* of five IMP. It is unfair to charge as errors unusual bids or plays that fail, without crediting "operations" that succeed. And, on the Italian side of the ledger, I put those five IMP in a special column for adverse swings caused, not by error, but by bad luck or by hands especially suited to the opponents' bidding style. I kept two of these "Act of God" columns, one for each team, and with all the results in, comparison would show if one team was substantially luckier than the other.

The final tabulation shows three types of notations in each player's column: charges for errors, credits for brilliance, and black marks for uncharged errors. The net figure is the player's total IMP charges, less IMP credits, plus (for I am a purist) a one-point charge for each black mark. This net figure, divided by the number of boards played, gives a fraction—actually, the number of IMP lost per board played—which, in my opinion, is a reliable index of general effectiveness.

Since this article will take the form of analysis of each player's per-formance, it will, inevitably, deal more with personalities than is the custom in bridge reports. I make no apology for this. My team has not done well enough to give us a chance to play for the U.S. next year; I am not in a glass house, and so I can afford to throw stones. But it is only fair to emphasize the obvious: opportunities for brilliance are few; for error, countless. In addition to the few brilliancies and many errors reported here, each player made thousands of sound, accurate decisions which go unheralded because the right play or bid is unspectacular.

The Italians

I was, I admit, very much surprised by my final tabulation on the Italian team:

	Charges	*Boards*	*Charges per Board*
Belladonna	13	92	.141
Avarelli	17	92	.185
Forquet	27	144	.188
Chiaradia	23	92	.250
Siniscalco	37	144	.257
D'Alelio	35	92	.380

I had always thought of Avarelli and Belladonna as the third-string Italian pair, and apparently the Italians agreed. In New York last year they played less than any of the others, and in Como they shared second billing with Chiaradia and D'Alelio. But they were clearly the best pair around this year.

My estimate is that fairly good play will lose one IMP every four boards. Par, then, is .250 (and it is not common to play well under the pressure of the World Championship match). So the record of Belladonna and Avarelli as a pair is truly remarkable.

There were very few charges against them. The only error in play that I noted was Avarelli's defense on Deal 71:

South dealer
Both sides vulnerable

NORTH
♠ J 5 3 2
♡ K
♢ Q 5 4 3
♣ 10 7 4 3

WEST
♠ Q 8 7 6
♡ 9 8 6 4 2
♢ A 9 6
♣ 9

EAST
♠ —
♡ A Q J 3
♢ J 10 8 2
♣ K Q 8 5 2

SOUTH
♠ A K 10 9 4
♡ 10 7 5
♢ K 7
♣ A J 6

72

SOUTH	WEST	NORTH	EAST
Avarelli	*Rapée*	*Belladonna*	*Silodor*
1 ♠	Pass	Pass	Double
Pass	2 ♡	2 ♠	3 ♡
Pass	4 ♡	Pass	Pass
Pass			

Rapée ruffed the opening spade lead in dummy and played the club queen. Avarelli won and led the spade king, forcing dummy to ruff again—the best defense. Now declarer led the diamond eight from the table, and Avarelli fell from grace: he ducked. Belladonna won with the diamond queen, and his spade continuation forced dummy to ruff with the heart queen, but now Rapée could cash the heart ace, discard his last spade on the club king, get back to his hand with the diamond ace (dropping South's king), and force out the master trump ten with his own nine. The defense could not prevent declarer from regaining the lead to draw the last trump.

If Avarelli had put up the king on the first diamond lead from dummy, Rapée would have had to go down. Dummy is pumped just the same with spade leads, but now South makes two trump tricks instead of one.

The swing was enormous, for in the other room Crawford opened the South hand with one notrump and played it there, down three, when Forquet elected not to reopen with the East cards.

The U.S. gained 320 total points, four IMP, instead of losing 400, five IMP—a charge of nine IMP for a slight slip in defense. Indeed, I concede that Avarelli has a legitimate howl coming to him on the grounds that a charge of nine IMP is excessive punishment for his mere misdemeanor.

I have a bidding charge against Avarelli for passing out Deal 96. He passed, fourth-hand, with:

♠ J 10 8 6 5　♡ 10 6 2　♢ K Q 7　♣ K Q

and lost three IMP, for his side was cold for three hearts.

On the very next board, Belladonna sinned. He held:

♠ K J 7 3 2   ♡ A 10 7 5 4   ◇ 6   ♣ 7 2

With neither side vulnerable, Belladonna passed as dealer, heard Silodor on his left open with one notrump (not the weak variety), heard Avarelli pass, and Rapée bid two clubs (Stayman). At this juncture, Belladonna came in with two hearts! He was doubled, ran to two spades, was doubled there, and went for a richly deserved 700, losing four IMP.

Belladonna cost Italy seven IMP on Deal 108:

West dealer; North-South vulnerable

NORTH
♠ 8 7 6 2
♡ K Q 10 7 4
◇ 3
♣ K J 9

WEST
♠ K 9 4
♡ 9 8 6
◇ 9 8 6 5 2
♣ 6 3

EAST
♠ Q J 3
♡ 5 3 2
◇ A K 10 7
♣ Q 7 2

SOUTH
♠ A 10 5
♡ A J
◇ Q J 4
♣ A 10 8 5 4

SOUTH	WEST	NORTH	EAST
Avarelli	*Rapée*	*Belladonna*	*Silodor*
—	Pass	Pass	1 ◇
Double	1 ♡ (!)	2 ◇	Pass
3 ♣	Pass	3 ♡	Pass
3 NT	Pass	4 ♣	Pass
4 ♡	Pass	Pass	Pass

Silodor led the diamond king and shifted to the spade queen. Belladonna ducked, took the spade continuation, and played a third round of spades himself, losing to West's king. Rapée returned a diamond, and declarer ruffed. Since the spades had split, the only problem was to guess the clubs. Belladonna cashed high cards, coming down to the king-jack-nine of clubs in his own hand, and ace-ten of clubs and the diamond queen in dummy. Silodor pitched the diamond ten and the club deuce, holding the diamond ace and the queen-seven of clubs, but Belladonna played him to be falsecarding and to have started out with:

♠ Q J 3   ♡ 5 3 2   ◇ A K 10 9 7   ♣ 7 2

Belladonna led to the club ace and finessed the club return, going down 200.

I charge Belladonna, not for going down, which is hard luck, but for disturbing the three-notrump contract. This is cold (Roth made three notrump in the other room without having to guess the clubs), and while four hearts is not a terrible contract, it is clearly inferior. At the same time, give Rapée a gold star for muddling the bidding.

Rapée also muddled up the opposing bidding on Deal 140:

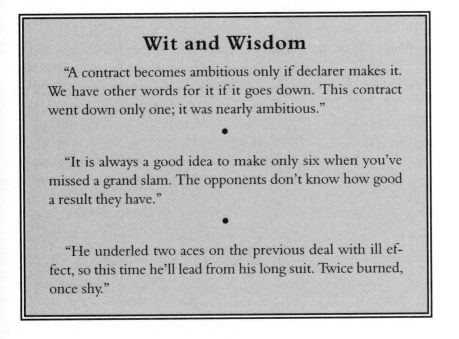

Wit and Wisdom

"A contract becomes ambitious only if declarer makes it. We have other words for it if it goes down. This contract went down only one; it was nearly ambitious."

•

"It is always a good idea to make only six when you've missed a grand slam. The opponents don't know how good a result they have."

•

"He underled two aces on the previous deal with ill effect, so this time he'll lead from his long suit. Twice burned, once shy."

West dealer; North-South vulnerable

NORTH
♠ A K 7 2
♡ Q 10 5
♢ J 8 2
♣ A K 5

WEST
♠ 10 9 5
♡ J 6
♢ K 10 7 6
♣ 10 9 8 3

EAST
♠ Q 8 6
♡ A 8
♢ A 5 3
♣ Q 7 6 4 2

SOUTH
♠ J 4 3
♡ K 9 7 4 3 2
♢ Q 9 4
♣ J

SOUTH	WEST	NORTH	EAST
Avarelli	*Rapée*	*Belladonna*	*Silodor*
—	1 ◇ (!)	Double	Redouble
2 ♣	Pass	2 ◇	Pass
2 ♡	Pass	Pass	Pass

In the other room, Crawford and Becker, unopposed, bid one notrump — three hearts — four hearts, and as both Souths easily won 10 tricks, the U.S. gained five IMP.

Who goofed? Well, I know a little about the Roman bidding system but not enough to answer this question. Avarelli's two-club bid meant that he was short in clubs, but was it a free bid, or would a pass have been a penalty pass of one diamond redoubled? If it was a constructive bid, Belladonna erred in passing two hearts; if it was a forced bid, then Avarelli should have jumped to three hearts on Round 2.

I simply split the charge between Avarelli and Belladonna, and gave Rapée a credit for his psychic. (The Americans psyched a good deal, with general effectiveness in that they kept the Italians out of normal contracts. However, quite a few of these very contracts went down at the other table when reached by the American pair, and so there was a net loss from the psychics. Unlucky, I say.)

System cost Belladonna and Avarelli a small loss on Deal 94, when they reached the wrong partial, but almost all of their infrequent bidding troubles seemed to arise after takeout doubles. Two examples have already been cited, a third arose on Deal 107, a fourth on Deal 68:

West dealer; both sides vulnerable

NORTH
♠ 6
♡ K Q 10 8 6 5
♢ K J
♣ A 10 7 6

WEST
♠ A 10 7 5
♡ 7 3 2
♢ A Q 10 8 4
♣ 3

EAST
♠ 9
♡ A 9
♢ 7 6 5 3
♣ K Q J 9 4 2

SOUTH
♠ K Q J 8 4 3 2
♡ J 4
♢ 9 2
♣ 8 5

SOUTH	WEST	NORTH	EAST
Avarelli	Rapée	Belladonna	Silodor
—	1 ♢	Double	Redouble
4 ♠	Double	(All Pass)	

On the singleton-club lead Avarelli had to go down two, for 500.

At the other table, Crawford was down one in three spades, so the U.S. gained 5 IMP.

Here again I'm not sure whom to charge. It seems to me that Avarelli made a good bid, but, for all I know, takeout doubles of one diamond without any spades may be *de rigueur* in the Roman Club System. I know that editor Moyse believes in this sort of thing, and I can only hope that he learns from this horrible (and somewhat unlucky) example. Incidentally, the story would have had a happy ending (for the Italians) if East had taken out to five clubs or five diamonds. It must have been an authoritative double.

This is just about all I have against this Italian pair. Oh, I don't like their contract on Deal 29 (they should have been in five diamonds, not three notrump), or on Deal 130 (after Rapée's psychic they got to six spades instead of six diamonds), but they made both contracts. This is a mighty small crime sheet for 92 boards. So let me finish off Avarelli-Belladonna with a good deal of theirs—Deal 101:

North dealer; North-South vulnerable

```
                    NORTH
                    ♠ A 8
                    ♡ A K 9 8 7
                    ◇ K 9 4
                    ♣ Q 7 5
    WEST                                EAST
    ♠ 9 7 5                             ♠ J 10 6 2
    ♡ J                                 ♡ Q 10 6 4 3
    ◇ A 5 3 2                           ◇ J 10
    ♣ A K 10 4 2                        ♣ 6 3
                    SOUTH
                    ♠ K Q 4 3
                    ♡ 5 2
                    ◇ Q 8 7 6
                    ♣ J 9 8
```

SOUTH	WEST	NORTH	EAST
Avarelli	*Rapée*	*Belladonna*	*Silodor*
—	—	1 ♡	Pass
1 ♠	Double	Pass	1 NT
Pass	Pass	Double	Pass
Pass	2 ♣	Pass	Pass
Double	Pass	Pass	Pass

Although Rapée was allowed to ruff a diamond in dummy, he was set 300.

At the other table, North-South played quietly at two hearts, down one, so Italy gained 400 points, five IMP. Personally, I consider Rapée's double of one spade correct (although Siniscalco passed at the other table). Avarelli and Belladonna created a swing by their adroitness in nailing the Americans for the set.

Forquet and Siniscalco were the anchor pair of the Italian team—they played 144 of the 164 boards. And they were an effective pair, though somewhat erratic. A few of their errors were shameful—e.g., on Deal 69 they played the hand in a cue-bid, on this auction:

SOUTH	WEST	NORTH	EAST
Crawford	Siniscalco	Becker	Forquet
—	—	1 ◊	1 ♠
Pass	2 ◊	Pass	Pass
Pass			

Siniscalco had the blank ace-queen of diamonds, and Forquet had the blank ten-nine. At the other table, Rapée and Silodor got to four spades and made five-odd. This was a total swing of 600 points, six IMP.

On Deal 67, Siniscalco played in three hearts with a trump suit of jack-seven-six-five opposite ace-queen-blank, when there was a laydown for five clubs. (Unfortunately, however, Silodor and Rapée landed in three notrump instead and went down one.)

And there was Forquet's incredible auction on Deal 58. He held:

♠ 8 6   ♡ Q J 4   ◊ A J 10 7   ♣ J 10 9 4

With both sides vulnerable, Siniscalco opened with one spade. Forquet responded one notrump. Siniscalco rebid two spades. Forquet rebid two notrump. Opener ran to three spades, and, so help me, Forquet persisted with three notrump and went for 500. I know a few players who bid like that, but they are all either occasional club players or dentists, not world champions.

The single most expensive error was Siniscalco's on Deal 18. He held:

Wit and Wisdom

"Today's players come from duplicate, which encourages bidding skills. Yesteryear's players came from rubber bridge, which encouraged playing skills and retrieving potential disasters."

♠ A Q 7 2   ♡ K   ♢ 10 6 5   ♣ 9 7 5 4 2

SOUTH	WEST	NORTH	EAST
Crawford	*Siniscalco*	*Becker*	*Forquet*
—	—	—	Pass
1 ♠	Pass	2 ♡	Pass
3 ♡	Pass	4 NT	Pass
5 ♢	Pass	6 ♡	Pass
Pass	Pass(!)		

Forquet did not lead a spade, and Becker made his vulnerable slam—a reasonable but only fair contract. Had Siniscalco doubled for a spade lead, Italy would have gained seven IMP instead of losing seven, a swing of 14 IMP, for game was bid and made at the other table.

Forquet recovered his reputation as an opening leader on Deal 40:

West dealer; neither side vulnerable

NORTH
♠ 7
♡ K Q J 8 4
♢ 9 6
♣ 10 9 7 3 2

WEST
♠ Q J 9
♡ 10 5
♢ K Q 2
♣ K Q 6 5 4

EAST
♠ 10 6 5 3 2
♡ 9
♢ A J 10 8 7 4 3
♣ —

SOUTH
♠ A K 8 4
♡ A 7 6 3 2
♢ 5
♣ A J 8

WEST	NORTH	EAST	SOUTH
Siniscalco	*Roth*	*Forquet*	*Stone*
1 NT	2 ♡	2 ♠	3 ♠
Pass	3 NT	5 ♢	5 ♡
Pass	Pass	Double	(All Pass)

Forquet led the diamond three! Siniscalco returned the club king, and Forquet ruffed. There was no way for Roth to avoid another club loser.

And this defense was necessary, too. At the other table D'Alelio was in five hearts also (on his own steam, not pushed there). Silodor led the ace of diamonds and shifted to a spade. D'Alelio pulled trumps, stripped out the spades and diamonds, and then endplayed West in clubs.

Siniscalco and Forquet were a little rocky in their slam bidding. They were very lucky on Deal 158:

East dealer
Neither side vulnerable

NORTH
♠ 10 7 5 4
♡ 10 6 4
◇ —
♣ J 10 7 5 4 2

WEST
♠ 9 8 6
♡ A 9 8 7 5
◇ 10 8
♣ Q 8 6

EAST
♠ A
♡ K Q 3
◇ A K Q 9 4 3 2
♣ K 3

SOUTH
♠ K Q J 3 2
♡ J 2
◇ J 7 6 5
♣ A 9

SOUTH	WEST	NORTH	EAST
Rapée	Forquet	Silodor	Siniscalco
—	—	—	1 ♣*
1 ♠	2 ♣	3 ♠	3 NT
Pass	Pass	Pass	

*big club

Siniscalco's three notrump is surely an error, because Forquet's two-club bid shows an ace. But it was a fortunate error, for there were nine tricks at notrump, whereas the four-zero diamond split (with the length in the wrong hand to boot) beats any slam. Crawford and Becker bid up to six hearts on the East-West cards—not quite as good a slam as six diamonds, but one that has a chance even as the cards lie. But Chiaradia opened a spade, and Becker had to play well to go down only one.

Forquet and Siniscalco lost quite a few IMP overbidding to dubious game contracts. Deals 34 and 152 are examples. Another is Deal 120:

West dealer; neither side vulnerable

```
                        NORTH
                        ♠ 7 5 3
                        ♡ Q
                        ◇ Q 8 7 5 4
                        ♣ 10 6 5 2
WEST                                        EAST
♠ 10 4 2                                    ♠ A J 9 8
♡ A 8 6 5                                   ♡ K 10 4 2
◇ J 3                                       ◇ A K 6 2
♣ Q 7 4 3                                   ♣ 9
                        SOUTH
                        ♠ K Q 6
                        ♡ J 9 7 3
                        ◇ 10 9
                        ♣ A K J 8
```

Siniscalco, East, landed at a four-heart contract, doubled by Becker, South.

Now, I don't say that four hearts is a terrible spot, but it needs a few things to be right, and then it still has handling charges. But Siniscalco actually could have made his contract!

Becker, South, led the club king and shifted to the king of spades. Siniscalco won and led to the heart ace. So he had to lose two hearts, a spade, and a club, for down one.

If Siniscalco, on winning with the spade ace, had led a spade right back, an interesting position would have developed. Becker would probably take this spade and continue the suit (or shift to the diamond ten, which makes no difference). Declarer wins the third spade, cashes the two top diamonds and leads a diamond. South must pitch a club; dummy ruffs and then leads a club for declarer to ruff.

This leaves:

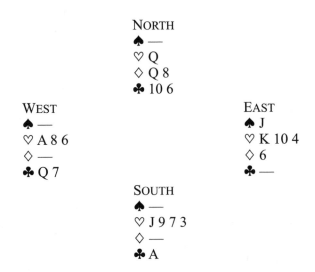

NORTH
♠ —
♡ Q
♦ Q 8
♣ 10 6

WEST
♠ —
♡ A 8 6
♦ —
♣ Q 7

EAST
♠ J
♡ K 10 4
♦ 6
♣ —

SOUTH
♠ —
♡ J 9 7 3
♦ —
♣ A

East leads his last diamond, and South's goose is cooked. If he throws off the club ace, dummy ruffs, cashes the heart ace and leads the club queen, East throwing his spade. South must ruff, and he must then lead from the jack-nine of trumps up to declarer's king-ten. If South ruffs the lead of the diamond six with the heart nine, dummy overruffs with the ace. The trump six is then led to the king, and declarer leads the spade jack. The eight of trumps on the table brings home the contract. (To anticipate: Yes, the contract could have been beaten by a different early shift, but I am not inclined to criticize Becker's defense.)

At the other table the auction was:

SOUTH	WEST	NORTH	EAST
Avarelli	*Stone*	*Belladonna*	*Roth*
—	Pass	Pass	1 ♦
Double	Pass	1 ♡*	Pass
1 ♠	Pass	2 ♣	(All Pass)

*short suit

The two-club contract was set one (though Belladonna might conceivably have made it if he hadn't touched trumps), and so the U.S. picked up 150, three IMP, on the board. I must say, however, that I would 100 times rather play the East-West cards at four hearts, for better or worse, than timidly sell out to two clubs.

Both teams missed a good slam in clubs on Deal 112:

WEST	EAST
♠ A 6	♠ J 10 9
♡ A Q 7 6 3 2	♡ 4
◊ A 7 3	◊ Q 10 8
♣ Q 7	♣ A K J 10 6 3

WEST	EAST
Rapée	*Silodor*
1 ♡	2 ♣
3 ♡	3 NT
Pass	

WEST	EAST
Siniscalco	*Forquet*
1 ♡	2 ♣
2 ♡	3 ♣
3 NT	Pass

I blame Rapée and Siniscalco. The West hand is so powerful for a club slam—club queen, all other controls, and the easily establishable six-card suit—that they should have been sniffing around for a grand.

Pretty bad errors of evaluation by Forquet cost games on Deals 162 and 150, and the Neapolitans lost other games on Deals 78 and 50, it seems to me, by violations of their own system. Forquet opened a solid 18-point hand with one heart instead of one club (on Deal 78); and Siniscalco opened with two clubs (on Deal 50) when he might well have bid one diamond. This led Forquet to try for five clubs instead of three notrump. Finally, Forquet and Siniscalco clearly misdefended on Deals 13 and 118, although both contracts were defeated. They made up for this, however, with a pretty defense on Deal 14: [*See next page.*]

Forquet led a high club and shifted to his singleton diamond. Stone won in dummy and led the heart ten, which was allowed to hold. Now he played a club from dummy, and Siniscalco did not rise with his queen or duck—he played the club *ten*. When this held, he gave Forquet a diamond ruff, was put back in by the marked underlead in clubs to his queen, and gave Forquet another ruff to set the contract. Nicely done.

Stone had made the defense easier than was necessary. Instead of playing a club from dummy he should ruff a spade and play the heart king. To beat the contract, Forquet must lead the club *jack* to be over-taken by the queen, and after ruffing a diamond must underlead again.

NORTH
♠ —
♡ K Q J 7 6 5 4
♢ Q 9 8
♣ 9 6 2

WEST
♠ A K J 6 3
♡ —
♢ 6 4 3 2
♣ Q 10 8 3

EAST
♠ 10 5 2
♡ A 9 8 3 2
♢ 5
♣ A K J 5

SOUTH
♠ Q 9 8 7 4
♡ 10
♢ A K J 10 7
♣ 7 4

SOUTH	WEST	NORTH	EAST
Roth	*Siniscalco*	*Stone*	*Forquet*
—	—	—	1 ♡
1 ♠	Double	2 ♡	Double
Pass	Pass	Pass	

It was ungenerous of Stone not to give Forquet the opportunity for such brilliance.

I can start my discussion of Chiaradia and D'Alelio with this same deal, No. 14, for at the other table the auction went:

SOUTH	WEST	NORTH	EAST
D'Alelio	*Becker*	*Chiaradia*	*Crawford*
—	—	—	1 ♡
1 ♠	Double	2 ♡	Double
3 ♢	Double	(All Pass)	

Becker led a trump, and D'Alelio was lucky to make five trump tricks, a spade ruff and one other trick, down 300, a loss of three IMP.

In my view, the three-diamond bid is a clear violation of partnership. North has heard the opening heart bid by East, and he knows that his run-out to two hearts shuts out possible contracts of two clubs or two diamonds; he could bid one notrump if he so chose. D'Alelio should pass two hearts doubled even with a void; his singleton ten is a bonanza.

I have some costly errors in play charged to D'Alelio. He should have picked up a swing by making his game contract on Deal 7, which he was playing, luckily, from the right side; and he misdefended on Deal 38:

East dealer; East-West vulnerable

NORTH
♠ K J 5 3
♡ Q 8 2
♢ A 6
♣ Q 10 7 5

WEST
♠ A 10 8 7 2
♡ A 10 3
♢ —
♣ A K 6 3 2

EAST
♠ Q 9 4
♡ J 6 5 4
♢ J 10 9 7 5 2
♣ —

SOUTH
♠ 6
♡ K 9 7
♢ K Q 8 4 3
♣ J 9 8 4

SOUTH *Chiaradia*	WEST *Crawford*	NORTH *D'Alelio*	EAST *Silodor*
—	—	—	Pass
Pass	1 ♠	Pass	2 ♠
Pass	3 ♡	Pass	4 ♡
Pass	4 ♠	(All Pass)	

D'Alelio, North, opened a low club, ruffed in dummy. A low heart was passed to D'Alelio's queen. Now he laid down the diamond ace. Crawford ruffed and was home. He cashed the two top clubs, pitching hearts from dummy, then cashed the heart ace and ruffed a heart. Declarer crossruffed a diamond and a club. Now North was reduced to trumps, while declarer had ace-ten-eight of trumps and the long club. So Crawford had to make two more trump tricks, and his contract, on the cold end-play.

If D'Alelio shifts to a trump when he gets in with the heart queen—and, looking at that dummy, he most certainly should—declarer is one trick short, no matter how he plays. Roth, at a comparable point in the defense, shifted to the king of trumps, a pretty play, but (it seems to me) pointless in view of his trump spots. Forquet-Siniscalco stopped at two spades and were held to three. Had D'Alelio beaten Crawford, Italy would have gained four IMP; as it was, Italy lost five.

Other charges against D'Alelio include his failure to double on Deal 89. He sat North with:

♠ 6 2   ♡ A J 10 7 5 2   ◇ —   ♣ A 8 5 4 2

With only East-West vulnerable, the bidding went:

SOUTH	WEST	NORTH	EAST
Chiaradia	*Stone*	*D'Alelio*	*Roth*
—	—	1 ♡	Double
3 ◇	4 ♠	(All Pass)	

Chiaradia had a diamond bust, with eight to the jack-ten and the singleton king of clubs, without a singleton heart, but the contract was still beaten two tricks. On virtually the same auction, Silodor did double on the North hand in the other room and collected a 500-point penalty, for a gain of four IMP.

There was also D'Alelio's failure to enter the auction on Deal 73. With only the opposition vulnerable, he dealt and passed with:

♠ K 10 9 5 4   ♡ 10 7 4 3   ◇ A   ♣ Q 8 6

The bidding went:

SOUTH	WEST	NORTH	EAST
Siniscalco	*Stone*	*D'Alelio*	*Roth*
—	—	Pass	1 ♣
Pass	1 ◇	Pass	1 ♡
Pass	1 NT	(All Pass)	

As a result of D'Alelio's continued passing, the U.S. made one notrump in this room, and, since Becker made two spades on the North hand in the other room, we gained three IMP.

Chiaradia and D'Alelio had a partnership mix-up over a strong jump-overcall on Deal 51; and they had a lot of trouble with slams. On Deal 88, they held:

NORTH
♠ A K 9 7 5
♡ A Q 7 5 2
◇ Q 7
♣ A

SOUTH
♠ Q 10 8 3
♡ 8 3
◇ K 10 9 8 6 2
♣ 4

With neither side vulnerable, the bidding went:

SOUTH	WEST	NORTH	EAST
Chiaradia	*Stone*	*D'Alelio*	*Roth*
—	1 ♡	Double	4 ♣
4 ◇	5 ♣	5 ♠	(All Pass)

Roth-Stone made things tough (Stone had an honest bid, but Roth had only eight clubs to the jack-ten, a singleton heart, and the doubleton jack of diamonds), but (1) Chiaradia might have bid four spades instead of four diamonds, and (2) D'Alelio might have bid six clubs instead of five spades, and (3) Chiaradia might have bid the slam anyway, as the auction went.

There was no loss to Italy, however, because at the other table Becker (South) passed over the same four-club call by East, and bid only four spades when Silodor again doubled in his turn.

These same two pairs, D'Alelio-Chiaradia and Becker-Silodor, missed the "cold" small slam in diamonds on Deal 90, but here they were both lucky—the trumps broke five-zero.

Deal 147 was D'Alelio's low point in slam bidding: he reached six diamonds, down five. However, in a way, Deal 160 was worse:

West dealer
East-West vulnerable

NORTH
♠ A K 10 9
♡ A 10 9 3
◇ J 4
♣ K Q 4

WEST
♠ Q 7 3 2
♡ K J
◇ 6 5
♣ J 10 7 3 2

EAST
♠ 6 5 4
♡ 6
◇ K Q 8 7
♣ A 9 8 6 5

SOUTH
♠ J 8
♡ Q 8 7 5 4 2
◇ A 10 9 3 2
♣ —

SOUTH D'Alelio	WEST Becker	NORTH Chiaradia	EAST Crawford
—	Pass	1 ♣	Pass
1 ♡	Pass	3 ♡	Pass
4 ◇	Pass	4 ♠	Pass
4 NT	Pass	5 ♡	Pass
6 ♡	Pass	Pass	Pass

The six-heart contract is bad on the particular cards but is awfully hard to stay out of. Chiaradia might not have bid four spades after his not-very-strong three-heart jump, but his hand had a lot of body. The really terrible feature was that D'Alelio could have made the contract and muffed it.

Becker led the *deuce* of clubs, and D'Alelio went wrong then and there: he put up the club queen from dummy. The ace covered; declarer ruffed and led a trump to the ace. When the king failed to drop, he conceded down one, for he had to lose a trump and a diamond.

But did D'Alelio have to lose the diamond? With the spade queen onside, he had two pitches. If he had ducked the club-deuce opening in dummy, it was 100 to 0 that Crawford would have gone up with the ace and given him two discards on clubs. The point is that one pitch on the

89

(*Repeated for convenience*)

NORTH
♠ A K 10 9
♡ A 10 9 3
◇ J 4
♣ K Q 4

WEST
♠ Q 7 3 2
♡ K J
◇ 6 5
♣ J 10 7 3 2

EAST
♠ 6 5 4
♡ 6
◇ K Q 8 7
♣ A 9 8 6 5

SOUTH
♠ J 8
♡ Q 8 7 5 4 2
◇ A 10 9 3 2
♣ —

clubs is worthless, and that two might be vital; so the club four must be the right play at Trick 1. Becker's deceptive lead (not the usual fourth highest) would have insured the success of this maneuver.

Here again there was no swing, for Rapée was in the same contract, down one also. Forquet, West, opened a diamond. Rapée won with the ace, led to the heart ace, and then conceded down one.

Perhaps Siniscalco would have ducked if the club four had been led from dummy—I think he should duck. But he didn't get the chance to go wrong. Apparently, neither D'Alelio nor Rapée considered the possibility of getting rid of four diamonds.

Chiaradia has a few serious charges on his own. His pass to two diamonds on Deal 139 (see page 94), and his fantastic phantom save on Deal 86 (see page 110) will be discussed in the section on the Americans, for these actions were partially duplicated at the other table.

Strangely, so was Chiaradia's play of Deal 87 (my last charge against the Italians): [*See next page.*]

Stone opened the spade jack and continued with the ten when he was allowed to hold the first trick. Chiaradia won with the spade ace and cashed the ace and king of diamonds, discarding a club. He then ruffed a diamond, led to the club ace, and ruffed a club, but he still had

South dealer; both sides vulnerable

```
                       NORTH
                       ♠ A 9 8
                       ♡ 5
                       ◇ A K 9 8
                       ♣ A Q 9 8 3
        WEST                            EAST
        ♠ J 10                          ♠ K Q 5 3
        ♡ J 10 7 4                      ♡ A 2
        ◇ Q J 6 5                       ◇ 10 7 4 2
        ♣ K 10 4                        ♣ J 7 5
                       SOUTH
                       ♠ 7 6 4 2
                       ♡ K Q 9 8 6 3
                       ◇ 3
                       ♣ 6 2
```

SOUTH	WEST	NORTH	EAST
Chiaradia	*Stone*	*D'Alelio*	*Roth*
Pass	Pass	1 ♣	Pass
1 ♡	Pass	2 ◇	Pass
2 ♡	Pass	2 NT	Pass
3 ♡	Pass	Pass	Pass

to lose two spades and two hearts, for down one. (He was lucky not to lose three hearts.) Becker, in the same contract on a similar auction (Silodor bid one diamond and then clubs, not the reverse), also ducked the spade-jack opening lead and went up with the ace on the continuation, but he then led the singleton trump from dummy, won with the king, and continued with a low trump, driving out East's ace. It was a nice guess, but not tremendously effective. East cashed his two high spades and West still had a trump trick to defeat the contract.

Perhaps the reader will understand these lines of play—I don't. Actually, ten tricks can be made by routine play. Win the second spade, cash the top diamonds, pitching a spade, and ruff a diamond. Take the club finesse and ruff another diamond. Cash the second club trick, ruff a club, and exit with South's last spade. West, down to trumps, must ruff and lead a trump, so South makes both of his high trumps. Even if you don't want to do all this, any variation brings in nine tricks—and four IMP.

The Americans

My final tabulation of the performance of the individual Americans confirmed my preconceptions in some respects but startled me in others.

	Charges	*Boards*	*Charges per Board*
Rapée	15	92	.163
Becker	25	124	.202
Stone	19	92	.207
Roth	25	92	.272
Silodor	41	132	.311
Crawford	55	124	.444

I had rather expected Rapée to finish on top; in previous World Championship records I have studied he has seemed to me to have turned in the most consistently good performances. He made errors in Como, of course—even Reese in New York did not play flawlessly throughout the long match—but Rapée, here as ever, produced his best when it counted most.

Let me start his short crime list with his much-criticized action on Deal 60. He held:

♠ Q ♡ — ◇ 9 7 6 5 4 2 ♣ Q J 9 8 7 5

Not vulnerable vs. vulnerable, he opened with three clubs. This resulted, it may be recalled, in a five-club sacrifice, down 700, when five diamonds might well have been made.

I charged Rapée with a substantial loss, but I have sympathy for his bid. The alternative is to pass (planning on backing in later with an unusual notrump overcall), and it seems to me that, first-hand in this vulnerability situation, the terribly weak freak holding calls for some sort of drastic preemptive action.

Rapée played a very active style in Como; he was always on the move, trying to create favorable swings; yet this was the only one of his "operations" that ended in American disaster. He psyched repeatedly and was never punished. On Deal 130, he jostled the Italians into a six-spade contract that needed a three-three trump split—they got it—while the Americans played in a cold six-diamond spot after an unimpeded auction; and on Deals 108 and 140, previously discussed, his psychics gained heavily. Moreover, the unsettling effect on opponents should not be discounted.

I charged Rapée for the rather ludicrous result on Deal 139:

South dealer
Neither side vulnerable

```
                        NORTH
                        ♠ K 9 3
                        ♡ J 8 6
                        ◇ A J 8 4 2
                        ♣ K 6
        WEST                            EAST
        ♠ Q 10 8 7 6 4                  ♠ 2
        ♡ A 4 3 2                       ♡ K Q 5
        ◇ 10 9 6                        ◇ K Q 7
        ♣ —                             ♣ Q 8 5 4 3 2
                        SOUTH
                        ♠ A J 5
                        ♡ 10 9 7
                        ◇ 5 3
                        ♣ A J 10 9 7
```

SOUTH	WEST	NORTH	EAST
Avarelli	*Rapée*	*Belladonna*	*Silodor*
Pass	Pass	1 ◇	2 ♣
Double	2 ◇	(All Pass)	

Surely, if two clubs had not been doubled, Rapée would have bid two spades with the expectation of making it. (Actually, an overtrick is available.) I don't think he should take such a dim view of his prospects because of the double. And, if he was afraid of a disaster at spades, why not run to two hearts first? I imagine he intended two diamonds as takeout for the majors, but I think that Silodor was right to play it to be a suit, at least until the bid got doubled. (These Italian partners frequently

(*Repeated for convenience*)

```
                        NORTH
                        ♠ K 9 3
                        ♡ J 8 6
                        ◇ A J 8 4 2
                        ♣ K 6
WEST                                        EAST
♠ Q 10 8 7 6 4                              ♠ 2
♡ A 4 3 2                                    ♡ K Q 5
◇ 10 9 6                                     ◇ K Q 7
♣ —                                          ♣ Q 8 5 4 3 2
                        SOUTH
                        ♠ A J 5
                        ♡ 10 9 7
                        ◇ 5 3
                        ♣ A J 10 9 7
```

bid short diamond suits, for their one-club opening is artificial, and their one-notrump opening is very strong.)

However, the U.S. gained one IMP on the deal, for at the other table this was the auction:

SOUTH	WEST	NORTH	EAST
Becker	*Chiaradia*	*Crawford*	*D'Alelio*
Pass	Pass	1 ◇	2 ♣
Double	Redouble	Pass	2 ◇
Pass	Pass	Pass	

Seemingly, East-West are inextricably trapped into a diamond contract by North's diabolical one-diamond opening. The Americans cleverly played with West as declarer and didn't get a diamond lead away from the ace-jack fifth, while the Italians foolishly played the hand from the East position, and South's trump lead beat them an extra trick.

On Deal 21, Rapée gave a very heavy raise from one spade to two spades on:

♠ J 6 4 3   ♡ Q 10 3   ◇ K 2   ♣ K 10 9 7

and missed a good game contract that the Italians bid. Luckily for the U.S., however, all the missing key-cards were offside, and we actually gained three IMP.

To counterbalance this there was Deal 67. Here, Rapée gave a strange raise from one club to two clubs and got to a fair three-notrump contract, down one, whereas the Italians played a ridiculous partial and gained four IMP. (More about this deal later.)

Rapée's bidding on Deal 112 (page 84) and his play of Deal 160 (page 90) have been mentioned; the final exhibit for the prosecution in his case is Deal 131:

South dealer; East-West vulnerable

NORTH
♠ J 9 7
♡ A 9 5 4
◇ A 8 7 5 4
♣ 6

WEST
♠ K 10 4 2
♡ K Q 8
◇ 2
♣ J 10 9 8 7

EAST
♠ —
♡ J 7 6 3
◇ K Q J 3
♣ A Q 5 4 2

SOUTH
♠ A Q 8 6 5 3
♡ 10 2
◇ 10 9 6
♣ K 3

SOUTH	WEST	NORTH	EAST
Avarelli	*Rapée*	*Belladonna*	*Silodor*
Pass	Pass	1 ◇	Pass
1 ♠	Pass	Pass	Double
2 ♠	Double	(All Pass)	

I don't much like the two-spade double, but it's the defense that I charge against Rapée. He led his singleton diamond; dummy won with the ace and played a club. Silodor rose with the ace, cashed two high diamonds (West discarding clubs), and shifted to a low heart. Dummy took the queen with the ace, and declarer finessed the queen of spades, losing to West's king. Rapée now cashed the heart king (his side's fifth trick), leaving this end-position:

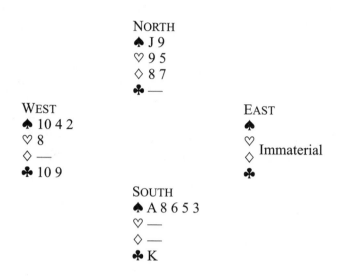

NORTH
♠ J 9
♡ 9 5
◇ 8 7
♣ —

WEST
♠ 10 4 2
♡ 8
◇ —
♣ 10 9

EAST
♠
♡
◇ Immaterial
♣

SOUTH
♠ A 8 6 5 3
♡ —
◇ —
♣ K

"Declarer easily took the remainder of the tricks," says the official record. Well, I don't know exactly what happened, but Rapée must have led a club or (more likely) a trump, because if he had led the eight of hearts he would have beaten the contract. Declarer could finesse the spade nine and cash the jack, but he could not then get out of dummy without letting Rapée make his trump ten.

At the other table, Becker opened the South hand with a weak two-bid in spades, and Crawford raised him to four spades. East-West did not get into the auction. On the lead of the club jack, the contract could be beaten by only two tricks (no loss against par, as four clubs is cold the other way, but the U.S. lost six IMP).

Incidentally, weak two-bids were almost a total loss for the Americans throughout this (as throughout every other world championship) match. Only one of them gained, and the net average was two IMP lost for each weak two-bid used.

I'll start my dossier on Crawford with one of these losses, on Deal No. 25: [*See next page.*]

Forquet, East, cashed two top spades and then led the ten of spades for partner to trump. Siniscalco did not give Forquet the club ruff he was angling for, but Becker had to lose a club anyway, for down 300. Since four spades was doubled and set 200 at the other table, the U.S. lost 500 points—six IMP.

North dealer; East-West vulnerable

NORTH
♠ 9 6 4
♡ K Q 8 4 3
◇ 8
♣ A 8 6 4

WEST
♠ Q
♡ 10 7 6 2
◇ J 7 5
♣ Q J 10 9 3

EAST
♠ A K J 10 8 5
♡ J
◇ Q 10 6 4 3 2
♣ —

SOUTH
♠ 7 3 2
♡ A 9 5
◇ A K 9
♣ K 7 5 2

SOUTH	WEST	NORTH	EAST
Crawford	*Siniscalco*	*Becker*	*Forquet*
—	—	2 ♡	4 ♠
5 ♡	Double	(All Pass)	

Now, I don't admire Becker's two-heart opening, but I have charged the whole loss to Crawford. The vagueness of the requirements for a weak two-bid and the liberties taken within even these hazy limits cause many a loss. But why here? It seems to me that Crawford should expect to beat four spades, perhaps a lot; and just as clearly he should expect five hearts to go down, no matter what sort of two-heart bid partner has. A decision like that five-heart bid can be justified only by success, and this one wasn't so justified.

In general, Crawford's performance, especially in the first half of the match, was astonishing. Some of his errors were of the sort you just don't expect from one of the world's greatest players. On Deal No. 23, he handed Italy a vulnerable game, going out of his way to make a strange, even inexplicable, defensive play. On Deal 60 (the one in which Rapée opened three clubs with six-six in the minors), Crawford, at the other table, vulnerable against non-vulnerable, held:

♠ J 10 9 6 5 2   ♡ A K Q 8 2   ◇ K   ♣ 6

The bidding was opened two diamonds (weak: a club-diamond two-suiter) at his left; pass from partner, two notrump at his right. He overcalled three *hearts*, and wound up in four hearts doubled, down one—cold for four and likely five spades.

And on Deal 64, nonvulnerable against vulnerable, he held:

♠ K 6   ♡ Q 4 2   ◇ K 7 6 4 3 2   ♣ J 7

One club (artificial, strong) was opened at his left; pass from partner; two clubs (artificial, strong) at his right. "Three diamonds," bid Crawford, undaunted by the minimum of 17 points at his left, and an ace and a king or three kings at his right. Down 1300. It's hard to believe.

However, most of Crawford's charges are far more reasonable (although, in my opinion, mistaken) decisions. On Deal 53, vulnerable against nonvulnerable, he held:

♠ J 10 8 6   ♡ K 6   ◇ Q J   ♣ A Q 9 6 5

His partner passed; one heart was opened at his right; and he chose to pass. As a result, the Italians played three hearts and made it, with three spades cold the other way. At the other table, the U.S. was forced to four hearts, down one.

Similarly, on Deal 161, none vulnerable, Crawford held:

♠ K Q J 10 4   ♡ A 7 6   ◇ 7 2   ♣ A 6 4

One spade was opened at his right, and he passed. One notrump at his left; pass from partner. Two hearts at his right, and Crawford passed again. Two hearts was the final contract, down 100. At the other table, the Italians bid three notrump and made four with the cards held by Crawford and partner.

Crawford passed first hand on Deal 113, holding:

♠ J 10 8   ♡ K Q 8 4   ◇ 10   ♣ K Q J 9 8

and when Becker opened one diamond, he responded two clubs. This was passed out, making five. The Italians opened his hand, then bid and made three notrump.

Likewise, he passed first hand on Deal 145 with:

♠ 8 2   ♡ 10 9 3   ◇ A 8 6 4 2   ♣ A Q 4

Becker opened one spade; Crawford responded two diamonds; Becker rebid two spades; and Crawford passed! A cold game was missed (but not by the Italians), for Becker's hand was:

♠ A K J 10 9 4 3   ♡ Q 7   ◇ 7   ♣ J 10 3

I have more sympathy for Crawford and Becker on Deal 66:

WEST	EAST
♠ A K 8	♠ Q 9 7 4
♡ 8 4 3	♡ 7 6 5 2
◇ A K 10 6	◇ Q J
♣ K J 10	♣ A 6 5

Crawford	*Becker*
1 ◇	1 ♠
2 ♣	3 ♣
4 ♠	Pass

The Italians opened one notrump and arrived briskly at three notrump, making five. Four spades was down two. A rather silly result, but neither American did anything terrible. Crawford's hand is top-heavy for a one-notrump opening (Avarelli-Belladonna play theirs as 17-20 points). I would respond one heart with Becker's hand, but one spade is surely reasonable. Crawford's rebid is a problem—perhaps a two-spade underbid or a three-spade overbid would be better, but two clubs looks all right. And by now the Americans were on the hook, for no one wanted to bid notrump without a heart stopper. Oh, Becker might bid two diamonds, not three clubs; Crawford might bid three, not four, spades. But I'm not sure it would help. A bad hand for Old Science.

On Deal 29, this pair, having a sort of heart stopper this time, decided to play notrump.

North dealer; both sides vulnerable

```
                        NORTH
                        ♠ A 5
                        ♡ Q 10 9
                        ◊ A Q J 7 6 5
                        ♣ 10 4
      WEST                              EAST
      ♠ Q J 7 6                        ♠ 10 9 8 3
      ♡ K J 6 4 2                      ♡ A 7 5
      ◊ 10 4                           ◊ 8
      ♣ Q 5                            ♣ J 9 6 3 2
                        SOUTH
                        ♠ K 4 2
                        ♡ 8 3
                        ◊ K 9 3 2
                        ♣ A K 8 7
```

SOUTH	WEST	NORTH	EAST
Crawford	*Siniscalco*	*Becker*	*Forquet*
—	—	1 ◊	Pass
2 ♣	Pass	2 ◊	Pass
2 ♠	Pass	2 NT	Pass
3 NT	Pass	Pass	Pass

Forquet, East, led the five of hearts; Siniscalco won with his king and returned a low heart. Becker had to guess whether to put in his nine or his queen, and he went wrong—he chose the queen, and the Italians cashed five heart tricks, for down one.

Actually, I think Becker's play is correct. If the hearts are four-four, or if East has five, Becker's play makes relatively little difference; only if the lead was from three is it crucial. And a lead from three to a jack seems a little more attractive than from three to an ace. [In contrast, if you assume a heart would always be led, it is twice as likely that the opening leader's honor is not the jack than that it is.—*Editor*]

The Italians also played in three notrump, but South, with two low hearts, was declarer. With a low heart lead, declarer has no option—he must put in the nine. So Italy picked up a lucky nine IMP by playing from the "wrong" side.

But it wasn't all luck; five diamonds is on ice, and at IMP scoring there is little excuse for being in notrump. Surely Crawford should have contrived to show his diamond fit.

Crawford and Becker missed a good slam on Deal 144:

WEST	EAST
♠ A 2	♠ K Q J 9
♡ 4 2	♡ A Q 9
◇ A K 9 6	◇ Q 8 4 2
♣ Q J 6 5 2	♣ K 4

WEST	EAST
Crawford	*Becker*
1 ◇	2 ♠
3 ♣	3 NT
Pass	

I like Becker's two-spade response, but not his three-notrump rebid. (Maybe this pair just doesn't believe in diamonds.) Still, I think that Crawford should certainly bid again over three notrump. The Italians did reach six diamonds—but the clubs were five-one, and a club and a ruff beat the slam!

Crawford was lucky on Deal 122 also, when he failed to jump-shift over partner's one-club opening with:

♠ A 3   ♡ A K J 6 5 3   ◇ K 10 7   ♣ 9 8

He bid only one heart, with the usual result: trying to make up for the underbid, he later got to five hearts. He just managed to scramble home, due to a fortunate lie of cards.

My last charge against Crawford is on one of the most publicized deals of the match. You may recall this deal as the one in which Siniscalco switched into an ace-queen tenace in dummy, found partner void, and beat a game contract. In the welter of speculation as to how Siniscalco managed to find the shift, it has hardly been noted that, on the auction at his table, Crawford should easily have made the winning play, but didn't.

B. Jay Becker's record at Como I would call good, but not up to his usual standard. I have only one charge against his dummy play: Deal 87, analyzed earlier (page 91); none against his defense; but quite a few against his bidding. One minor charge was on Deal 2, when he held, nonvulnerable vs. vulnerable:

$$ \spadesuit\ — \qquad \heartsuit\ A\,10\,6\,2 \qquad \diamondsuit\ 9\,8\,3 \qquad \clubsuit\ Q\,8\,6\,5\,4\,2 $$

One spade was opened to his right, and Becker passed. As a result, the Italians bid and made their vulnerable game without opposition, although a five-level save was available in hearts or clubs. It is hard to find the sacrifice even if you bid, but surely it is wrong to stay out of the auction on this vulnerability.

I think Becker was again a little timid on Deal 88. With no one vulnerable, he held:

$$ \spadesuit\ Q\,10\,8\,3 \qquad \heartsuit\ 8\,3 \qquad \diamondsuit\ K\,10\,9\,8\,6\,2 \qquad \clubsuit\ 4 $$

One heart was opened to his left, Silodor doubled, four clubs was preempted to his right. And Becker passed. When Silodor reopened by doubling again, Becker made the right decision to bid spades, not diamonds, but a good slam was missed.

However, Becker bid too much on my next two deals. On Deal 118 he held, nonvulnerable vs. vulnerable:

$$ \spadesuit\ 7\,6 \qquad \heartsuit\ A\,6\,3 \qquad \diamondsuit\ A\,K\,7 \qquad \clubsuit\ K\,J\,6\,4\,3 $$

He opened one club, and there was a one-spade overcall at his left, passed back to him. Becker doubled. Pass to his left; one notrump from Crawford; two spades to his right. And now Becker bid two notrump, a dangerous overbid, in my view. Crawford quite properly carried on to three notrump with his six points, and I do not understand (even from the description in the official record) how declarer was allowed to go down only one.

And on Deal 155, Becker overbid to a terrible slam contract, which went down two.

WEST	EAST
♠ A 9 6 2	♠ 5 3
♡ Q J 8 5 4	♡ K 9 6
◇ K 9	◇ A Q J 10 2
♣ K 9	♣ A J 10

WEST	EAST
Becker	*Crawford*
1 ♡	2 ◇
2 ♡	3 ♣
3 ♠	4 ♡
5 ♡	6 ♡
Pass	

That five-heart bid does seem unduly optimistic. However, it should be noted that this was late in the match, with the sands running out, and so Mr. B. may have been swinging.

I suppose I should give him a credit for producing a favorable swing on Deal 147. First hand, nonvulnerable vs. vulnerable, he opened three clubs on:

♠ —   ♡ 7 5 2   ◇ A 9 4 2   ♣ Q J 10 9 8 7

Chiaradia, West, doubled; Crawford bid four clubs, and D'Alelio jumped to five diamonds. Becker passed, Chiaradia bid five hearts, Crawford passed, and D'Alelio went on to six diamonds. Why Mr. Becker didn't double, I'll never know, but he passed and so did everyone else—down five. Now, at IMP scoring the difference between 500 and 1400 is relatively slight—only three IMP—but that final pass outrages me anyway. So I'll be hanged if I'll hand out a credit for bidding like that.

On Deal 115, Becker lost three IMP by opening with one club instead

103

of one diamond on:

♠ 9 3   ♡ 7 5   ◇ A J 7 3   ♣ A K 10 5 4

Crawford responded one heart, and Becker had to rebid two clubs. Down one, with two diamonds cold (and bid by the Italians).

No record of Becker's performance would be complete without Deal 6. He held:

♠ J 10 9 8 7 5 4   ♡ J 10 6   ◇ A 2   ♣ A

Crawford opened one club; Becker responded one spade. Crawford raised to two spades, and now Becker control-bid three hearts! *Hearts,* that is. Picked up an IMP, too, by stopping the lead. Nowadays, Mr. B. is seen playing all sorts of modern gadgets, like Stayman, and here he is psyching! Don't tell me about old dogs.

Silodor, on his record in Nationals over the past few years, is very likely the finest player in the U.S. And he was the key man on the team: he had three partners and played more boards than any of the others. So it was disappointing and costly that he was not at the top of his usually magnificent game.

I just don't understand his bidding of Deal 61. With both sides vulnerable, he held:

♠ K Q 9 8   ♡ Q 7 6 5   ◇ 9 8   ♣ K Q 10

Dealer passed at his right; Silodor passed also (I would open); third hand passed, and Rapée opened one club. Dealer bid one heart, and Silodor, perhaps suspecting a skinny "Italian overcall," doubled. LHO ran out to two diamonds, passed back to Silodor, who now bid two spades. LHO persisted with three diamonds, and Rapée raised to three spades. Believe it or not, Silodor passed! I checked up on the record, and it's true. As you might imagine, game was bid and made at the other table, so we lost five IMP.

It seems to me that Silodor's action on Deal 129 was as clear an underbid, if less spectacular. With no one vulnerable he held:

♠ A 3   ♡ Q 10 4 3   ◇ K 10 5 3 2   ♣ J 2

Dealer at his right opened one club—artificial; either a very strong hand or a weak notrump—Silodor passed, LHO responded one heart, and Rapée overcalled two clubs. Pass by opener, pass also by Silodor. Four clubs made, but three notrump made at the other table.

Deal 136 brings up an unusual bidding point:

Wit and Wisdom

Unknown except to his closest associates, Edgar was a practical joker. Indeed, he excelled at this art, because his stunts amused or perplexed but didn't sting. His most common type of thrust was the "personal double entendre," a phrase or sentence that meant different things to different readers, but he ranged widely. One of his most effective gags was pulled on Peter Leventritt, one of his partners in The Card School in New York.

Peter had long been complaining about the major annoyance of bridge teaching: The need to duplicate lesson deals to be played simultaneously at many tables, a procedure that is tedious and boring, yet must be done exactly right. One day, Edgar explained that Peter's problem was failure to use the correct deals. To demonstrate, Edgar, pretending to make it up as he went along, wrote out a four-hand diagram. He noted the interesting points to make about the bidding and play; Peter agreed it was a useful layout.

"Then," Edgar said, "For the next lesson, simply switch the North and East hands, like this . . . " Lo and behold, there was another suitable instructional deal. Peter's mouth fell open, and, as far as anyone else knows, Edgar never revealed that it had taken him the better part of a day and a half to construct that exhibit.

West dealer
Neither side vulnerable

```
                      NORTH
                      ♠ A K 5 2
                      ♡ Q 10 3 2
                      ◇ A 9 2
                      ♣ 9 6
WEST                                      EAST
♠ 9 8 4 3                                 ♠ —
♡ 8 7                                     ♡ A K 9 5 4
◇ 8 7 6                                   ◇ J 10 5 4
♣ Q J 10 5                                ♣ A K 3 2
                      SOUTH
                      ♠ Q J 10 7 6
                      ♡ J 6
                      ◇ K Q 3
                      ♣ 8 7 4
```

At one table, Crawford opened one diamond on the North hand, East doubled, and Becker bid one spade. Crawford raised to two spades, and Becker passed.

There was more action at the other table:

SOUTH	WEST	NORTH	EAST
Avarelli	*Rapée*	*Belladonna*	*Silodor*
—	1 ♣	Double	1 ♡
Double	Pass	1 ♠	2 ♠
3 ♠	Pass	4 ♠	5 ♣
Pass	Pass	Double	(All Pass)

Silodor had an interesting and rather novel problem. He knew that Rapée must be psyching, and after his own two-spade cue-bid, that Rapée must know that he knew. But could Silodor beat four spades? Could East-West make five clubs or find a profitable sacrifice there? At total points, it would surely be right to take out insurance by bidding five clubs—the loss should not be great. But at IMP the premium you pay for insurance is much, much higher. In my view, there are two reasonable ways to handle the East cards: (1) Decide that you will not let the enemy play four spades and so bid five clubs right over one spade. There is an excellent chance that South, whose double of one heart was responsive, not business, can be stampeded into five spades; in any event, this is certainly better than letting him show his support and then taking the save. (2) Make Silodor's fine spade cue-bid, which should convey: "Even though you're psyching, partner, we may still belong in five clubs, but I have too much defense to bid it directly." However, if you do bid two spades, you must leave the final decision to your partner.

Since Belladonna opened the spade king against five clubs doubled, Rapée was able to peel off 10 tricks on a crossruff. Down 100, for a gain of one IMP, as 140 was made at the other table. Silodor's phantom sacrifice cost only two IMP, but had Rapée gone for 300—as he would have with a trump lead—it would have cost six IMP.

I consider Silodor responsible for the terrible game contract reached on Deal 37. Second-hand, nonvulnerable vs. vulnerable, he opened two diamonds, holding:

♠ K   ♡ 10 8 4   ◇ K Q J 6 4   ♣ Q 6 3 2

Crawford responded two notrump, and Silodor raised to three notrump. Since the opponents' spades split four-four, this contract was set only two, for a three IMP loss. (Crawford had four low spades and three aces.) Again, the lack of a clear agreement on what is a weak two-bid cost our team. Opener bid as though he had a maximum, while responder was clearly hoping for a better hand.

In my opinion, Silodor also overbid on Deal 19. He held:

♠ A Q J 10 8   ♡ K   ◇ A 2   ♣ K J 8 6 4

and opened one spade in fourth position. When Rapée responded one notrump, Silodor forced with three clubs. The result was a very poor three-notrump contract and a four IMP loss. True, Rapée could have made three notrump, but the winning line of play depends on a near-miraculous lie of cards and is obvious only when looking at all four hands.

I have twice before mentioned Deal 67. Here are all the cards:

South dealer
East-West vulnerable

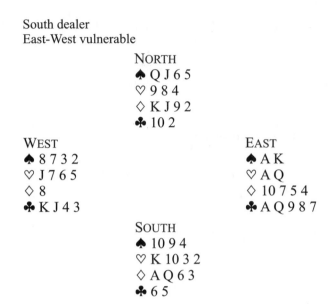

NORTH
♠ Q J 6 5
♡ 9 8 4
♢ K J 9 2
♣ 10 2

WEST
♠ 8 7 3 2
♡ J 7 6 5
♢ 8
♣ K J 4 3

EAST
♠ A K
♡ A Q
♢ 10 7 5 4
♣ A Q 9 8 7

SOUTH
♠ 10 9 4
♡ K 10 3 2
♢ A Q 6 3
♣ 6 5

It was with these East-West cards that Forquet and Siniscalco played in three hearts. On a diamond lead, they made nine tricks—three diamond ruffs, two high clubs, two high spades, a spade ruff, and the ace of trumps—and gained four IMP. The auction at the other table went:

SOUTH	WEST	NORTH	EAST
Avarelli	*Rapée*	*Belladonna*	*Silodor*
Pass	Pass	Pass	1 ♣
Pass	2 ♣	Pass	3 NT
Pass	Pass	Pass	

Avarelli led a diamond, and, even though that suit split four-four, Silodor needed the heart finesse for nine tricks and went down one. I must say that I would rather be in three notrump than in three hearts, but surely the ironclad five-club contract should be reached.

I don't care much for Rapée's two-club bid, personally, but it was a step in the right direction. If Silodor bids his hand more delicately, he will find the right spot. A two-diamond rebid would be answered with two hearts. If Silodor next bids two spades, Rapée will raise to three spades. And now West's singleton diamond is well marked. A five-club contract would gain nine IMP—a pickup of five against a loss of four.

Silodor lost even more—14 IMP—through his one error in play. On Deal 156, near the end of the match, he pulled a wrong card in a six-notrump contract and went down just when he had it made. This was frightfully expensive, because Crawford had psyched the Italians out of the slam in the other room. (It should be noted that without this lapse Silodor would have had quite a respectable record under my scoring system.)

Now for some double trouble. On Deal 79, Silodor held, vulnerable vs. nonvulnerable:

♠ A K 9 5 4 3   ♡ 9 6 4   ◊ J 7 3   ♣ Q

and overcalled with one spade when one heart was opened at his right. This was passed back to the opener, who rebid two clubs. Silodor and next hand passed, and Becker competed with two spades. Pass by dealer, pass by Silodor, three clubs by responder. "Double," said Mr. Becker. Three clubs could be beaten one trick—Mr. B. had a close double—but Silodor ran to three spades, got doubled, and went down himself. It cost five IMP.

Silodor's decision in a competitive auction was even more costly on Deal 86:

Wit and Wisdom

"Freddy Sheinwold and I told a publisher who was interested in a book we wanted to write about our system that it was highly specialized and about eight people would want to buy it. He thought he knew more about it than we did, and he was right. The book sold over 50,000 copies in hardcover. Never overestimate the business intelligence of bridge players."

East dealer; East-West vulnerable

NORTH
♠ K 4
♡ A Q J 9 5 3
◇ K 8 7 5
♣ Q

WEST
♠ J 9 8 6 5 3
♡ K 6 2
◇ Q J 9
♣ 7

EAST
♠ A Q 7 2
♡ 10 7 4
◇ A 10 3
♣ K 10 9

SOUTH
♠ 10
♡ 8
◇ 6 4 2
♣ A J 8 6 5 4 3 2

SOUTH	WEST	NORTH	EAST
Becker	*Siniscalco*	*Silodor*	*Forquet*
—	—	—	1 ♠
4 ♣	4 ♠	5 ♣	Double
Pass	Pass	Pass	

The diamond queen was led, and Becker had to lose three diamonds, one spade, and one club, for down 500. The Italians' four-spade contract would also have gone for 500—North-South would get two hearts and a ruff, the ace of clubs, and a club overruff.

I'm not sure that Silodor should double four spades, but I know he shouldn't save against it. In my view, to push the opponents into a contract and then sacrifice against it is one of the gravest bidding crimes.

However, there was no actual swing on this deal. At the other table the auction went:

SOUTH	WEST	NORTH	EAST
Chiaradia	*Stone*	*D'Alelio*	*Roth*
—	—	—	1 ♣
3 ♣	Pass	3 ♡	Pass
4 ♣	4 ♠	Double	Pass
5 ♣	Double	(All Pass)	

Just as Stone was about to pay the penalty for his rashness—the difference between a rash bid and a courageous one is a matter of result—Chiaradia came to his rescue with a five-club bid much worse than Silodor's.

In contrast, Silodor made a fine double in a similar position on Deal 89. He opened the bidding with one heart, first hand, nonvulnerable vs. vulnerable, holding:

♠ 6 2　　♡ A J 10 7 5 2　　♢ —　　♣ A 8 5 4 2

It went double at his left; Becker preempted four diamonds; four spades to his right. "Double," said Silodor, foreseeing the crossruff that beat the sound game contract 500. On a similar auction, D'Alelio did not take this imaginative action and lost four IMP.

Against Italy, Roth and Stone did not play except as partners (Roth played briefly with Crawford, but against Argentina), so it is convenient to treat their records jointly. They were, in general, an effective pair, tossing away a little more than their share of points, especially early in the match, but playing a very active style and earning back many points. Stone, particularly, created many favorable swings for the U.S.

On the whole, the Roth-Stone System was less successful than Roth and Stone were as individuals. Unluckily, many of their specialized bids and conventions simply didn't come up. Take the negative double for example. Roth made a sort of "positive" negative double on Deal 1, holding:

♠ A Q 9 4 2　　♡ 10 7 3　　♢ J 7 6　　♣ J 9

Stone opened one heart; Forquet overcalled one spade; and Roth doubled! Stone had opened on:

♠ K　　♡ A 9 6 5 4 2　　♢ A 8 3　　♣ K Q 4

and now cue-bid two spades over the supposed negative double. The result was a shaky, though not unreasonable, four-heart contract, which went down for a three-IMP loss on a diamond lead. Perhaps you think that Roth just forgot his shiny new gadget, but he says no—he was simply trying to make the Italians worry a little through the rest of the match as to what negative doubles really were.

Well, it turned out that this three-IMP investment was wasted, for negative double opportunities came up only twice more and had little bearing on the results. Moreover, negative inferences from a negative double that wasn't made may have hurt Roth-Stone on Deal 77:

North dealer; both sides vulnerable

```
                    NORTH
                    ♠ J 10 8 7 3 2
                    ♡ 4 3
                    ◊ 7 6
                    ♣ Q 9 3
WEST                                    EAST
♠ Q 5                                   ♠ A 9 6 4
♡ Q J                                   ♡ K 9 2
◊ Q 10 8 5 2                            ◊ K 9
♣ A 7 6 5                               ♣ K J 10 8
                    SOUTH
                    ♠ K
                    ♡ A 10 8 7 6 5
                    ◊ A J 4 3
                    ♣ 4 2
```

SOUTH	WEST	NORTH	EAST
Chiaradia	*Stone*	*D'Alelio*	*Roth*
—	—	Pass	1 ♣
2 ♡	Pass	Pass	Pass

I'm pretty sure that in the old, pre-Sputnik days, Roth would have bid again over Chiaradia's strange-looking strong jump-overcall; the fact that Stone had not bid freely would not have diminished game prospects, it would merely have made slam unlikely. Now, however, Roth could conclude from Stone's failure to double that his side should make no high contract.

Why didn't Stone double? [not promising spades in 1958—*Editor*] Perhaps he didn't like his doubleton spade; possibly one ace and no king isn't enough by his standards. (Stone is not an enthusiastic point-counter.) In any event, the cold and (apparently) easily biddable three-notrump game was missed.

Luckily, the Italians, for once, had system trouble too:

SOUTH	WEST	NORTH	EAST
Becker	*Siniscalco*	*Silodor*	*Forquet*
—	—	Pass	1 ♠
2 ♡	3 ◇	(All Pass)	

Siniscalco's response was nonforcing but invitational; he denied the strength to bid two notrump (artificial), which would be forcing. Forquet's decision to pass was reasonable, with one heart stopper, no great fit, and a minimum. The four-card-major opening had so crowded the auction that opener had to guess what to do, and he guessed wrong. So, in the end, the U.S. gained two IMP! Three diamonds just made, while Roth and Stone defeated two hearts two tricks, 200, although chucking a trick on defense.

It was not only negative doubles that were few and far between. The cards at Como stubbornly refused to accommodate themselves to most of the Roth-Stone special bids. They had no preemptive jump-responses at all; their two-club balancing device never came up (in fact, believe it or not, they had only one balancing auction of any sort); they had only one weak two-bid, one psychic, no psychic controls, only one strong single raise of a major, and even the forcing response of one notrump to a major-suit opening seldom occurred. Infuriating!

They did have quite a few weak jump-overcalls. But here again the cards played them false; the preempts had little effect, good or bad. It does seem to me, though, that they should have picked up on Deal 76:

Wit and Wisdom

It was a rare day that Edgar would reply to a seriously-intended question with a simple answer. Once, when asked to classify a misguided action, he considered for 15-20 seconds before saying, "Execrable, but not obscene."

West dealer
North-South vulnerable

NORTH
♠ A K 4
♡ K 6
◇ A 7 5
♣ Q 10 9 8 2

WEST
♠ Q 8
♡ 10 5 4
◇ K 4 3
♣ A 7 6 5 3

EAST
♠ J 10 7 6 5 2
♡ A 9 8 7
◇ J 9 8
♣ —

SOUTH
♠ 9 3
♡ Q J 3 2
◇ Q 10 6 2
♣ K J 4

SOUTH	WEST	NORTH	EAST
Chiaradia	*Stone*	*D'Alelio*	*Roth*
—	Pass	1 ♣	2 ♠
Pass	Pass	2 NT	Pass
3 NT	Pass	Pass	Pass

Here was the perfect setup. Had Stone raised to three spades (as I think he should have), the Italians would pretty surely have been frozen out. At the other table, three notrump was bid without opposition, so all that was lost was the potential gain (and the potential systemic triumph if Stone had brought it off).

There was a big loss after a weak jump-overcall on Deal 16. Only North-South vulnerable:

WEST
Stone
♠ K 5
♡ A Q 7 6 5 4 2
◇ Q 4 3
♣ 4

EAST
Roth
♠ Q J 9 4 3
♡ K 10 3
◇ 10
♣ K 8 7 6

Dealer [South] passed, and Stone, second-hand, passed also! Third hand opened one diamond, and Roth jumped to two spades. Everyone passed, so Roth had bought himself a contract. He made it with an overtrick, too, because the spades split; but of course the Italians bid four hearts at the other table and made it easily. Who was responsible for the four IMP loss?

Roth's jump-overcall is certainly atypical, but I don't think it is unreasonable on this vulnerability, facing a passed hand. Obviously, he must have felt that the deal belonged to the enemy and that it was worth a little risk to disrupt their communications. Probably the danger of his missing four hearts never occurred to him. Personally, I consider Stone to be the guilty party. Granted that he believes in "sound" opening bids; surely he could "take his life in his hands" and open this holding.

The concept of supersound openings was costly to Roth and Stone on other deals. They passed out Deal 127: luckily, the Italians bid only two notrump, making three. And the very next deal, No. 128, was even more expensive:

Wit and Wisdom

When the American Contract Bridge League's **Bulletin** made a futile attempt to explain the organization's announced policy on psychic bidding, Edgar expressed the membership's widespread confusion with this poem to the editor:

Thanks for the Bulletin's clever
Clarification endeavor:
It's legal to psych
As much as you like,
So long as you like to psych never.

West dealer
East-West vulnerable

NORTH
♠ A 3
♡ 10 9 8 7 5
◇ K Q 6 5
♣ 9 6

WEST
♠ Q 10 6 5
♡ 2
◇ A J 10
♣ K Q 4 3 2

EAST
♠ K J 9
♡ A Q 4 3
◇ 7 4 3
♣ A 8 5

SOUTH
♠ 8 7 4 2
♡ K J 6
◇ 9 8 2
♣ J 10 7

SOUTH	WEST	NORTH	EAST
Avarelli	*Stone*	*Belladonna*	*Roth*
—	Pass	1 ♡	Pass
1 ♠	Pass	2 ♡	Pass
Pass	Double	(All Pass)	

Roth led a diamond, which made the hand easy for declarer, who lost one diamond, one spade, two clubs, and two hearts, for down 100. Actually, it is not simple to stop seven tricks on any defense, though it can be done. But even a 300 set would have been a big loss, for the Italians opened the West hand, naturally enough, at the other table and romped into three notrump, which is unbeatable.

True, Roth-Stone were fixed up by Belladonna's gay opening bid. I must admit that while I would surely open Stone's hand, it would not occur to me to open Belladonna's. But would Roth-Stone have had such an easy time getting to game anyway, after an original pass by West? Roth would open one heart, presumably, and Stone might respond two clubs. Would Roth bid again with his minny, and if so, what?

Against these losses must be set the gain when Stone passed this holding in Deal 84:

♠ K 7 2   ♡ K Q 5 4 3   ◇ A 10 2   ♣ 9 4

The Italians opened this hand at the other table and went down 300 in two spades (they could have made two diamonds, but elected to play in a Moysian four-three fit). At Stone's table, Italy bid two notrump and made 120, so the super-sound-opening thesis gained three IMP. But it lost heavily on balance.

Roth-Stone paid for their solid openings in a different way when they overbid to doubtful games on Deals 33 and 106. In both cases, a passed hand jumped to two notrump over a third-hand opening, and both times the original passes were normal, with 11- and 12-point hands. But in each case opener carried on to three notrump with a skinny minimum opening:

♠ K J 8 5   ♡ J 3   ◇ K J 10   ♣ A 9 4 3

and

♠ A J 9 4 2   ♡ J 4 2   ◇ Q J 2   ♣ A 7

clearly hoping for a strictly "Roth-Stone" passed hand of 13 points or better. The result? Down one; down one. Six IMP lost.

Do you suppose that opener went on in these instances because he hadn't opened a very light "third-hand" bid? But Roth and Stone weren't opening light hands in third or fourth seat. Stone passed, third hand, with:

♠ A 6 3   ♡ Q J 9 4   ◇ A 8 6   ♣ 7 6 4

And Roth, fourth hand, passed out:

♠ 10 8 6 5   ♡ A 10 9   ◇ A 6   ♣ K 9 5 4

Maybe I'm wrong, but it seems to me that either hand above might make game opposite the sort of monsters they pass in first and second seat. Game? Why, they would pass out:

WEST	EAST
Stone	*Roth*
♠ A Q x x x x x	♠ 10 x x x
♡ K x	♡ A 10 9
◊ x	◊ A x
♣ Q x x	♣ K 9 x x

even though they have a fighting chance for slam!

Another Roth-Stone quirk, a reluctance to reverse, cost twice. On Deal 10, they held:

WEST	EAST
♠ A K 6	♠ Q J 7 5
♡ K Q 4 2	♡ A 8 5
◊ A Q 6 3	◊ K J 5 2
♣ Q 3	♣ 8 6

WEST	EAST
Roth	*Stone*
1 ◊	1 ♠
2 NT	3 ◊
3 ♠	3 NT
Pass	

Eleven tricks can be made in spades or diamonds, ten in hearts. But three notrump was down two when Siniscalco found the club lead. (Stone's suspicions notwithstanding, a charge based on this opening lead could scarcely be made to stick, for Siniscalco had ace-ten-nine-sixth!) Roth could not duplicate the one-heart opening at the other table (where the Italians bid one heart — one spade — three diamonds — four hearts), since he plays five-card majors. But why he didn't bid two hearts over one spade, with his strong spades and hearts and weak clubs, I'll never know. Maybe 20 high-card points is not enough.

Well, if Roth couldn't reverse on Deal 10, he certainly couldn't here:

WEST	EAST
♠ A 3	♠ Q 10 9 8 7 5
♡ A Q 7 5	♡ J 9 4
◇ K Q 6 5 2	◇ J
♣ K 7	♣ 8 6 3

Roth	*Stone*
1 ♡	1 NT (!)
2 NT	4 ♡ (!)
Pass	

For a full explanation of this remarkable auction, I must refer you to the perpetrators. All I can contribute is that Stone must have felt it unnecessary to bid spades when he had already (presumably) found an "eight-card" fit in hearts; and that Roth deemed it preferable to "violate" by bidding a four-card major than by reversing with such a "miserable" hand. It may seem a little unfair to blame this three-IMP loss (we were lucky to lose only three; unaccountably, Forquet opened the big hand with one heart instead of one club, his system's strong bid, and missed the spade game also; but the Italians made a partial while we went down) on the Roth-Stone System, but it seems to me that the original sin was the unwillingness to bid the hand naturally and reverse.

Perhaps the system was also responsible for the four-IMP loss on Deal 93; I don't know.

WEST	EAST
♠ A 6	♠ 5 4 3
♡ 9 7	♡ K Q 3
◇ K 9 6 4	◇ 7 3
♣ A Q 9 3 2	♣ K J 8 7 5

SOUTH	WEST	NORTH	EAST
	Stone		*Roth*
—	1 ◇	Pass	1 ♡
1 ♠	2 ♣	2 ♠	Pass(!)
Pass	Pass		

Two spades made, while four clubs made the other way at the other table. I don't pretend to understand Roth's pass. Perhaps Stone's free rebid promised another bid; perhaps Roth needed more for a free bid.

119

Apart from his complicity in these systemic troubles, there are few charges against Roth. The "nullos" defense on Deal 100, described earlier (pages 68-69), was partly his fault, and he timed his bids wrong on Deal 121, when he held:

♠ J 10 7 5   ♡ Q J 9 7   ◇ Q 7   ♣ Q J 2

One heart was opened at his left; Stone doubled, and Roth advanced one spade. Opener rebid two clubs, passed around to Roth; he now bid two notrump. Stone held:

♠ A Q 8 2   ♡ K 2   ◇ 8 4 3 2   ♣ A 8 5

and passed two notrump, which went down one. Two spades, bid at the other table, came home without difficulty.

However, Roth picked up with a good penalty double on Deal 111, already discussed (page 70); and I like his action on Deal 34, where, vulnerable vs. nonvulnerable, he held:

♠ K 10 3   ♡ A Q 7   ◇ Q 10 4   ♣ A Q 9 3

Dealer, at his left, opened one diamond; Stone passed; one spade at his right. And Roth passed. The Italians now overbid to four spades, down one. At the other table, D'Alelio doubled with Roth's hand, and the Americans stopped at a partial.

Roth worked hard on Deal 99, both in the bidding and the play:

Wit and Wisdom

"The marvelous thing about bridge is that it is impossible to learn; it is impossible to know how to play it. It has this absolutely enormous variety. True, there is a great deal of skill in bridge; but even after playing regularly for over 50 years, I see something new every time I sit down at the table."

South dealer
East-West vulnerable

NORTH
♠ A 10
♡ Q 5 4 3
◇ K J 10 7
♣ A Q 6

WEST
♠ K 7 2
♡ K 10 9
◇ A 6 5
♣ K 9 5 4

EAST
♠ Q J 8 4
♡ J 8 6
◇ Q 4
♣ J 10 7 2

SOUTH
♠ 9 6 5 3
♡ A 7 2
◇ 9 8 3 2
♣ 8 3

SOUTH	WEST	NORTH	EAST
Roth	*Siniscalco*	*Stone*	*Forquet*
1 ♡ (!)	Pass	3 ♡	(All Pass)

Siniscalco did well not to be trapped into the bidding, and now Roth had to struggle with his unnatural contract. West led a low club, and dummy's queen held. Dummy played the ten of spades, ducked to West, who shifted to a cunning five of diamonds. Roth hopped up with the king and played a diamond right back. East won and knocked out the club ace. Dummy played a third diamond; West won and led a spade to dummy's ace. Roth ruffed dummy's low club, played ace of hearts and a heart, and was home free—he lost one heart, two diamonds, and one spade.

All this gained little, for the Italians played in a peaceful two diamonds, making three. But it was exciting.

Stone, too, has few non-systemic charges. Like Roth, he must share the blame for the fiasco on Deal 100; he might well have made one notrump on Deal 36; and he lost a bushel of IMP with his opening lead on Deal 117:

121

North dealer; North-South vulnerable

NORTH
♠ 6 5 4
♡ 10 5 4 2
◇ 7
♣ A J 10 6 5

WEST
♠ 3
♡ A 9 8 7
◇ K 9 5 2
♣ 9 8 7 2

EAST
♠ 10 7 2
♡ Q J 6
◇ Q 10 8 6
♣ Q 4 3

SOUTH
♠ A K Q J 9 8
♡ K 3
◇ A J 4 3
♣ K

SOUTH	WEST	NORTH	EAST
Avarelli	*Stone*	*Belladonna*	*Roth*
—	—	Pass	Pass
1 ◇	Pass	1 ♡	Pass
2 ♠	Pass	3 ♠	Pass
4 ♠	Pass	5 ◇	Pass
6 ♠	Pass	Pass	Pass

Stone, West, led the ace of hearts—and the defense was finished. His trump shift was too late; declarer could ruff two diamonds and pitch one on the high club.

The slam can be made against a club or a diamond lead, but probably wouldn't be, for declarer would more likely play for the heart ace onside than for the involved set of circumstances that makes it possible to ruff out three diamonds. And a trump lead beats six spades automatically.

What does the Italian auction mean? One diamond followed by two spades shows a powerful hand with long spades and shorter diamonds. The one-heart response was an artificial denial, the three-spade raise natural; and North's five-diamond bid showed a control in diamonds and slam interest. Since Stone was looking at the diamond king, it was odds-on that dummy was coming down with the singleton, so a trump lead was not far-fetched. (At the other table, Becker-Crawford bid an uninspired one spade — one notrump — four spades, and made five.)

Stone got half this loss back by finding the killing lead against three notrump on Deal 76; Forquet, with Stone's cards, guessed wrong. And Stone gained 7 IMP on Deal 39, at a three-notrump contract, by guessing to finesse against a queen with seven to the ace-king-jack-ten opposite a doubleton. He made five; Italy went down three.

On Deal 75, Stone held, with no one vulnerable:

♠ 8 4　♡ 7 4　♢ Q 3 2　♣ A Q J 9 7 4

Dealer, at his right, passed, and Stone preempted three clubs. As a result, he stole the deal from his opponents, neither of whom could enter the auction although cold for three hearts. A favorable lead let Stone make 12 tricks, while at the other table his hand was pushed to four clubs and set one.

Similarly, Stone picked up points on Deal 96. He held, nonvulnerable vs. vulnerable:

♠ 3　♡ A K J 7 5　♢ 10 6 5　♣ 9 7 6 5

Dealer passed at his right, and he opened two hearts, weak. This closed the auction, and Stone made three, for a three-IMP gain, as the deal was passed out at the other table.

General Conclusions

After all I have written, it may come as a surprise that I consider the Italy-United States match to have been played quite well. Technically, the match was on a very high plane indeed—there were few errors of dummy play or defense; of these few, not more than three or four were really glaring. And the bidding errors were generally ones involving fine judgment, not gross overbids or underbids.

Slam bidding was the worst department for both teams. The U.S. bid twelve slams—five made, seven went down. We missed four good slams that would have made, and one good one that wouldn't. One of the U.S. slams that made should have been beaten; conversely, one of those beaten should have been made. All in all, a miserable showing.

The Italians were no better. They bid only eight slams—four made, four didn't. That looks almost respectable, but they missed five good slams, and, of the four they bid and made, two were in the wrong contract and one should have been beaten. One of the slams they bid and went down on was a good contract, but they luckily stayed out of another good one that only failed because of stacked cards.

I came to no conclusions about the "battle of the systems." Somehow, there were very few strictly systemic swings—either pickups or losses—for the Neapolitan or Roman systems. Roth-Stone seemed to have quite a few systemic losses, but the results are inconclusive. The other Americans did fairly well with psychics, unimpressively with preempts and jump-overcalls, disastrously with weak two-bids. I saw no signs that anyone was losing points through unfamiliarity with the meaning of his opponents' bidding. The swings were due to judgment, rarely to system at all.

Over the long match luck was fairly even. The Americans lost, on my reckoning, 51 IMP through unlucky swings. They gained 44 IMP in lucky ones. (By luck, I mean good contracts going down, bad ones making; slams on finesses, guess situations on lead, etc.) We were, then, slightly unlucky, but not enough to make the difference.

We lost because we were outplayed; we did a few more good things than the Italians did, but a lot more bad things. But don't believe that vague impression floating around (at least here in New York) that the U.S. players performed miserably in Como. That's not true. I think they played better than almost any of our previous World Championship teams. According to my calculations, our teams would have won in 1955, 1956 and 1957 if they had played as well as the U.S. team this year. It's just that the Italians put on a real championship performance and played better still.

But wait till next time.

SYSTEM BUILDING

Edgar was one of the leading bidding theorists in bridge history. This section focuses on some of his early expositions of pet treatments, including both methods that were cornerstones of the Kaplan-Sheinwold System and gadgets that can be mixed and matched within other general approaches.

The championing of the weak notrump can be read to advantage both to gain understanding of the general advantages of this approach and to learn how it fits into the K-S orientation. (Those who find Edgar's customizations—five-card majors, opener's strong single-raise rebids, and responder's weakness rebid of one notrump—attractive are potential K-S players.) In later years, Edgar slightly relaxed the requirements for his major-suit openings, but the foundations of his original theory stayed firm.

Most bridge methods evolve over time, and it is striking that although all of the articles gathered in this section were published before 1960, except for some supporting details they are still in wide use today. K-S loyalists remain a significant part of the tournament world and include some of the leading experts. And Edgar's gadgetry has retained strong popularity; some has even become standard American expert practice.

The Weak Notrump

More and more, players throughout the country are abandoning the strong 16-to-18-count opening one notrump and returning to the weak 12-to-14-point variety. There are many sound reasons for this.

1. The opening bid of one notrump is mildly preemptive in effect, forcing the opponents to act at the two level. You want this preemption on your balanced minimum—not on your balanced strong hand, with which you welcome a little healthy competition from the enemy.

2. The weak notrump sets a dangerous trap for the opponents, especially for fourth hand when one notrump is passed around to him. What is he to do with about 13 points? If he passes, he may miss a game; if he bids, he may find the notrumper's partner with an 11-point hand, and take a 500-point set against a partial. Of course, fourth hand is entitled to guess right a fair share of the time, but when he does, he gets merely his normal result. When he guesses wrong, he gets his head handed to him.

3. Certain purely descriptive features of the weak notrump work to one's advantage. On deals where the strength is split evenly between two partners (12-12, 12-13), game is very often made but seldom bid when the opening has been in a suit. Using the weak notrump, you bid one notrump—three notrump. When the partnership strength is 13-11 or 11-12 (the 11-point hand having passed originally and the 12-pointer having opened), it is virtually impossible to stay out of two notrump unless, using the weak variety, you bid one notrump—pass.

4. The greatest advantage of the weak notrump does not show up on paper, however. You have to see it at the table. Nothing in bridge is as tough as defending accurately when the bidding has gone:

SOUTH	WEST	NORTH	EAST
1 NT	Pass	Pass	Pass

or

SOUTH	WEST	NORTH	EAST
1 NT	Pass	Pass	Double
Pass	Pass	Pass	

or

SOUTH	WEST	NORTH	EAST
1 NT	Pass	3 NT	(All Pass)

Much of the effectiveness of weak notrumps, both at matchpoints and rubber bridge, is due to this; many a theoretically lost position is turned into a winning one by the full trick or more you can count on picking up from inaccurate defense.

Obviously, this advantage—from not bidding any suits—also applies to strong notrumps, but you are dealt a lot more weak ones, and the lighter your hand, the more likely you are to need help from the defense.

Weak notrumps are very easy to use. Responder, with a balanced hand, bids three notrump with 12 points or more, and passes with less. (The response of two notrump is very rare. It is normally better to pass doubtful holdings and hope that fourth hand will balance.) With an unbalanced hand, responder can sign off with two of his suit, or jump in his suit if he has the equivalent of an opening bid. Normally, some form of Stayman is employed to find major-suit fits and also for delicate handling of problem hands.

In all auctions, the responder controls. He signs off; he bids game. He will be the one to double the opponents if they step into the auction; he will be the one to balance in a competitive situation. After all, he knows vastly more about opener's hand than opener can know about his.

How do you handle stronger balanced hands that might normally be opened with one notrump? You simply open with one in a suit, and when, at any subsequent stage in the auction, you show a balanced hand by making a minimum rebid in notrump, partner knows you have 15, 16 or 17 points, for otherwise, you would have opened with a weak notrump. This means that in the following auction, the one-notrump call shows a strong hand:

SOUTH	WEST	NORTH	EAST
1 ♣	Pass	1 ♡	Pass
1 NT			

It does not mean, however, that you must rebid one notrump immediately to show strength. Holding:

♠ A Q x x   ♡ K x x   ◇ K x x   ♣ A J x

and having opened with one club, if partner responds with one heart, your immediate rebid should be one spade, not one notrump. If partner has 8 points or under, he will then either pass or bid one notrump (which you will pass). With more, he will make some other bid that will enable you to bid two notrump at your next opportunity.

This also means that you must open all balanced minimums with one notrump, even if you have a weak doubleton. You cannot open:

♠ x x　♡ K J x x　◇ A x x　♣ K Q x x

with one club, for you would have no rebid over the expected one-spade response. The one-notrump rebid is denied you: you are too weak.

The opening notrump with a weak doubleton does not work out as badly in practice as you might imagine from theory. You will still reach the proper game contracts. Occasionally, you'll play one notrump when you have a safer partscore contract, but remember that most of the time you will do a lot better in one notrump than you are entitled to do on your combined hands.

Playing the weak notrump, you had better lower your two-notrump jump-rebids to 18-20 points. This will give you a continuous range of notrump bids for all balanced hands: 12-14 points, an opening one notrump; 15-17, an opening in a suit, with minimum notrump rebid; 18-20, an opening in a suit, with jump notrump rebid; 21 up, opening two notrump or three notrump.

The weak notrump has a marked effect on the whole complex of bidding. The tendency now is to open only sound hands with one of a suit, for the light balanced hands are all opened with one notrump, and the light unbalanced hands are easy to back in with, once you've passed. For example, I would hate to pass:

♠ Q 10 x　♡ K x x　◇ A J 10 x　♣ Q x x

for I am not likely to get another chance to bid safely; but I don't mind passing:

♠ A Q 10 x x x　♡ x　◇ x x　♣ K x x x

because now I can back into the auction at almost any level. In my opinion, it is best to preserve the inference that any opening other than one notrump is a solid bid.

If all your opening bids in a suit are to be sound, you do not need the preemptive value of the opening four-card major. The one-spade opening, which Adam Meredith of the championship British team uses like a *shillelagh*, is displaced by the opening one notrump. Therefore,

you sacrifice very little by playing five-card majors in conjunction
with weak notrumps, and you gain a secure foundation for your strong
hands. In addition, you eliminate, once and for all, the annoying rebidding problems of 4-4-3-2 hands.

Think of all the various 4-4-3-2 patterns, and you will see what I
mean. The only rebidding problem you will ever have is whether to
raise partner's major-suit response with three. Playing weak notrumps,
you will almost always be able to avoid doing this, for you have available the strong one-notrump rebid. For example, if you, South, held:

♠ A x x   ♡ A J x   ◇ A Q 10 x x   ♣ J x

the bidding, if your side were using strong notrumps, would go:

SOUTH	WEST	NORTH	EAST
1 ◇	Pass	1 ♠	Pass
2 ♠			

[Opening one notrump on a hand with a weak doubleton that presented
no apparent rebid problem was not popular when this article was written.—*Editor*] Your hand would be too strong for a one-notrump rebid.
But with this same holding, when you are using the weak notrump, you
can convey a quite adequate picture of your hand by starting with one
diamond and rebidding one notrump over partner's one spade.

Remember that you are less reluctant to show your support second-
arily, now that your one-notrump rebid is constructive, which means
that your partner will more probably give you another chance to bid.
Consider how an auction such as the following is clarified:

SOUTH	WEST	NORTH	EAST
1 ♣	Pass	1 ♠	Pass
2 ♠			

As generally played today, this two-spade rebid has a tremendous
range, both in strength and in trump support. However, if you are using
the weak notrump, this two-spade rebid should mean fair trumps and a
hand unsuitable for a weak notrump because of distributional features

or because of high-card content—in either case, a strong hand in support of spades.

If you play weak notrumps, you will quickly become accustomed to these changes and will doubtless find many other auctions in which the shade of meaning is changed. The main concept to grasp is that of the preemptive opening of one notrump on light hands, along with sound opening bids of one in a suit. This combination, in my opinion, will give you the maximum offensive-defensive effectiveness.

Responding to the Weak Notrump

In this discussion of responses to an opening weak notrump, it is assumed that a 12-14-point one notrump is being used in conjunction with Stayman.

Several variations of Stayman are possible, but it is important that there be no two-notrump reply to two clubs. Without a major, the two-diamond reply should be automatic, irrespective of maximum or minimum strength.

Tactical considerations induce you to bid two clubs over one notrump with certain very weak hands. Suppose you hold:

♠ x x x   ♡ J x x x   ◇ J 10 x x   ♣ x x

Partner, first hand, opens one notrump, and second hand passes. Unquestionably, you are in trouble. If you pass, your left-hand opponent will surely double; his partner will leave it in, and the set may be more expensive than the game the enemy could have made.

Instead of waiting for the lightning to strike, bid two clubs and pass partner's reply. This will be much tougher for the opponents to punish, as a double is now a balancing double for takeout, not for penalties. You will be very unlucky to find the specific adverse holding that will hurt you.

Occasionally, you will be able to do better than merely get out of trouble—you may be able to steal the whole pot. Here is a spectacular example taken from actual play:

Wit and Wisdom

"There's a certain amount of tension in any husband-and-wife partnership, as I probably don't have to tell you. I have come to the conclusion that there is absolutely no way to play happily with your spouse at the bridge table over a long period of time."

North dealer; East-West vulnerable

NORTH
♠ A 7
♡ K Q 6 4
◇ A 8 4
♣ 10 5 3 2

WEST
♠ Q 10 8 3
♡ A 9 5
◇ Q 7
♣ K Q 8 6

EAST
♠ K J 4 2
♡ 10 3
◇ K 9 6 5
♣ A J 7

SOUTH
♠ 9 6 5
♡ J 8 7 2
◇ J 10 3 2
♣ 9 4

SOUTH	WEST	NORTH	EAST
—	—	1 NT	Pass
2 ♣	Pass	2 ♡	Pass
4 ♡(!)	Pass	Pass	Pass

The result was a puny 100-point set. It could have been 150, but this hardly would have compensated East-West for their cold vulnerable game.

Actually, it is hard to see how East or West could enter the auction. Each assumed that South held the remaining strength, in which case competition would be disastrous. When South jumped to four hearts, each opponent congratulated himself on staying out of trouble.

The four-heart bid, of course, is not recommended standard action—don't complain to me if you try it and go down 900. But it does illustrate what you can accomplish with a yarborough opposite a weak notrump.

Holding any unbalanced hand, with no real chance for game, responder takes out to two in a suit. The two-spade response to one notrump, varies from:

♠ J x x x x x   ♡ x x   ◊ x x   ♣ x x x

to

♠ A K x x x   ♡ x x x   ◊ x   ♣ Q x x x

This wide range is dangerous to the opponents, for though you have given up on game, you may have enough to crush any opposing three-level contract. This additional preemptive effect, along with considerations of safety, should lead you to take out to the two level rather than pass one notrump whenever you hold a five-card major. Even with:

♠ J 10 x x x   ♡ K J x   ◊ A J x   ♣ 10 x

you should (in my opinion) bid two spades over one notrump.

This last hand comes very close to the game range. Strengthen it a little, to:

♠ Q 10 x x x   ♡ K J x   ◊ A J x   ♣ 10 x

and I would bid two clubs, not two spades. Over my partner's two-diamond or two-heart reply, I rebid two spades. This I play nonforcing but invitational, and the sequence describes a hand with five spades and 11-12 points, or six spades and 10-11 points. I want to be in game if facing a sound one notrump with some spade fit.

Thus, you have a sign-off and an invitation. With game-going hands you can bid two clubs and then jump in your suit, or jump to three in your suit, or jump all the way to game. The method you choose should depend on the strength of your suit and the amount of room you wish to leave for slam investigation. These are the same standard Stayman sequences used with strong notrumps, except that you need about a king more. Why only a king more when the opening weak notrump averages four points less than standard? Because with the strength more equally divided between the partnership hands, you need fewer points to make game—the increased transportation and flexibility are worth at least a jack.

Only rarely will the partner of the weak notrumper have problems in a competitive auction, but it does happen occasionally, especially at matchpoints. Suppose South opens one notrump, and you, North, hold:

♠ A 10 x x   ♡ x x   ◇ K x x   ♣ Q x x x

Too little for game, but enough for it to be "your partial." The bidding goes:

SOUTH	WEST	NORTH	EAST
1 NT	Pass	Pass	Double
Pass	2 ♡	?	

At rubber bridge, you would tend to pass. The opponents will probably go down a trick or two, and even if they make a partial when you could have made one yourself, there is no disaster. At matchpoints, however, you must act. Two spades is a fairly safe bid—partner will play you for a four-card suit and run if he holds only two. (You would have bid two spades directly over one notrump with a five-card suit.) If the opponents are vulnerable, however, you should go out for the 200 number, doubling two hearts. You will get an occasional zero this way, but on balance it must pay off. After all, the two-heart bid was not voluntary—West just couldn't stand one notrump doubled. In these balancing situations, it is very important to note whether the suit was bid under pressure or not. For example, had the auction gone:

SOUTH	WEST	NORTH	EAST
1 NT	Pass	Pass	2 ♡
Pass	Pass	?	

I would bid two spades, not double. East rates to have a good trump suit, while in the first auction West is probably gambling on catching his partner with support. Now transpose North's cards a little, to:

♠ x x   ♡ A 10 x x   ◇ K x x   ♣ Q x x x

and let the auction go:

SOUTH	WEST	NORTH	EAST
1 NT	Pass	Pass	2 ♠
Pass	Pass	?	

Now, at either matchpoints or rubber bridge, and regardless of vulnerability, North should bid two notrump. Obviously, he does not hold any length or much strength in spades, else he would have doubled. Logically, then, North is asking his partner to bid a suit at the three level, or to stand for two notrump if he holds two spade stoppers. This balancing two notrump by responder is a useful bid to remember.

When does the notrump opener himself balance? Almost never. About the only time he can do so is in an auction like:

SOUTH	WEST	NORTH	EAST
1 NT	2 ♡	Pass	Pass
Double			

The double means that South has a maximum notrump with a doubleton heart, and good support for the other suits, especially spades. Even here, the opener is on dangerous ground and should be prepared to apologize if the balancing double turns out badly. It is an almost inviolable rule that the responder is captain.

The last action by responder that I want to discuss is the penalty double. This would seem to need no elucidation, but there are two related points that I want to make.

Point 1: The penalty double is based primarily on high cards, not on trumps. Don't double the opponents if you know it is their deal in high cards even if you're sure they're going down at their present contract. They may run. A holding of:

♠ Q 10 9 x x   ♡ A x x   ◇ x x x   ♣ x x

is not a double of two spades after partner opens a weak notrump. Conversely, don't be afraid to double the opponents with three trumps if you have 10 or more high-card points. They have no business contracting

135

to take eight tricks when your side has 55-60 percent of the high cards and at least five cards in their trump suit.

This brings us to Point 2: You must be willing to let the opponents occasionally make a doubled contract against you. Obviously, when you double primarily on high cards, you will once in a while be wrecked by an eight-card suit, or by a key singleton in dummy, or by a six-five distribution against you.

But most of the time when an opponent steps into the auction after a weak-notrump opening he is gambling. If you have a strong hand, he has lost his gamble, but he has lost it only if you double. If you have a pathological horror of doubling the enemy into game, don't play the weak notrump, because you will lose most of its trapping effect. Let them make one time in eight—you will still show a big long-term profit.

One final word of caution. I have couched much of this article in terms of points. This is a little dangerous for penalty doubles: queens and jacks in side suit have little more than displacement value. Better to look for aces and kings.

Further Thoughts on the Weak Notrump

I read T. A. Lightner's article on the weak notrump with a great deal of interest. We both believe in weak notrumps, but our outlooks are quite dissimilar. Lightner puts his finger directly on the point of difference when he writes that with him the weak notrump is a gimmick, whereas I build a system around it.

Here is the central question: Are we to open all balanced minimums with one notrump? Lightner says No—he simply wants to be able to open the most suitable "minnies" with a weak notrump, when the mood seizes him or when the tactical situation seems right. I, however, answer the question Yes—all balanced light hands that I open, I open with one notrump; otherwise, I couldn't rebid accurately or consistently.

Consider: What is the auction:

SOUTH	WEST	NORTH	EAST
1 ♣	Pass	1 ♠	Pass
1 NT			

to mean? With me, it must be a balanced hand of 15-17 points, too strong to open one notrump. What is it with Lightner? This:

♠ A x   ♡ A Q x   ◇ J x x x   ♣ A Q x x

or

♠ x x   ♡ A J x   ◇ J x x x   ♣ A Q x x?

Too strong for an opening notrump or unsuitable for one? 12 points or 17?

If he doesn't rebid one notrump with strong, balanced hands, what does he do with them? If he jumps to two notrump with 17 points—one possible solution—what does he do with 16-point hands? He still can't treat them like 12-point hands. If his one-notrump rebid does show a strong hand, what does he rebid with the weak balanced hands that he has chosen not to open with his "gimmick" one notrump?

I strongly suspect that Lightner has no formula for rebidding these hands; that he "scrambles." Well, I don't doubt that he comes out with fine results—he's a wily scrambler. But only a Lightner could handle the weak notrump this way. I'm afraid I would find it unplayable.

Now, if you decide to open all your balanced minimums with one notrump, you will find yourself playing a new system—the great majority of your offensive auctions will be affected. This includes, in addition to all your weak-notrump openings, many hands that you open with one in a suit. Here are some of the principal types of auctions whose meaning is altered:

SOUTH	WEST	NORTH	EAST
1 ♣	Pass	1 ♢	Pass
1 NT			

or

SOUTH	WEST	NORTH	EAST
1 ♢	Pass	1 ♠	Pass
1 NT			

or

SOUTH	WEST	NORTH	EAST
1 ♣	Pass	1 ♡	Pass
1 NT			

This type of auction, as I said above, defines a hand too strong to open with a weak notrump, but not strong enough for a jump to two notrump. It denies a four-card major that you could bid at the one level—you should never suppress a suit merely to let partner know you have a good hand; he'll find that out shortly.

However, you should choose the one-notrump rebid rather than a three-card raise of partner's suit. Holding:

♠ K x   ♡ K J x   ◇ A Q x x x   ♣ K x x

open one diamond and, over one heart, rebid one notrump, not two hearts. It may become difficult for you to describe a balanced hand later.

Playing weak notrumps, you needn't fear being dropped in one notrump when you should be in two of partner's suit. On an auction like:

SOUTH	WEST	NORTH	EAST
1 ◇	Pass	1 ♡	Pass
1 NT	Pass	?	

responder will take out with a weak, unbalanced hand. Remember, your one-notrump rebid now shows a fine hand, so partner will not be reluctant to go to the two level with a little distribution and very few high cards.

What about this next sequence?

SOUTH	WEST	NORTH	EAST
1 ♣	Pass	1 ◇	Pass
1 ♠	Pass	1 NT	Pass
?			

Should you raise on this auction if you hold the 15-17 point hand? If you do, you will find yourself in unplayable and dangerous two-notrump contracts when, using strong notrumps, you would open one notrump and be passed out there.

The answer is that responder's one-notrump rebid must be limited to a weak hand—one with which he would pass a strong one-notrump opening. Regardless of his pattern, responder may not rebid one notrump if he has even as much as a good-looking 8 points. Therefore, in this sequence opener passes with the balanced 15-17 points. If he raises to two notrump, he announces 18 or 19 points, and should be raised with about 7 points.

Another sequence:

SOUTH	WEST	NORTH	EAST
1 ♣	Pass	1 ♦	Pass
1 ♠	Pass	2 ♣ or 2 ♦ or 2 ♠	

Since responder's one-notrump rebid is a signoff, these bids should be considered progressive. They are responder's "intermediate" rebids: he is too strong to rebid one notrump, not strong enough to force to game.

The two-club bid above might very well be on 3=3=4=3, intended to let opener describe his hand. Responder might hold:

♠ Q x x   ♡ K x x   ◇ K J x x   ♣ x x x

With an unbalanced hand, the opening bidder will show his strength and distribution by some bid (or jump) in a suit, or by passing. If opener has a balanced hand, he will rebid two notrump with 15 or 16 points, three notrump with 17 or more.

Obviously, then, responder cannot give a "preference" to the two level without holding "intermediate" strength—he's liable to hear partner jump to three notrump. What does he do after:

SOUTH	WEST	NORTH	EAST
1 ♣	Pass	1 ◇	Pass
1 ♠	Pass	?	

holding:

♠ x   ♡ J x x   ◇ K 10 x x x   ♣ J x x x?

He bids one notrump, not two clubs. And with a singleton in the unbid suit, say:

♠ J x x   ♡ x   ◇ K 10 x x x   ♣ J x x x

North just passes one spade.

Even when his second suit has been raised, as in:

SOUTH	WEST	NORTH	EAST
1 ♣	Pass	1 ◇	Pass
1 ♠	Pass	2 ♠	

opener should rebid two notrump with a balanced hand that includes something in the unbid suit. Responder may have raised with three trumps. For example, holding:

♠ K x x   ♡ Q x x   ◇ A J x x x   ♣ x x

responder would bid:

SOUTH	WEST	NORTH	EAST
1 ♣	Pass	1 ◇	Pass
1 ♠	Pass	2 ♠	

Take another sequence:

SOUTH	WEST	NORTH	EAST
1 ♣	Pass	1 ♡	Pass
2 ♡			

This should become a very specifically-defined auction when you play weak notrumps. Since (as discussed earlier) opener will rebid one notrump rather than raise with three trumps, this major-suit raise is almost always on four. It says: "Partner, I have a hand too strong for a weak-notrump opening and four cards in your suit."

Obviously, opener may instead have an unbalanced minimum, like:

♠ x ♡ K Q x x ◇ Q x x ♣ A Q x x x

and bid the same. However, the distribution lifts this sort of hand to about the same overall strength as a balanced 15-17. The raise of responder's major suit is a strong, forward-going bid. Note that all your balanced minimums, which normally provide the bulk of the hands for this raise, are opened one notrump, not one of a suit.

What does responder need to bid again over the raise? He should move with any hand with which he would have tried for game over a strong one-notrump opening. These are equivalent auctions:

Using the weak notrump:

SOUTH	WEST	NORTH	EAST
1 ♣	Pass	1 ♡	Pass
2 ♡			

Using the strong notrump:

SOUTH	WEST	NORTH	EAST
1 NT	Pass	2 ♣	Pass
2 ♡			

Another sequence:

SOUTH	WEST	NORTH	EAST
1 ♣	Pass	1 ♡	Pass
2 NT			

The limits of this sequence are changed slightly by the weak notrump. Instead of 19-21 points, you must play 18-20. Consequently, your opening two-notrump bid must start at 21 points.

One further change: The two-notrump jump virtually denies a four-card major. Whereas, normally, you must make a close decision with:

♠ A Q x x   ♡ K x   ◊ A J x   ♣ A J x x

whether to rebid one spade or two notrump after one club — pass — one heart — pass — ?, you should now automatically bid one spade. Partner is not going to pass one spade with any hand that will produce game, for he has available the negative one-notrump rebid.

The opening bid of one in a major is not automatically affected by the weak notrump, but I would advise playing five-card majors as an adjunct. The case for four-card majors is based on preemptive effect and ease in rebidding minimum hands. Both considerations are rendered meaningless by the weak notrump, because (1) you have no rebidding problems, as all light 4-4-3-2 hands are opened one notrump; and (2) one notrump is a more effective preempt than one heart or one spade.

These changes induced by the weak notrump are quite far-reaching. Most of them spring from the conception that the opening bid in a suit can no longer be a balanced minimum; with this head start, the opening bidder can now delimit his hand much more precisely at a low level.

The weak-notrump opening sacrifices scientific investigation of the best partscore contract in order to gain preemptive and trapping effects. You also get this handsome extra dividend: greatly increased accuracy when you do not open with one notrump.

Double Raises in the Minors

A few years ago, with one of my favorite partners, I started playing that a jump-raise of a minor-suit opening bid (one club — three clubs, or one diamond — three diamonds) was preemptive, while a single raise (one club — two clubs, or one diamond — two diamonds) was a strong bid, forcing for one round. Lately, I've been using this with almost all partners, and it has worked so well that, in all conscience, I should let everyone in on it.

The theory is this: On weak hands with length in partner's suit, you want the preemptive effect of the jump; on strong hands with a fit for partner's minor, you need the extra round of bidding that the single raise gives you, to determine whether or not to play three notrump.

Suppose partner opens the bidding with one diamond, and you hold either (a):

♠ x x x   ♡ x   ◇ K x x x x   ♣ Q x x x

or (b):

♠ x x x   ♡ x   ◇ K x x x x   ♣ A K J x

Standard practice is to bid two diamonds on (a) and three diamonds, forcing, on (b), yet wouldn't you love to be able to bid three diamonds with the weak hand and make life tough for the enemy? Two diamonds is a filthy bid—it invites the opponents to enter the auction just when you hope they won't.

Now look what the standard three-diamond bid does for you (or to you) on (b), the strong hand. The trouble is that most of the time partner will rebid three notrump. He may be stabbing; he may not be. He may be cold for three notrump; he may have no play. He may be spread for six diamonds; he may be down at four diamonds. What can you do except pass and pray?

Remember, partner has opened one diamond; you have bid three diamonds with:

♠ x x x ♡ x ◊ K x x x x ♣ A K J x

and partner has rebid three notrump. If partner's hand is:

♠ Q J x ♡ K J x ◊ A Q x x ♣ Q x x

you're right to pass three notrump. If his hand is:

♠ Q x ♡ K J x ◊ A Q J x x ♣ x x x

you're wrong, but you can't make any game.

However, if his hand is:

♠ A x ♡ Q x x ◊ A Q x x x ♣ Q x x

three notrump is a horrible contract, while six diamonds is laydown.

How can you tell what to do? Partner would bid three notrump with all three hands.

The answer is that you desperately need the extra round of bidding that the strong two-diamond response affords. Partner can still jump to three notrump over your two-diamond raise, if he wants to play three notrump and nothing else. But he can also bid two notrump; now you bid three clubs. If partner persists in notrump, you're in the right spot. But if he doesn't bid three notrump, you have the chance to stop at a diamond partial, or go on to a diamond game (or even investigate slam).

You will notice that I am emphasizing the strong single raise, not the preemptive jump. The weak jump is a useful adjunct, but it seldom comes up and, like all preempts, can cut both ways. The strong raise, in contrast, occurs more often and has produced no bad results and all sorts of good ones.

It does more than help you get to minor-suit games. Here is a deal from our Vanderbilt semifinal match, where it enabled us to play three notrump:

NORTH
♠ —
♡ A J x x
◇ J x x
♣ Q J x x x x

SOUTH
♠ Q J x
♡ K x x
◇ Q x x
♣ A K x x

Our auction went:

SOUTH	WEST	NORTH	EAST
1 ♣	Pass	2 ♣	Pass
3 NT	Pass	Pass	Pass

Ralph Hirschberg, with the North hand, passed three notrump cheerfully, as he knew from the auction that we would have a poor play for five clubs and an excellent play for three notrump. At the other table, the North player had no such assurance, and, not unnaturally, drove to five clubs, going down.

In another deal from this match, the strong minor-suit raise gained 410 points simply by letting us play in a partial.

NORTH
♠ J x
♡ K x x
◇ Q J x x
♣ K Q x x

SOUTH
♠ A x x x
♡ x
◇ A K x x
♣ J x x x

Our auction was:

SOUTH	WEST	NORTH	EAST
1 ◇	Pass	2 ◇	Pass
2 ♠	Pass	2 NT	Pass
3 ◇	Pass	Pass	Pass

Their auction was:

SOUTH	WEST	NORTH	EAST
1 ◇	Pass	3 ◇	Pass
3 ♠	Pass	3 NT	(All Pass)

Note how vital that extra round of bidding was. Three notrump went down 300, undoubled, with virtually no play for a make, and yet this contract is almost invariably reached by "normal" bidding. You just don't have room to stop.

The innovation I am suggesting seems radical, as it virtually interchanges the meanings of the single raise and the jump-raise. Actually, however, it is a very simple changeover. There are almost no side effects; other auctions are not affected; there are no subtle inferences. It is very easy to announce to the opponents and can be used without any feeling that you are taking advantage of the element of surprise. No deception is involved—the bids stand entirely on their own merits.

Try them and see.

The Kaplan-Sheinwold Philosophy

W hy do we establish our requirements? What do we gain by such a major alteration in opening-bid style?

Primarily, we gain accuracy in bidding games and slams. This increased accuracy stems directly from the fact that the opening bid carries with it so much more information. Take, for example, the opening one-spade bid in "standard bidding." It can be made with either of two quite dissimilar types of hand.

Type 1: ♠ A K 10 x   ♡ Q x x   ◇ K x x x   ♣ x x

Type 2: ♠ K Q J x x   ♡ A J x   ◇ x   ♣ Q x x x

We, however, open Type-1 hands with one notrump, thereby eliminating some 40 percent of all "standard bidding" one-spade openings. With such a tremendous head start, we can be a great deal more precise in our handling of the other 60 percent, the Type-2 hands, which we do open with one spade.

Now examine these two "standard bidding" auctions:

WEST	EAST
♠ A x x	♠ J x x x
♡ x x	♡ Q J x
◇ K Q x x x	◇ x x
♣ K x x	♣ A Q x x

OPENER	RESPONDER
1 ◇	1 ♠
2 ♠	

What should responder do over two spades? Well, if you go by the result, he had better pass, as he may be too high already. But what if opener, for the identical sequence, held:

WEST	EAST
♠ K Q x x	♠ J x x x
♡ K x	♡ Q J x
◇ A Q x x x	◇ x x
♣ x x	♣ A Q x x

OPENER	RESPONDER
1 ◇	1 ♠
2 ♠	

With a little luck, 11 tricks can be made. Clearly, if this is opener's hand, responder must bid over two spades. How can responder make an intelligent decision when his partner, in "standard bidding," might have either hand? The fault lies in the too-broad range of the opening diamond bid. Opener simply does not have enough rebids available to tell partner which of the many different "standard" one-diamond openings he holds.

We, however, don't have this problem, for the range of our one-diamond opening is narrower. With opener's first hand, we would have opened with one notrump, not one diamond, and that would have been the end of the auction. With the second opener's hand, our bidding would start as shown, and responder would proceed confidently to game. He would not be gambling on finding opener with a good hand. He would know how strong opener was.

You will see in the further description of our system just how we manage to convert the narrower meaning we have given to the opening bids of one in a suit into more accurate bidding sequences—more games and slams bid and made. This is the greatest gift of the weak one-notrump opening—you will have fine results when you use it, but its most striking benefits come when you open in a suit. For it is the weak notrump that makes our whole system possible, cutting down the broad ranges of the opening suit bids by eliminating all balanced minimum hands.

The weak notrump itself, in contrast to most of our bids, does not always aim at precision. Of course, in game-going and slam auctions, you can bid as delicately as you want. However, when responder is too weak to look for game, you sacrifice almost all chance to investigate the best fit for a suit contract when you open one notrump. For example, in "standard bidding," a partnership could reach a contract of two hearts with these cards:

WEST	EAST
♠ A x	♠ x x x
♡ K Q x x	♡ A J x x
◇ J x x	◇ x x
♣ K x x x	♣ Q J x x

WEST	EAST
1 ♣	1 ♡
2 ♡	Pass

Two hearts is a fine contract; with normal splits, you will make an overtrick. We, however, would bid one notrump with opener's hand and be passed out there. With a spade or diamond opening lead, we could be set two tricks.

Now, on the surface this looks like a major defeat for the weak notrump—one notrump, down two, instead of two hearts, making three. But look at the complete deal, which is taken from a team-of-four match we played in the National Championships last year:

West dealer; North-South vulnerable

NORTH
♠ K x x x
♡ 10 9 8 x
◇ A K 10
♣ x x

WEST	EAST
♠ A x	♠ x x x
♡ K Q x x	♡ A J x x
◇ J x x	◇ x x
♣ K x x x	♣ Q J x x

SOUTH
♠ Q J 10 x
♡ x
◇ Q x x x x
♣ A x x

SOUTH	WEST	NORTH	EAST
—	1 ♣	Double	Pass
2 ♣	Pass	2 ♠	3 ♣
4 ♠	Pass	Pass	Pass

The auction is given as it occurred with our teammates sitting North and South, and our opponents East and West. Our teammates made their vulnerable game contract with ease, losing one trick each in spades, hearts and clubs. However, when the deal was replayed at our table, where we sat East-West, this was the auction:

SOUTH	WEST	NORTH	EAST
—	1 NT	(All Pass)	

Neither of our vulnerable opponents could risk a bid at the two level. We would cheerfully have given them the 100 points for setting us two tricks when they could have scored a vulnerable game worth 620 points. But they didn't even get that. Who can blame North for leading the heart ten against one notrump? He had a blind lead to make, with no auction to guide him, and he guessed wrong. So we made our one-notrump contract. South shifted to diamonds on winning the club ace, but our opponents could now take only six tricks before we took seven.

This deal points up two features that work in favor of the weak notrump. The first is preemption. When you have a minimum balanced opening, you should want to make it as difficult as possible for the opponents to enter the auction. It is all very well to explore carefully to find a suit fit with partner, but you will discover, in general, that if you and your partner have good fitting hands, so have your opponents. With a light opening bid, your first concern must be buying the contract cheap, not reaching your maximum spot. Only with a strong hand can you afford to probe delicately for a fit, safe in the knowledge that you can outbid the enemy. And yet a strong 16-18-point hand is opened one notrump in "standard bidding," making it difficult to find your fit, while the weak 12-14-point hand is opened one club, making it easy for the opponents to compete.

The second feature of the weak notrump that shows up in our example deal is the trouble it gives the opponents on defense. When no suits have been bid, declarer has a tremendous advantage over the defenders—he knows which suits to attack and which to avoid, while they must guess. Even against the most expert opponents, it is worth, on average, between one and two tricks in the play to reach your final contract without bidding any suits (e.g., one notrump — three notrump; or one notrump — pass).

Naturally, this is just as true of the strong 16-to-18-point notrump opening. But you hold far fewer 17-point hands than 13-point hands. And it is with the weaker hands that you are more likely to need a little friendly defense.

This, then, is the gist of our system: We give up accuracy in our partscore bidding when we have balanced, minimum openings; in return, we gain accuracy for slam, game and part-score bidding when we have strong and unbalanced openings. In addition, we gain preemption for our weak hands.

You will find this theme repeated many times and in many ways throughout our bidding system: *high, preemptive bidding for weaker hands; "keep-it-low," precise bidding for stronger hands.*

Short-Suit Tries for Game

For the past few years I (along with Freddy Sheinwold, Lenny Harmon, and Ivar Stakgold) have been experimenting with a new kind of try for game. It arises out of a specialized situation: A trump suit has been firmly established at a low level, and the auction has limited both hands to the extent that there are no slam prospects—only game is being considered.

The most common of these auctions is:

SOUTH	WEST	NORTH	EAST
1 ♠	Pass	2 ♠	Pass

Other instances are:

SOUTH	WEST	NORTH	EAST
1 NT	Pass	2 ♠	Pass

SOUTH	WEST	NORTH	EAST
—	1 ♣	Double	Pass
1 ♠	Pass	2 ♠	Pass

In each example, a bid of three spades by South would be a straightforward game-try, saying: "Go on if you have a maximum; stop if you have nothing extra." Often, however, the question is not of maximum or minimum points, but of fit—of how well the partnership hands mesh.

Here, the standard treatment is to bid the longest side suit. Partner is expected to "encourage" if he fits the second suit also. With each of the following five example hands, opener, having bid one spade and been given a single raise to two spades, might well bid three diamonds:

1. ♠ A K x x x ♡ K J x ◇ K 10 9 x ♣ x

2. ♠ K Q x x x ♡ K Q x ◇ A x x x ♣ x

3. ♠ A K J x x ♡ A J x ◇ J x x x ♣ x

4. ♠ A J x x x ♡ x x x ◇ A K J x ♣ x

5. ♠ K Q x x x ♡ x x x ◇ A K Q x ♣ x

But does this three-diamond bid really do the job of finding out how well the hands fit?

Suppose responder has three diamonds to the queen. Is that good or bad? Well, it's good facing Hand 1; fair, facing No. 2; terrible, facing No. 3; and magnificent, facing No. 4.

Suppose responder has a singleton diamond. That's tremendous, facing No. 2 or 3; pretty fair opposite No. 1; but it warns of dangerous duplication facing No. 4 or 5.

Actually, responder is just guessing on these auctions, for except when opener has a freakish two-suiter, the fit of a pair of hands is not largely determined by responder's holding in his partner's second suit. It is determined by how much waste strength and distribution responder has opposite opener's singleton.

This is the central point. Good, fitting hands are those with little duplication, either of strength (honors opposite singletons or voids) or of distribution (short suits opposite short suits).

Look at these two cases:

(a)

WEST	EAST
♠ A Q x x x	♠ J x x
♡ K Q x	♡ x x x
◇ Q x x x	◇ K x x
♣ x	♣ K J x x

(b)

WEST	EAST
♠ A Q x x x	♠ K x x
♡ K Q x	♡ J x x
◇ Q x x x	◇ K J x x
♣ x	♣ x x x

The reason that (b) has a decent play for 10 tricks, while (a) has a struggle for eight tricks, is not so much the superior diamond fit as it is the absence of waste in clubs. Partnership hands with three low cards of a suit facing a singleton will take at least a trick more than their points warrant.

The next pair of partnership hands illustrate the other factor involved in "fit":

(c)

WEST	EAST
♠ A Q x x x	♠ K J x x
♡ x x x	♡ Q x x
◇ A K J x	◇ 10 x x x
♣ x	♣ x x

(d)

WEST	EAST
♠ A Q x x x	♠ K J x x
♡ x x x	♡ x x
◇ A K J x	◇ 10 x x x
♣ x	♣ Q x x

Combination (d) offers a fair play for game, while (c) needs a miracle. It is not a matter of diamond fit but of duplicated distribution. In (c) both partners are short in the same suit, clubs. (Make that doubleton in responder's hand a singleton, and it becomes a two-trick difference whether it's in clubs or hearts.)

Well, what's the solution? Simply to have opener rebid in his shortest side suit! It doesn't help responder much in gauging the fit to know what opener's second-longest suit is, but learning what opener's short suit is answers all questions.

On the auction:

SOUTH	WEST	NORTH	EAST
1 ♠	Pass	2 ♠	Pass
3 ♣			

as we use this club bid, the meaning is that opener is short in clubs. Responder goes to game at spades with:

♠ Q x x x   ♡ K 10 x   ◇ Q J x   ♣ x x x

because all his values are working; but he signs off at three spades with:

♠ Q x x x   ♡ K 10 x   ◇ x x x   ♣ Q J x

because of the duplication in the club suit.

On the same auction, with:

♠ Q x x x   ♡ A x x x   ◇ x x   ♣ x x x

responder jumps to four spades over three clubs—the hand patterns fit well. But with:

♠ Q x x x   ♡ A x x x   ◇ x x x   ♣ x x

responder signs off. In effect, the hand with the doubleton diamond is a full ace stronger than the hand with the doubleton club, because opener's rebid announced club shortness of his own.

Almost always, finding opener's shortest suit tells responder (1) whether his high cards are where they will do the most good, and (2) whether his own short-suit values are useful.

If you decide to use short-suit tries, be sure to remember that they should not be used indiscriminately whenever the auction goes one spade — two spades, or one heart — two hearts. Of the following four opening bids of one spade, only the first is suitable for a three-club game-try if partner raises to two spades:

♠ A Q x x x   ♡ K J x x   ◇ K Q x   ♣ x

♠ A Q x x x   ♡ Q J x x   ◇ K x x   ♣ x

♠ A Q J x x   ♡ K J x x   ◇ A K x   ♣ x

♠ A Q x x x   ♡ K J x   ◇ Q 10 x   ♣ A x

The second hand is too weak—even if the fit is good, game is too unlikely. Just pass.

With the third hand, bid four spades directly over partner's two spades; you should be willing to play at game even if there is some duplication of values. The fourth hand is the right strength for a game-try, but three clubs is the wrong try. You need points from partner, not fit; just about any old points will do. Bid two notrump or three spades to show that you are looking for game on power, not on fit.

Incidentally, when playing against opponents who tend to trap and balance, it pays to use the auctions one spade — two spades — three spades and one heart — two hearts — three hearts as substantially preemptive, like the raise of a weak two-bid. When looking for a game on power, rebid two notrump; when looking for a good fit, rebid in a short suit.

Remember also that short-suit tries have nothing whatever to do with auctions like these:

WEST	EAST
1 ◇	1 ♠
2 ♠	3 ♣

WEST	EAST
1 ♠	3 ♡
4 ◇	

Why not? Because the three-club bid in the first case and the four-diamond bid in the second may well be slam-tries. The rebid in a short suit must not be confused with a control-showing bid that suggests a slam. Only if the auction indicates that game is all that's in view—generally, because the bidder has limited his hand—are short-suit signals on.

Here is a sampling of deals from play that feature the short-suit game-try:

WEST	EAST
♠ K 10 7 6 5 4	♠ J 8 3
♡ K 4	♡ Q J 7 5
◇ A Q 10 6	◇ K 5 2
♣ 3	♣ 10 7 5

Our bidding went:

WEST	EAST
1 ♠	2 ♠
3 ♣	4 ♠
Pass	

Responder had a flat, unexciting raise on Round 1, but bid game anyway, since he knew that there was no duplication of values.

WEST	EAST
♠ Q 6 4	♠ 7 5 2
♡ A K J 6 3	♡ Q 10 5 4 2
◇ 7	◇ Q 8
♣ A J 6 4	♣ K 7 5

Our bidding went:

WEST	EAST
1 ♡	2 ♡
3 ◇	3 ♡
Pass	

Here, responder had a far stronger initial raise—a tip-top maximum as we play the single raise—but he signed off because of the double-duplication of his wasted points and shortness in diamonds. Actually, three hearts went down, since the club finesse was off, but our counterparts at the other table (in team-of-four with IMP scoring) bid four hearts and went down two. So we picked up two IMP anyway.

Another case:

WEST	EAST
♠ A Q 5 3	♠ K J 10 7 2
♡ K 6 2	♡ 8 7 5
◇ A J 7 4	◇ K 3 2
♣ 8 4	♣ K 6

Our bidding went:

WEST	EAST
1 NT	2 ♠
3 ♣	3 ♠
Pass	

As will be seen, we were playing weak notrumps. Initially, responder did not have enough strength to envision game, but opener was excited by the spade response. Perhaps there might be a game on fit if not on points. But West's short-suit try—obviously, any bid over the two spade sign-off must be based on a big spade fit—did not encourage East despite his maximum. He knew that the distributional mesh was wrong and that there were not enough high cards to compensate.

Our opposite numbers reached game, down one. (The club ace and the diamond queen were right, but the heart ace was wrong.) Their bidding went:

WEST	EAST
1 ◇	1 ♠
2 ♠	3 ♠
4 ♠	Pass

Still another case:

WEST	EAST
♠ K Q J 6 5	♠ 10 9 7 4 2
♡ A J 5 3	♡ 4
◊ K J 10	◊ Q 7 3
♣ 6	♣ 8 7 5 2

Our bidding went:

WEST	EAST
1 ♠	2 ♠
3 ♣	3 ♡
4 ♠	Pass

Responder's three-heart bid said: "I have a singleton heart but such a miserable hand that I can't afford to bid game. Is it enough?" It was just what opener needed, and an excellent game contract was reached with less than half the high cards in the deck. The two short-suit tries disclosed the hand-in-glove fit.

Of course, our results have not always been so pretty. These game-tries deal with close situations, and plenty of judgment is involved. My recollection is that over the years we have had an overwhelming preponderance of good results over bad, but perhaps this is partly due to a tendency to ascribe an occasional bad result, not to the bidding device, but to (1) partner's poor judgment or (2) an unlucky position of cards, according to circumstances.

Still, I, and all the other hardy experimenters, know this for certain: We have been able to get exactly the information we want in these occasional situations. We have made informed decisions, not guesses. When we made errors, we could have known better. And we have had a lot of fun, getting to those game contracts with 17 or so high-card points in the combined hands—the kind of game contracts which, if they make, leave the opponents gnashing their teeth.

A New Approach to Slam Bidding

S lam bidding is the greatest single weakness of virtually all American expert partnerships. This is not just my notion—it is an opinion shared by most authorities, and there is solid evidence to back it up.

Year after year in the World's Championship, America's slam record has been miserable. In the early years, when we were winning, our opponents' slam bidding was, luckily, as bad as ours. But lately theirs has been much better. In the 1959 match, the Italian superiority in this department accounted for nearly the entire 50-IMP margin of victory.

This generally inept slam bidding is obvious in our own tournaments. In the Master Pairs, you will score about 22 matchpoints out of 25 for bidding a "tough" slam—one predicated on fit, not power. And even a "baby" slam, with 12 tricks off the top, will generally receive 17 or so matchpoints. Team competition, even in top-level matches, is no different. When you bid and make a slam, you rather expect to gain on the deal; and when your opponents make the slam, you are likely to be nervous about the result at the other table.

Why is American slam bidding so poor? One reason, in my opinion, is the general inaccuracy of standard bidding methods. The game zone is very wide, and the broad, vague limits of the early rounds in standard bidding are not too great a handicap in hitting so wide a target. But the slam zone is narrow, so that systems that provide more specific meanings to opening bids, responses and rebids have a big advantage in this department, where precision is of prime importance. But that is another story. I do not want to beat the drum here for the Kaplan-Sheinwold, Roth-Stone, Acol, Neapolitan Club or Roman Club systems, any one of which, in my opinion, provides a firmer base for slam bidding than does American Standard. I do want to discuss the slam investigation itself.

For here is the greatest weakness in our slam bidding: We simply do not have the tools to do the job effectively. Our main reliance is on Blackwood, with some undisciplined control-bidding thrown in. (Is a control-showing bid always an ace? Do you show lower or higher-ranking controls first? Must you respond to a control-bid with one of your own if you have an ace to show?) And Blackwood is not a precision instrument. It's good enough for a club rubber-bridge game, just so that you can find out something for sure about the hand that the so-and-so opposite you holds. But an expert partnership should want to use Blackwood for no more than one slam in ten. Location of honors, distribution, hand quality, trump strength—these are the factors that make or break most slams, and we have no specific methods for exchanging information of this sort.

In contrast, when Signor Forquet is aware of the slam possibilities in a deal, he has seven different ways to exchange information with, or extract information from, Signor Siniscalco. He has a four-notrump bid that announces certain values and asks about hand quality and controls; he has an organized control-bidding series; he has asking-bids; he has bids to check on trump quality for both small and grand slams; and he even has Blackwood and Gerber available for rare specific situations. I've heard of top-ranking golfers who, as a gag, go around a course using only a five-iron. In effect, that is what we have been trying to do in our slam bidding, and it hasn't worked well against opponents who have a full set of clubs.

Freddy Sheinwold and I used to be just as complacent as most American pairs about our slam-bidding techniques, but we have learned from the Italians. We have adapted several of the Neapolitan and Roman conventions to our own use, and worked out an integrated method which assures us of getting the information we want. In the future, if we miss good slams or bid poor ones, it will be, at any rate, the fault of our judgment, not of our equipment. The Italian devices that we have borrowed are the Neapolitan D.I. (declarative-interrogative) four notrump, the Roman modifications of Blackwood and the Grand-Slam Force, and the simplified asking-bids used in both systems.

The D.I. four-notrump bid resembles the old Culbertson Four-Five Notrump convention. It is not a "captain-private" device like Blackwood, in which one partner must make all decisions; instead, it allows full scope for partnership interplay and judgment. The four-notrump bidder promises certain values and asks for other values (hence declarative-interrogative). He promises an interest in slam and at least two aces. (Exceptionally, the D.I. four notrump may be bid with one ace, but only by a rigidly limited hand.) The four-notrump bidder is unlikely to have two losers in an unbid suit, for then he would tend to show a control he has (in order to suggest weakness in the danger suit) rather than bid four notrump. The bidder is interested in partner's quality and controls.

There are three types of replies to the D.I. four notrump: negative, encouraging, and positive. The negative response is, of course, the return to the agreed trump suit. An encouraging response is the bid of a control or feature lower-ranking than the agreed trump suit. A positive response is the bid of a control or feature higher-ranking than the trump suit, or a jump to slam in the trump suit (which warns partner not to bid seven), or a bid of five notrump (a grand-slam-try that announces possession of the other two aces, plus maximum values for previous bidding).

OPENER	RESPONDER
♠ K x	♠ A Q x
♡ A Q x x x x	♡ J x x
◇ A x x	◇ K x x
♣ K x	♣ Q J x x

OPENER	RESPONDER
1 ♡	2 NT
3 ♡	4 ♡
4 NT	5 ♡
Pass	

When opener's suit is supported, he makes a generalized slam-try with the D.I. four notrump. Responder signs off, for he has a minimum, poor support, and no low-ranking control to show. Opener then passes, knowing that he is missing the ace of clubs and either the ace of spades or king of trumps.

If, instead of the hand shown, responder held:

♠ Q J x   ♡ J x x   ◇ K x x   ♣ A Q x x

he would bid five clubs over four notrump. He should show his ace, even with a minimum, so long as it does not commit the partnership to slam. Now opener would bid only five hearts; he has made his slam-try and, with a hole in trumps, must leave the final decision to partner, who would pass.

If responder's hand were:

♠ A x x ♡ K J x ◇ K x x ♣ A x x x

he would bid five notrump over four notrump—two aces, a maximum, good values for seven. But opener would sign off with six hearts or six notrump.

Normally, a grand slam will be bid only after a five-notrump reply to the D.I. four notrump. But the four-notrump bidder may try for seven over any other reply by bidding five notrump himself. This promises one more ace than his four-notrump bid announced and asks partner's views on grand-slam prospects. Again, the negative response is the return to the trump suit; a bid of six in a lower-ranking suit is encouraging; and a bid in a higher-ranking suit or a jump to seven is obviously positive.

OPENER	RESPONDER
♠ A K J x x x	♠ Q x
♡ A x	♡ K Q 10 x x
◇ K x x	◇ A x x
♣ A x	♣ x x x

OPENER	RESPONDER
1 ♠	2 ♡
3 ♠	4 ♠
4 NT	5 ◇
5 NT	6 ♡
7 ♠	Pass

Responder shows his diamond ace in answer to the D.I. four notrump, and opener tries for seven with five notrump. Responder cannot jump to seven for fear that opener's hand is:

♠ A J 10 x x x x ♡ A x ◇ K x ♣ A x

but he confirms the quality of his hearts and indicates a lively interest in a grand slam by bidding six hearts, refusing to sign off with six spades.

Now opener can comfortably bid seven, for responder would not dare encourage without a trump honor.

Note that none of the D.I. sequences described are automatic, cut-and-dried questions and answers. At every stage, judgment is required. It is this flexible partnership element that makes the convention ideal for expert partners who have confidence in each other's decisions.

We do not give up either Blackwood or quantitative raises to four notrump in order to use the D.I. convention. Our understanding is this: If four notrump is bid directly over any notrump bid:

OPENER	RESPONDER
1 ♡	2 NT
4 NT	

it is quantitative, a request to go on to six notrump with maximum point-count.

If four notrump is bid as a *jump* over three or lower in a suit:

OPENER	RESPONDER
1 ♡	3 ♡
4 NT	

it is Blackwood.

Only if four notrump is bid over four of a suit is it D.I. And even then, we consider four notrump to be Blackwood when bid by responder at his first turn or by opener at his second turn:

OPENER	RESPONDER
4 ♠	4 NT

OPENER	RESPONDER
1 ♡	4 ♡
4 NT	

We do not sneer at Blackwood; it is a very useful convention for an occasional slam deal, so we retain it without depending upon it exclusively. In replying to Blackwood, any regular partnership should adopt the Roman modification, which gives information about which aces, as well as how many aces, are held. Over the Blackwood four notrump:

Five clubs shows no aces or three aces.

Five diamonds shows one ace or four aces.

Five hearts shows two aces: both red or both black or both major or both minor.

Five spades shows two aces, different both in color and rank of suit. The same replies are used at the six-level over a five-notrump request for kings.

OPENER	RESPONDER
♠ A K J x x	♠ Q 10 x x
♡ K Q J x	♡ A
◇ K Q x	◇ J 10 x x x
♣ K	♣ A x x

OPENER	RESPONDER
1 ♠	3 ♠
4 NT	5 ♠
6 NT	Pass

The five-spade reply shows two aces, different in color, one in a major suit, the other in a minor. Since opener holds the spade ace himself, he knows that partner holds the club and heart aces, and 12 tricks at notrump are virtually guaranteed. Without the modification, opener would have to bid the slam at spades, risking a diamond ruff, for fear that responder did not hold the club ace. (A five-heart response would not be so illuminating; it could be either hearts and diamonds—both red—or clubs and diamonds—both minor. All opener could tell for sure would be that responder holds the ace of diamonds.)

It is pure laziness not to use this Roman improvement. All it can do is help; it cannot hurt, even by telling the opening leader which ace his partner holds, for only a player with an ace himself can get any useful information.

Control-bidding, as Freddy Sheinwold and I use it, has two primary functions. When a trump suit has been established early in the auction, we use control-bids under the game level to suggest slam possibilities, to find out whether or not partner is slam-minded, too. Over the game level, we use control-bids to locate a control in a danger suit in which we have losers. Thus, replies to control-bids differ according to the particular bidding level at which the bid is made.

When the control-bid is made under game:

OPENER	RESPONDER
1 ♡	3 ♡
4 ♣	

partner is under no obligation to answer with a control-bid of his own merely because he holds an ace in an unbid suit. If the control-bidder wanted to know only about aces, he would have used Blackwood; and if he were looking for only one specific control, he could use the asking-bid described in the next section. Partner control-bids in reply only if he has good values for slam; otherwise, he signs off by returning to the trump suit. (The control-bidder can now persist in slam investigation with the D.I. four notrump—his control-bid may have been marking time until the proper level for the D.I. bid was reached—or with another control-bid over the game level.)

Control-bids under game do not unconditionally promise first-round controls, although they suggest them. The initial control-bid is made to test for slam, and the answering control-bid is made to encourage—sometimes, no side-suit first-round control is available to be bid.

Wit and Wisdom

"In an effort to improve, I studied records of late rounds of major events. Among other things, this led me to give up overcalling on marginal hands. With a light, distributional hand, it is better to pass unless you have enough playing strength to jump preemptively. If you bid on a light hand, partner may put you overboard; and when an opponent becomes declarer, he may play better than you would like."

OPENER	RESPONDER
♠ K J x x x	♠ A Q x x
♡ K x	♡ x x
◇ A x	◇ K Q J x x
♣ A x x x	♣ x x

OPENER	RESPONDER
1 ♠	3 ♠
4 ♣	4 ◇
4 NT	5 ◇
6 ♠	Pass

Over the forcing jump-response, opener puts out a tentative feeler for slam—he will pass a sign-off reply. But responder has slammish values and shows a second-round control for lack of a side ace. This encourages opener to try again with a D.I. four notrump. Once again, responder refuses to sign off; he shows extra values in diamonds. (Responder is not worried about aces; opener has promised two.) Now opener, with excellent controls, bids the laydown slam. (He, too, is not worried about aces; responder would surely not encourage twice if aceless.)

Control-bids over the game level should be used to find a specific control. In reply, no option may be exercised—the control partner is seeking *must* be shown, regardless of hand quality. In this auction:

OPENER	RESPONDER
1 ♠	2 ♡
4 ♡	5 ♣

opener must now show a diamond control if he has one—the ace or a void by bidding five diamonds, the king by bidding five notrump, a singleton by jumping to six hearts. If responder were interested in general strength, he would have bid four notrump (D.I.) His only concern must be the unbid suit.

OPENER	RESPONDER
♠ K J x x x	♠ —
♡ x x	♡ A K Q x
◇ K J x x	◇ A Q 10 x x x x x
♣ A x	♣ x

OPENER	RESPONDER
1 ♠	3 ◇
4 ◇	4 ♡
5 ◇	5 ♡
6 ♣	7 ◇
Pass	

Note that opener does not show his ace in reply to the four-heart control-bid under game—he shows his minimum by signing off. But the second control-bid—over game—gives him no choice, and responder finds out what he wants to know.

We have added to our arsenal of slam weapons a second method of locating specific controls: asking-bids. These are jumps in a new suit after a trump suit has been established.

OPENER	RESPONDER
1 ♠	3 ♠
5 ◇ (?)	

They ask for first- or second-round control in the suit jumped in. The replies (borrowed from the Italians) are by steps; each possible bid skipped shows more control in the asked suit.

One step (five hearts in the example auction) shows neither first- nor second-round control.

Two steps (five spades): king or singleton.

Three steps (five notrump): ace or void.

Four steps (six clubs): ace and king. (When the deal is clearly going to play in a trump suit, and with an abundance of trumps, the four-step answer may be given at discretion with a void or singleton ace.)

Wit and Wisdom

"It is easy to see how declarer could lose by that play; it is more difficult to see how he could gain. As is so often demonstrated, the declarer can always defeat the contract."

OPENER	RESPONDER
♠ A K J x x	♠ Q x x
♡ Q x x	♡ x x x
◇ A K J x x	◇ x
♣ —	♣ A K J x x x

OPENER	RESPONDER
1 ♠	2 ♣
2 ◇	2 ♠
4 ♡	4 ♠
Pass	

The asking-bid of four hearts enables the partnership to stay safely at the four level. The one-step reply tells opener that slam is impossible, and he can avoid going to five, which would jeopardize game.

These asking-bids must be handled with great care, for they use up a good deal of bidding space. Particular attention must be paid to the level of safety in the event of an unsatisfactory response. For instance, in the last example on control-bidding, responder dare not "ask" with a jump to six clubs over opener's four-diamond rebid; a two-step answer, showing second-round control, would put the partnership overboard.

But, within safe limits, the asking-bid is a magnificent device for rare appropriate hands. For example:

OPENER	RESPONDER
♠ A Q J x x x	♠ K 10 x x x
♡ Q J x x x	♡ A
◇ A	◇ K x x x
♣ A	♣ x x x

OPENER	RESPONDER
1 ♠	3 ♠
5 ♡ (?)	6 ◇
7 ♠	Pass

After the jump-raise, opener is concerned only with responder's heart holding, so he asks with a jump. He will pass a one-step reply, or bid six spades over a two- or three-step answer. But when responder skips three bids to give a four-step reply, showing first- and second-round control, opener bids the cold grand slam. Observe that he bids seven spades, not seven notrump, allowing for the possibility of a heart void or singleton ace.

If bidding economy permits, an asking-bid may be repeated in order to locate third-round control, A one-step answer denies holding the queen or a doubleton in the asked suit, while a two-step answer affirms such a holding.

OPENER	RESPONDER
♠ A K Q 10 x x x	♠ J x x x
♡ —	♡ K x x
◇ A K x x	◇ x x x
♣ A K	♣ 10 x x

OPENER	RESPONDER
2 ♣	2 ◇
2 ♠	3 ♠
5 ◇ (?)	5 ♡
6 ◇	6 ♡
6 ♠	Pass

After his spades are raised, opener asks in diamonds. He will bid seven spades over a two-step reply showing a singleton. Over responder's denial, opener asks in diamonds again—the diamond queen or even a doubleton will make the grand slam odds-on. But responder denies once more, and that's that.

The final Italian device that we have adopted is the Roman modification of the Grand-Slam Force. As most American expert partnerships play, a jump to five notrump after a trump suit has been established, as in:

OPENER	RESPONDER
1 ♠	3 ♠
5 NT	

demands that partner bid seven in the agreed suit if he has two of the three top trump honors; otherwise, he must bid six.

The Romans have added a third reply. In answer to five notrump, six clubs denies holding any of the three top honors; six in the trump suit announces one honor; and seven in the trump suit promises two. (Obviously, if the trump suit is clubs, no distinction can be made between no honor and one.)

OPENER	RESPONDER
♠ K Q x x x	♠ J 10 9 x x
♡ —	♡ A K x
◇ A K Q J x	◇ x
♣ A x x	♣ K 10 x x

OPENER	RESPONDER
1 ♠	3 ♠
5 NT	6 ♣
6 ♠	Pass

Here, the Roman modification allows the partnership to avoid an undignified grand slam. So far as I can see, it has no disadvantages.

I don't think that anyone would dispute the fact that the set of tools for slam investigation described in this article represents a considerable improvement over standard equipment. However, one reasonable objection can be made: each of these devices is fine by itself, but taken together they are a formidable list to remember. Is there not a grave danger of confusion, of human error?

Of course there is. If you were to sit down to play rubber bridge with some other *Bridge World* reader, and said to one another, "Let's play all that stuff in Kaplan's article," you would be asking for trouble. These slam devices are meant not for casual play but for steady partnerships. And if you have a regular partner for set games or for tournament play, you should be anxious to use delicate bidding methods.

So, at your club, stick to Blackwood and prayer. But don't be surprised if these don't win any world championships.

NATIONAL CHAMPIONSHIPS

Edgar's reports of national championships covered a wide range. Most were descriptions of the major team events—the national knockouts and the trials to select international representatives—but there were also pair events (at IMPs when the international trials were on a pair basis, and at matchpoints), other team events (such as the national board-a-match championship, at which Edgar excelled beyond even his usual fine results), and, remarkably, after his long-shot triumph in what was far from his favorite event, a report of the (Life) Masters Individual. The last-named was his first tournament report.

Life Masters Individual

While I enthusiastically approve of the result of this year's [1957] Masters Individual, I can't say that I had a very good time playing in it. And I usually do. This is a nerve-shattering tournament if you're in a good position to win. I could never relax and really enjoy the mad scramble. [*Editor's note (by Sonny Moyse): It has, perhaps, been subtly indicated that Mr. Kaplan was the winner of this year's Masters Individual, with its record-breaking field of 136, but we like to make everything pellucidly clear: He was.*]

There are three factors in the winning of this event: you must play reasonably well; you need a lot of fortitude; and you must be enormously lucky. Luck is the theme of this article, as it should be in one about the Individual.

There are many kinds of good luck in bridge, and I had all of them. In this first deal, I was lucky enough to have my partner make an excellent play. (In this event, in which even the best players produce their worst bridge, this is the very height of luck.)

East dealer; neither side vulnerable

NORTH
♠ 7 5
♡ 8 5
◇ A 7 3
♣ A Q 10 8 6 5

WEST
♠ A Q 9 6 2
♡ K 3
◇ K 10 6 2
♣ J 4

EAST
♠ K J 8 4 3
♡ A J 9 4
◇ J 8 4
♣ 2

SOUTH
♠ 10
♡ Q 10 7 6 2
◇ Q 9 5
♣ K 9 7 3

I was South, playing with Geoffrion, of Montreal.

SOUTH	WEST	NORTH	EAST
—	—	—	Pass
Pass	1 ♠	2 ♣	3 ♠
4 ♣	4 ♠	5 ♣	Pass
Pass	Double	Pass	5 ♠
Pass	Pass	Pass	

Geoffrion opened the club ace against the five-spade contract and shifted to the eight of hearts. Declarer pulled one round of trumps, played a heart to the ace and ruffed a heart, then went back to the trump king to ruff the fourth heart. Now he ruffed his club jack in dummy, and this was the position:

Wit and Wisdom

"Which method you choose is not as critical as the decision to select some complex method. The chief benefit is that it forces partnership discussion of many sequences. In the end, you pick a method that fits your personality."

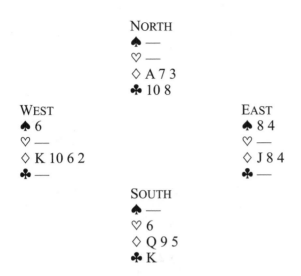

NORTH
♠ —
♡ —
◇ A 7 3
♣ 10 8

WEST
♠ 6
♡ —
◇ K 10 6 2
♣ —

EAST
♠ 8 4
♡ —
◇ J 8 4
♣ —

SOUTH
♠ —
♡ 6
◇ Q 9 5
♣ K

Declarer led the diamond jack from dummy. I covered with the queen, and West played the king.

On winning with the ace, North is endplayed. A club return affords a ruff-and-sluff; and the lead of either diamond is fatal, with declarer's combined eight-six "tenace" over North's seven-spot picking up my nine. Talk about a battle of spots!

But Geoffrion didn't take the diamond trick. He valued his seven correctly and let West hold the trick with the king. Now declarer had to continue the suit for himself and had to lose two tricks in it. Down one, and a well-deserved top for my partner, a lucky top for me.

Another Canadian, Eric Murray, of Toronto, also earned an excellent score for me with accurate play, but he was my opponent:

Wit and Wisdom

"Don't have your business in your house, because you will never get away from your work. I never have a clear conscience. I always have a vast pile of work to be done, right at my elbow, so I can't do anything else with an easy conscience—I do it anyway, but not with a clear conscience."

NORTH
♠ Q
♡ 10 9 5 3
◇ K J 6
♣ Q J 10 6 4

WEST
♠ A K 3
♡ K 8 4
◇ A 2
♣ A K 9 8 5

EAST
♠ 10 8 7 5 4 2
♡ Q J 6
◇ 10 4 3
♣ 7

SOUTH
♠ J 9 6
♡ A 7 2
◇ Q 9 8 7 5
♣ 3 2

Murray was East; I was South. The bidding went:

SOUTH	WEST	NORTH	EAST
—	2 NT	Pass	4 ♠
Pass	Pass	Pass	

I led a low diamond. The ace was played, followed by the club ace. Murray then ruffed a club, led to the trump ace and tried to ruff another club. I overruffed, led a diamond to partner's king, and made my trump jack for the setting trick when my partner returned another club.

Now, superficially it seems that Murray blew a cold contract, but I'm sure that his play was correct at matchpoints. Obviously, it is no feat to make four spades; but to make five, Murray had to establish dummy's fifth club. He can't afford to draw two rounds of trumps before going after the clubs; he needs both high trumps in dummy for entries. In short, he should go down one in the try for an overtrick [moot at best—*Editor*]. It was simply my good luck to have a capable declarer playing this deal against me.

One of my most interesting results came when I held this hand:

♠ K 7 5 2   ♡ —   ◇ 8 4 3   ♣ A Q J 9 7 6

With both sides vulnerable, my LHO opened with one heart, which was passed by my partner and my RHO. I decided not to double (despite my quite respectable high-card strength) for fear of a leave-in; so I balanced with two clubs. The opener now bid two diamonds, my partner doubled, and two hearts was bid at my right. I strongly suspected that partner's double of two diamonds was based on a slew of hearts behind the opener, but I still wanted to warn against a heart double, and so I bid two spades. Who knows—partner might get a crack at three hearts. However, opener passed, and my partner went to two notrump. I happily raised to three notrump and wasn't too worried when the opener doubled, as I had a maximum for my bidding, with a long, strong, suit. As may be seen, we achieved an excellent result, for this was the full deal:

NORTH
♠ 10 6
♡ A 8 6 5
♢ Q J 9 7
♣ K 5 3

WEST
♠ A Q J
♡ K J 10 9 4
♢ A K 10 2
♣ 8

EAST
♠ 9 8 4 3
♡ Q 7 3 2
♢ 6 5
♣ 10 4 2

SOUTH
♠ K 7 5 2
♡ —
♢ 8 4 3
♣ A Q J 9 7 6

No, we didn't make three notrump doubled. East led a heart, and the best my partner could do was cash six clubs and one heart, for down 500. But we got 10 matchpoints out of 12 for this horrible contract—the opponents were cold for game at hearts.

This stroke of fortune was neatly counterbalanced in the next session, on this freak:

West dealer
Both sides vulnerable

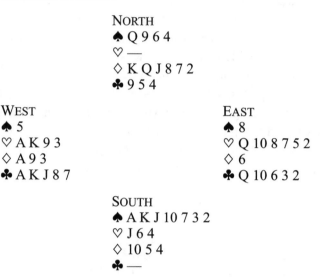

NORTH
♠ Q 9 6 4
♡ —
◇ K Q J 8 7 2
♣ 9 5 4

WEST
♠ 5
♡ A K 9 3
◇ A 9 3
♣ A K J 8 7

EAST
♠ 8
♡ Q 10 8 7 5 2
◇ 6
♣ Q 10 6 3 2

SOUTH
♠ A K J 10 7 3 2
♡ J 6 4
◇ 10 5 4
♣ —

West opened his monster with one club. North, my partner, over-called one diamond, and East passed, biding his time. I took a shot at four spades. West licked his chops and doubled. North passed happily, but, of course, East took out the double to five clubs. This was passed around to my partner, who bid five spades, undeterred by the double of four spades. East passed rather reluctantly, I just passed, and West blasted us all out of our seats with a *"Double!"* East simply had to leave that one in!

Since West made a normal lead, I lost only one trick—the diamond ace. Five spades, doubled, and made with an overtrick—pretty sweet. Oh sure. Out of 12 matchpoints we got two-and-a-half. Almost everyone bid six clubs on the East-West cards—a contract that certainly figured to come home looking only at their hands—and drove the North-South pairs into a spectacularly successful "save" at six spades.

This last deal was the luckiest of all. It came up in the final session, and the tournament hinged on the outcome.

West dealer; both sides vulnerable

```
                        NORTH
                        ♠ A K Q 7 5
                        ♡ A 7
                        ◇ K J 9 4
                        ♣ 9 7
    WEST                                    EAST
    ♠ J 6 3                                 ♠ 9 8 4 2
    ♡ Q J 9 6 4 2                           ♡ K
    ◇ Q 8 6                                 ◇ A 10 5 2
    ♣ A                                     ♣ 10 6 3 2
                        SOUTH
                        ♠ 10
                        ♡ 10 8 5 3
                        ◇ 7 3
                        ♣ K Q J 8 5 4
```

SOUTH	WEST	NORTH	EAST
—	Pass	1 ♠	Pass
1 NT	Pass	2 ◇	Pass
3 ♣	Pass	3 NT	(All Pass)

As South, I hold no brief for my partner's three-notrump bid, although it won the tournament for me. I had done my darndest to scream that my hand was worthless except at clubs. But there I was at three notrump, a foul contract which can make only if an opponent wins the first club trick, either injudiciously or because he has the singleton ace.

West opened the heart queen, which I won in dummy, East's king falling. I led the nine of clubs (not the seven) to my king, and West put on the ace. West shifted to a small diamond, and dummy's jack forced the ace. The diamond return rode to dummy's king. I led the club seven from the table, finessed my own eight, and made 10 tricks for a top.

You see, I was lucky enough to have Norman Kay on my left, in the West position. Never in his life has Norman been guilty of so bad a play as winning the first club if he could hold up, so the finesse was marked.

Obviously, the secret of winning Individuals is to make sure that your opponents are more expert than your partners.

Trials Quiz

The team that will represent North America in the 1967 World Championship will be: Sami Kehela and Eric Murray of Toronto; Edgar Kaplan of New York and Norman Kay of Philadelphia; Alvin Roth and William Root of New York. These three pairs finished one, two, three in the International Team Trials held in Pittsburgh in November [1966]. You can test yourself with these problems, taken from Edgar Kaplan's account of his own experiences in the Trials. IMP scoring in all cases. The results will be found in Trials Diary, which follows.

1. With both sides vulnerable, you hold:

♠ Q 9 6 5   ♡ Q 10 4   ◊ 10 9 4   ♣ Q 9 2

Partner opens one spade, and your RHO passes. What is your response? (*See page 187.*)

2. With both sides vulnerable, you hold:

♠ A K Q J 8 6 4   ♡ K   ◊ 8   ♣ 10 5 4 3

Partner opens one heart. With the opponents silent, you respond one spade, and partner rebids two diamonds. What now? Do you approve of the first response? (*See page 188.*)

3. You hold the East cards, sitting behind the dummy in this layout:

NORTH (*dummy*)
♠ J 6 4 2
♡ K 9 3
◊ K 7 6
♣ A 9 4

EAST (*you*)
♠ Q
♡ A J 6 2
◊ Q J 9 8 3
♣ K 7 6

SOUTH	WEST	NORTH	EAST
—	Pass	Pass	1 ♡
2 ♠	3 ♡	4 ♠	(All Pass)

South's jump-overcall was preemptive. Partner leads the heart four, dummy plays the three, and your jack wins the trick, declarer following with the eight. What do you return? (*See page 189.*)

4. Your right-hand opponent opens one notrump (12-14 points), you pass, and your left-hand opponent closes the auction with three notrump. What is your opening lead from this hand? (*See page 190.*)

♠ Q 8 3   ♡ A K 9 6 3   ◇ K 5 3   ♣ 6 2

5. Partner opens one diamond; you respond one spade, holding:

♠ A 10 7 4   ♡ K 10 4   ◇ J 9 8   ♣ K 8 3

Partner reverses to two hearts. What is your rebid? (*See page 193.*)

6. You hold, nonvulnerable against vulnerable opponents:

♠ K 7 3   ♡ 9 7 3   ◇ J 5 3 2   ♣ 10 4 2

Partner opens two spades (weak) in first seat; RHO passes. What is your action? What if partner had bid *three* spades? (*See page 196.*)

7. You are declarer in four spades with the cards below:

DECLARER	DUMMY
♠ A J 7 5	♠ 10 4 3 2
♡ A K 7	♡ J 4
◇ A 9 3 2	◇ J 7 6 5
♣ 9 8	♣ A K 10

Your left-hand opponent leads the heart three to dummy's jack, right-hand opponent playing the deuce. Plan your play. (*See page 197.*)

8. Again you are East, defending:

NORTH (*dummy*)
♠ A Q 10 8 3
♡ A 7
◇ 8
♣ K J 6 5 2

EAST (*you*)
♠ K 6 4
♡ 6 5 4 2
◇ J 10
♣ A Q 10 9

With the opponents vulnerable, the auction has gone:

SOUTH	WEST	NORTH	EAST
—	—	1 ♣	Pass
1 ♠	5 ◇	5 ♠	Double
Pass	Pass	Pass	

Partner leads the diamond ace, to dummy's eight, your ten, and declarer's queen. Partner shifts to the club four, you take dummy's jack with your queen, declarer follows with the three. Your next play, please. (*See page 194.*)

9. You are South, with both sides vulnerable, holding:

♠ J 5 3   ♡ K J 10 6 2   ◇ 10 4 2   ♣ A J

The auction goes:

SOUTH	WEST	NORTH	EAST
—	2 ◇*	Double	3 ◇
4 ♡	Pass	5 ◇	Pass
?			

*weak

What is your call? (*See page 198.*)

10. With the opponents vulnerable, you hold:

♠ 5   ♡ 8 6 4   ◇ A 9 6 4 3   ♣ 9 8 3 2

Partner opens with one heart, and right-hand opponent overcalls with one spade. What call do you make? (*See page 202.*)

11. With neither side vulnerable, you, South, hold:

♠ 7   ♡ A Q J 10 9 8 3   ◇ 5   ♣ A 9 7 5

SOUTH	WEST	NORTH	EAST
1 ♡	Pass	2 ◇	2 ♠
3 ♡	4 ♠	5 ♡	Pass
?			

Would you have chosen the same opening? What call do you make now? (*See page 205.*)

12. With your side vulnerable, you hold:

♠ K J 9 7 4   ♡ J 8 3   ◇ K 9 6   ♣ Q 5

After three passes, your partner opens with one diamond; your right-hand opponent doubles. What call do you make? (*See page 207.*)

13. You are declarer in six hearts:

DECLARER	DUMMY
♠ A Q J 10	♠ K 9 5
♡ A K 9 7 3 2	♡ 8 6 5
◇ A J 7	◇ Q 6
♣ —	♣ A K 7 6 5

Left-hand opponent leads the ten of diamonds, covered by queen, king and ace. How do you plan the play? (*See page 208.*)

14. With East-West vulnerable, you are sitting West with these cards:

♠ 9 2   ♡ Q J 5 4 3   ◇ 8 4   ♣ A J 5 3

The bidding proceeds as follows:

SOUTH	WEST	NORTH	EAST
1 ◇	1 ♡	Pass	1 ♠
2 ♣	Pass	2 ♡	Pass
2 ♠	Pass	3 NT	Pass
5 ♣	Pass	6 ◇	(All Pass)

What is your opening lead? (*See page 211.*)

15. With your side vulnerable, you hold:

♠ —   ♡ A K Q 10 9 8 7 5 4   ◇ 5   ♣ A K 2

Your left-hand opponent opens with one spade; partner passes, and there is a raise to two spades on your right. What action do you take? How do you plan to continue? (*See page 212.*)

16. With your side vulnerable, you hold:

♠ A 7 6 5 4   ♡ Q J 10 3 2   ◇ A 2   ♣ K

After two passes, your right-hand opponent opens with three diamonds. What call do you make? (*See page 216.*)

Trials Diary

O n Wednesday, November 9th [1966], the 16 pairs qualified for the Trials to select the team to represent North America in the 1967 Bermuda Bowl assemble in Pittsburgh. We draw for pair numbers, exchange system announcements, listen with only half an ear to speeches from Al Sobel, the head director, and Julius Rosenblum, the Captain of the team that will emerge after 10 days of struggle. We are eager to begin.

This year, the Trials are in two stages. First, there is a 15-session round-robin in which each pair plays a 14-board match against each other. Then, the ten high pairs qualify for a nine-session round-robin of 28-board matches. The carryover from the qualifying rounds into the finals is tiny, so the early objective is to sneak into the top 10; getting into the first three, to make the team, can wait.

The scoring of the qualifying matches is according to the usual Trials method. Of the eight results on each deal, the best and worst are discarded; the remaining six are averaged. This average is the "result at the other table" against which you figure your IMP score for the board. At the end of the match, you add up your IMP results, plus and minus. This final figure (plus 8, say, or minus 20) is converted into Victory Points—each pair starts with 21, and the first 14 imps won or lost are added or subtracted at full value; from 14 to 28 imps, you win or lose at half a Victory Point per imp. Thus, if you win by 8 imps you score 29 to the opponents' 13; if you lose by 20 imps you score 4 to the enemy 38.

Norman Kay and I start out against B. Jay Becker and Dorothy Hayden [now Truscott]. The boards are flat, producing only two big swings. One is in our favor, when I play three diamonds down 50, with four hearts or spades cold the other way. The other goes against us, when we fail to find the exact defense necessary to beat Dorothy in three notrump; most of the field plays the same contract from the other side of the table and goes down automatically.

Actually, the most interesting deal is a one-bid:

NORTH
♠ Q 10
♡ K 7 5 4
◇ J 9 7
♣ J 9 4 2

WEST
♠ J 8 6 4 2
♡ 9 2
◇ K 5
♣ A 10 8 7

EAST
♠ 9
♡ A Q J 10
◇ Q 10 8 6 4
♣ K 6 3

SOUTH
♠ A K 7 5 3
♡ 8 6 3
◇ A 3 2
♣ Q 5

As East, I open one heart in third seat; Dorothy, South, overcalls one spade, and everyone passes. I win the heart opening lead with my ten and return the six of diamonds to the king. Norman does well to continue diamonds; Dorothy wins with the ace and puts me back on lead with a diamond, Norman discarding a high club. I lead the club six, and Dorothy falsecards with the queen; Norman wins with his ace and shifts back to hearts. I cash the jack and ace of hearts, and the position is:

NORTH
♠ Q 10
♡ K
◇ —
♣ J 9 4

WEST
♠ J 8 6 4 2
♡ —
◇ —
♣ 10

EAST
♠ 9
♡ Q
◇ 8 4
♣ K 3

SOUTH
♠ A K 7 5 3
♡ —
◇ —
♣ 5

We have six tricks in, and the battle is over whether we score 100 or 200. Obviously, I will beat the contract two if I cash my club king, but Dorothy's queen-of-clubs play has fooled me—I play her for 6=3=3=1 and lead my heart queen.

To my embarrassment, she discards her club five and Norman ruffs. He returns the club ten; Dorothy plays dummy's four—she wants to see if my king will drop. So I can recover my lost face—I follow with the king, still concealing my three, and Dorothy ruffs. She counts me for 2=4=5=2 and plays for the drop in spades rather than finesse. Down 200, with equal honor, for we have fooled each other.

Alas, they have the last laugh, for we lose the match by 7 imps, scoring 14 V.P.'s to their 28.

Our second match is against Al Roth and Bill Root. Again, there are few swings. We pick up on a few partscore deals and when they miss a fair game. But Roth gets even with two well-judged doubles of thin game contracts. The match is decided when Norman opens a big hand with one spade and I hold:

♠ Q 9 6 5   ♡ Q 10 4   ◇ 10 9 4   ♣ Q 9 2

Luckily, I respond one notrump, not two spades, and we stay safely at a partscore; no game can make. Roth is furious. "All the idiots will bid one spade — two spades — four spades," he complains. I soothe him by explaining that I would have responded two spades also, but didn't dare to with the high-priest of sound major raises at the table. We gain 5 imps, and this gives us 26 V.P.'s to their 16.

Next, we play against Ira Rubin and Curt Smith. They play well against us, getting the better of many small boards. We gain only two minor swings, but hope for a big one on this vulnerable board:

Wit and Wisdom

Edgar frequently offered one form or another of this advice for how to approach a head-to-head match: "It is not necessary to play to win, only not to lose."

WEST	EAST
♠ 3	♠ A K Q J 8 6 4
♡ A J 9 5 2	♡ K
◇ A 9 5 3	◇ 8
♣ K Q 8	♣ 10 5 4 3

WEST	EAST
Smith	*Rubin*
1 ♡	1 ♠
2 ◇	4 ♠
Pass	

Slam is a spread, but there is no swing! This auction occurs with only minor variations at every table, and no one even makes a slam-try, much less bids a slam. This excessive timidity in slam bidding is to be typical of the whole Trials. So we lose by 16 imps, scoring only 6.5 V.P.'s.

Our fourth match is against Tobias Stone and Ivan Erdos. We get the worst of every swing up until the end, when we strike back and nail them for 500 on a wild deal, picking up 13 imps. We are lucky to lose by only 11 imps. Lucky! We stand fifteenth out of 16 pairs. Mathe-Hamman are riding high, way ahead of the field, with Lazard-Rapée second and Kehela-Murray third.

The sun finally breaks through the clouds when, in the fifth round, we meet Sami Kehela and Eric Murray, a redoubtable Canadian playing with an indubitable one. They go down in a slam on a finesse; they go down in another because five trumps are in one hand and side suits split badly; they lose 9 imps when we bid a cold five clubs; they lose 9 imps more when Norman finds the killing defense against a vulnerable game. And to cap it all, they lose a further 11 imps when Norman and I bid a laydown grand slam. Actually, they play an excellent session while Norman and I have our first two disasters of the tournament (a missed game on a Landy sequence, and a four-three major fit down 300 with three notrump icy); but we are washed clean of sin as we win 42 V.P.'s to 0. Have we found the formula for success in the Trials? Play badly? Play Canadians? Anyway, we have climbed into ninth place.

Here is the killing defense I mentioned earlier:

NORTH
♠ J 6 4 2
♡ K 9 3
◊ K 7 6
♣ A 9 4

WEST
♠ 5
♡ Q 5 4
◊ A 10 5 4
♣ Q 10 5 3 2

EAST
♠ Q
♡ A J 6 2
◊ Q J 9 8 3
♣ K 7 6

SOUTH
♠ A K 10 9 8 7 3
♡ 10 8 7
◊ 2
♣ J 8

SOUTH	WEST	NORTH	EAST
Murray	*Kaplan*	*Kehela*	*Kay*
—	Pass	Pass	1 ♡
2 ♠	3 ♡	4 ♠	(All Pass)

I lead the heart four, and Norman's jack wins (declarer drops the eight—the ten might be better). After long study, Norman finds the devastating club shift—I cover the jack, and dummy wins. A trump to the ace, and a low diamond towards dummy—now it is my turn to think. It is not hard for me to find the winning play, though, since declarer cannot have three diamonds, two hearts and one club; with that, he would first lead his heart ten to establish a discard. It is possible that Norman has opened a four-card heart suit (we merely promise five with our opening bids), so I take my ace and cash the club for down one.

Now we play Eddie Kantar and Marshall Miles. It is, as always with this pair, a wild match; you must play guessing games with these boys. This time, luckily, we are guessing better than they. The pattern is set on the first board, when Norman opens a weak notrump and buys the contract without competition although I have a bare six points. Norman plays with great skill against an exotic but unfortunate defense and takes an incredible eight tricks amid general hilarity. (Marshall and Eddie are anxious to forget this board, but are not allowed to. Al Sobel comes in an hour later to see if it is a scoring error; he cheers up our opponents by telling them that everyone else is making two notrump with their cards.)

We pick up a huge gain on another weak notrump, this time theirs. (Incidentally, our nonvulerable weak notrumps were consistent winners throughout. Not so our strong notrumps, vulnerable.)

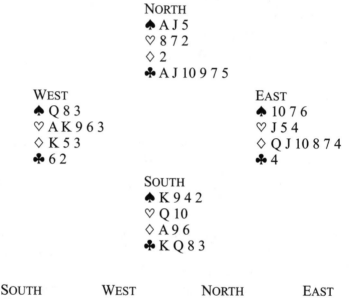

NORTH
♠ A J 5
♡ 8 7 2
♢ 2
♣ A J 10 9 7 5

WEST
♠ Q 8 3
♡ A K 9 6 3
♢ K 5 3
♣ 6 2

EAST
♠ 10 7 6
♡ J 5 4
♢ Q J 10 8 7 4
♣ 4

SOUTH
♠ K 9 4 2
♡ Q 10
♢ A 9 6
♣ K Q 8 3

SOUTH	WEST	NORTH	EAST
Kantar	Kaplan	Miles	Kay
—	—	—	Pass
1 NT	Pass	3 NT	(All Pass)

I guess to lead the heart ace, on the theory that if dummy has a balanced strong hand I want to avoid being thrown in later, and if dummy has a long club suit I must cash out quickly. This beats the contract as the cards lie, Norman unblocking the heart jack on the second round, but how impressed would you be by my logic if declarer held my partner's hearts and my partner his? Most pairs are in five clubs, after a club opening and a heart overcall, but three notrump on this auction is surely more likely to make.

The other big swing in our favor comes on a slam deal:

WEST	EAST
♠ A K J 9	♠ 10 8 6 4 3 2
♡ Q	♡ 10 8 4 3
◇ A 10 8 7 4	◇ K 5
♣ A K 5	♣ Q

Atypically, most East-West pairs reach the cold six-spade contract. Four West players bull their way into slam after a spade response to their one-diamond opening (two after a one-spade response, two after a weak jump-response of two spades); they just gamble that there are no minor-suit losers. Two auctions, however, are more sensible.

WEST	EAST
Lawrence	*Stansby*
1 ◇	1 ♠
3 ♣	3 ◇
4 ♠	4 NT
5 ♠	6 ♠
Pass	

On this sequence, Stansby is able to know that his weak hand is pure gold and that slam must be odds-on.

WEST	EAST
Roth	*Root*
1 ◇	2 ♠
2 NT	3 ♡
6 ♠	Pass

Here, Roth forces with two notrump, finds partner with ten major-suit cards, and is able to bid the slam with assurance.

Against us, Miles opens with two diamonds, his own variation of the Roman Two Diamonds, showing a strong three-suiter. The auction gets up too high too fast to disclose the perfect fit, and they stop in game. So we win the match 36-6. Suddenly, we are comfortably in sixth place.

Our seventh match, against Phil Feldesman and Dick Freeman, is nip and tuck, with neither pair gaining any large swings, and with equal ups and downs on the small deals. We nip them at the wire by 1 imp and win 22-20. As we head for the halfway mark, Mathe-Hamman are still leading, followed closely by Lazard-Rapée and Feldesman-Freeman. Two young California pairs, Kantar-Miles and Lawrence-Stansby, are fourth and fifth, we are sixth, Erdos-Stone seventh, Roth-Root eighth, Becker-Hayden ninth, and Schleifer-Baron have pulled up to tenth after a dismal start. Two highly regarded pairs are in trouble—Smith-Rubin are thirteenth and Murray-Kehela fourteenth.

Now we play Bill Grieve and Harold Ogust, who are not doing well. But they play excellently and win by 7 imps. We lose 5 imps on this deal, because our opponents, a relatively new partnership, have not had time to work up any two-diamond gadget response to one notrump:

```
                        NORTH
                        ♠ K J 6
                        ♡ K 9 2
                        ◇ A J 7 6
                        ♣ A J 3
        WEST                                EAST
        ♠ A 7 4 2                           ♠ 10 8 5 3
        ♡ A                                 ♡ Q 10 8 6 5
        ◇ K Q 10                            ◇ —
        ♣ K 9 7 6 4                         ♣ Q 10 8 5
                        SOUTH
                        ♠ Q 9
                        ♡ J 7 4 3
                        ◇ 9 8 5 4 3 2
                        ♣ 2
```

SOUTH	WEST	NORTH	EAST
Grieve	Kay	Ogust	Kaplan
—	—	1 NT	Pass
2 ◇	Pass	Pass	Pass

Grieve plays it well and makes three. Normal? No, because most of the other pairs cannot respond two diamonds to one notrump. They use the Murray Two Diamonds or the Stayman Two Diamonds or the Carter Two Diamonds or the Roth-Stone Two Diamonds. The most common result is one notrump passed out, down 200; several times, South responds three diamonds, which fetches a hopeful three notrump from North, down more. Ah well, I suppose I should balance instead of letting them play in their unsporting contract; we are cold for three spades or four clubs.

Our next opponents are Billy Eisenberg and Lenny Harmon, another pair with an uphill road toward qualification. They have not given up— in fact, they play better than any of our other opponents throughout the Trials. They gain 6 imps by bidding a good five clubs, and a further 6 imps by staying out of trouble on this deal:

```
                        NORTH
                        ♠ K 3 2
                        ♡ A Q J 5
                        ◇ A K 7 5 2
                        ♣ 2
        WEST                                EAST
        ♠ J 6                               ♠ Q 9 8 5
        ♡ 7 3 2                             ♡ 9 8 6
        ◇ Q 10 4 3                          ◇ 6
        ♣ A 10 9 6                          ♣ Q J 7 5 4
                        SOUTH
                        ♠ A 10 7 4
                        ♡ K 10 4
                        ◇ J 9 8
                        ♣ K 8 3
```

SOUTH	WEST	NORTH	EAST
Eisenberg	*Kay*	*Harmon*	*Kaplan*
—	—	—	Pass
Pass	Pass	1 ◇	Pass
1 ♠	Pass	2 ♡	Pass
3 NT	Pass	Pass	Pass

Norman makes the only lead, a heart, that does not give away the ninth trick. But Eisenberg makes his contract without jeopardy, for he can establish dummy's fifth diamond without ever giving me the lead. We lose heavily, because three pairs are in slam down two or three, and one pair is in five diamonds down two. The trouble comes when the auction starts one diamond — one spade — two hearts — two notrump. Now, when North bids three spades, South feels too strong to sign off at three notrump, so bids four diamonds and they're off. We lose this match by these 6 imps and drop to seventh place.

Now we come up against Bob Hamman and Lew Mathe, who have lost four matches in a row, dropping to sixth place. We pick up a big swing early when they reach a 22-point three-notrump contract and go down four. We gain on a number of small deals and have a commanding lead. But we lose almost all of it back on one board, when they push us to five spades and I go down one, misguessing a queen. So we win by only 4 imps.

Our eleventh match is with Sidney Lazard and George Rapée, who have been among the leaders all the way. I nearly have a great triumph over Lazard on one deal. You see, Sidney and I played together as a partnership for many years, and we had one serious disagreement over bidding theory: He insisted on opening a five-five spade-club two-suiter one club for ease in rebidding; I maintained that these hands must be opened one spade, and that he would one day go for 1100 when he had to introduce his spades at too high a level. Well:

North dealer; North-South vulnerable

NORTH
♠ A Q 10 8 3
♡ A 7
◇ 8
♣ K J 6 5 2

WEST
♠ —
♡ K J 9 3
◇ A 9 7 6 5 4 3 2
♣ 4

EAST
♠ K 6 4
♡ 6 5 4 2
◇ J 10
♣ A Q 10 9

SOUTH
♠ J 9 7 5 2
♡ Q 10 8
◇ K Q
♣ 8 7 3

SOUTH	WEST	NORTH	EAST
Rapée	Kaplan	Lazard	Kay
—	—	1 ♣	Pass
1 ♠	5 ◇	5 ♠	Double
Pass	Pass	Pass	

I lead the diamond ace and guess to shift to the club four, hoping to get Norman in for a heart lead through. If he plays a heart we collect my long-awaited 1100, since declarer cannot get to his hand in time to pitch dummy's heart. Alas, Norman cannot expect me to lead a singleton with a void in trumps, and he lays down the club ace—we lose our heart trick and a club trick both, and get only 500. Lucky Lazard! (On a high level, Norman's defense is wrong. Declarer is known to have only two diamonds; if he has three clubs and four spades, he has four hearts and would have responded one heart, not one spade. So I am void in trumps, and the heart play must be right.)

The match seems very close, and, sure enough, when we compute our scores from the averages on the wall in the players' lounge we find we are 1 imp behind with one result still to come in. This is the remaining deal:

WEST	EAST
♠ A 8 5 3 2	♠ J 10 9 7
♡ J	♡ A 9 4 3 2
◇ J 5 3 2	◇ —
♣ K Q J	♣ A 7 6 5

WEST	EAST
Rapée	*Lazard*
Pass	1 ♡
1 ♠	2 ♠
4 ♠	Pass

Twelve tricks are available. We will pick up imps if two pairs have bid the slam, possible if West opens, as I would. But when the average is posted we find that we have lost 4 imps. Why? Two pairs (Roth-Root and Smith-Rubin, of course) passed this slam out!

We have fallen to eighth place and are in jeopardy with four rounds to go. Feldesman-Freeman and Lawrence-Stansby are first and second, way ahead. Roth-Root and Lazard-Rapée are comfortable, as are Kantar-Miles. Hamman-Mathe should not be in trouble with their score but are sliding downhill fast. Baron-Schleifer, we, Erdos-Stone and Becker-Hayden round out the top 10. Kehela-Murray are lengths behind, and Rubin-Smith languish last.

195

In our twelfth match, we face John Moran and Chuck Henke, no longer a contending pair. They reach a number of excellent contracts that cost us imps, but most of the swings go our way. This deal saw wild results at many tables:

West dealer
North-South vulnerable

NORTH
♠ 5 4
♡ K J 4
◇ K 10 8
♣ K J 9 5 3

WEST
♠ Q J 10 9 8 2
♡ Q 10 8 6
◇ 9 4
♣ 7

EAST
♠ K 7 3
♡ 9 7 3
◇ J 5 3 2
♣ 10 4 2

SOUTH
♠ A 6
♡ A 5 2
◇ A Q 7 6
♣ A Q 8 6

SOUTH	WEST	NORTH	EAST
Moran	Kay	Henke	Kaplan
—	2 ♠	Pass	3 ♠
3 NT	Pass	Pass	Pass

At our table, Moran takes his 12 tricks for a substantial loss. The auctions throughout the field make an excellent object lesson in preemptive tactics. Almost always, West opens two or three spades; where East raises to four or five spades, North-South end up in six or seven clubs (seven was bid twice and made once). Six spades would probably buy the contract for an expensive sacrifice, but of the lower bids only three spades is likely to work. Should Moran double instead of bidding three notrump? He is, of course, afraid of hearts, a fear, that is borne out by the result at one table where, on this auction, North tries four hearts (and makes his bizarre contract too). Moran's action seems reasonable to me, but it cost him, and we win 35.5 V.P.'s to 6.5. We improve to seventh place with three rounds left.

We can climb to sixth in our next match, for we play Hermine Baron and Meyer Schleifer, who are just ahead of us. Instead, though, we play our first poor set and lose by 8 imps. An interesting deal from this match:

NORTH
♠ 10 4 3 2
♡ J 4
◇ J 7 6 5
♣ A K 10

WEST
♠ Q 9
♡ Q 9 8 3
◇ K 10 8
♣ Q 6 4 2

EAST
♠ K 8 6
♡ 10 6 5 2
◇ Q 4
♣ J 7 5 3

SOUTH
♠ A J 7 5
♡ A K 7
◇ A 9 3 2
♣ 9 8

Both Mathe and Roth play this deal in four spades, with a heart lead won by dummy's jack. Mathe cashes his remaining hearts, throwing a diamond from dummy, then takes the top clubs and ruffs a club. Finally, he plays ace and a small diamond for an endplay—the opponents must give him a ruff and sluff or guess the trumps for him.

In contrast, Roth disdains this technical play and backs his always magnificent table judgment of where the cards are. He leads the spade ten from dummy at trick two and makes his game in 10 seconds flat.

For our fourteenth match, we meet the leaders—Mike Lawrence and Lew Stansby. Nearly all the swings go our way. Our biggest pickup is on this deal:

West dealer
Both sides vulnerable

```
                        NORTH
                        ♠ A K Q 7 4
                        ♡ A Q 8 3
                        ◇ —
                        ♣ K 6 5 3
     WEST                                    EAST
     ♠ 8                                     ♠ 10 9 6 2
     ♡ 7 5                                   ♡ 9 4
     ◇ A Q 9 8 7 6                           ◇ K J 5 3
     ♣ Q 9 7 2                               ♣ 10 8 4
                        SOUTH
                        ♠ J 5 3
                        ♡ K J 10 6 2
                        ◇ 10 4 2
                        ♣ A J
```

SOUTH	WEST	NORTH	EAST
Kay	*Lawrence*	*Kaplan*	*Stansby*
—	2 ◇	Double	3 ◇
4 ♡	Pass	5 ◇	Pass
6 ♡	Pass	7 ♡	(All Pass)

We have a simple auction to reach the laydown grand slam. The only serious problem is Norman's reply to my five-diamond cue-bid: Should he sign off at five hearts, jump to six hearts, or show the club ace en passant? In my view, his middle course is best. He wants to accept if I am trying for a small slam, but he certainly does not want to encourage me to bid seven, and a control-bid of six clubs must be construed as a grand-slam-try. I, of course, have no difficulty realizing that Norman holds the club ace—what else can he have? This grand slam is worth a surprising 13 imps, since no other pair bids it. We win the match by the maximum—42 V.P.'s to 0—and are snug in sixth place, mathematically certain to qualify.

Going into the final qualifying session, there are three places open and five pairs fighting for them. Becker-Hayden will qualify if they are not slaughtered in their match against Eisenberg-Harmon; their opponents have a chance to make the top 10 if they win by the maximum (actually, Eisenberg-Harmon win 37 V.P.'s to 5, not enough to get them in or to keep Becker-Hayden out). Kehela-Murray play Kantar-Miles, and will qualify even with a small loss (in fact, the Canadians win by 3 imps). Hamman-Mathe play Henke-Moran and need a win to hold onto tenth place (they win by the maximum and gain a position for the first time in nine matches). Erdos-Stone are pitted against Roth-Root, needing a big win to qualify. (They do win 35 V.P.'s to 7, but fall just short.) Meanwhile, we win comfortably against Bobby Goldman and Paul Levitt, moving into the top five at last. The order of finish:

Qualifiers: 1st: Feldesman-Freeman, 405.5; 2nd: Lazard-Rapée, 394.5; 3rd: Kantar-Miles, 381; 4th: Lawrence-Stansby, 356.5; 5th: Kaplan-Kay, 352.5; 6th: Roth-Root, 330.5; 7th: Baron-Schleifer, 330; 8th: Kehela-Murray, 326; 9th: Hamman-Mathe, 316; 10th: Becker-Hayden, 312.5. We have all been playing hard for five days, yet our real work starts tomorrow.

The Finals

After a gruelling 15-session round-robin of 14-board matches, 10 pairs have survived to battle for the three positions on the International Team. We have had Sunday night off, but it is perhaps an exaggeration to say that everyone is fresh and rested for Monday's struggles.

In the finals, we will play nine matches—one against each other pair. Here, though, each match will be a long one, 28 boards played straight through without a break. The scoring will again be by Victory Points (V.P.'s), but now 84 V.P.'s are at stake in each match. Both sides start with 42 V.P.'s, and points are added or subtracted according to the final IMP result of the match: the first 28 imps won or lost at full value, the next 28 imps at 50 percent. Thus, if we win a match by 10 imps, we score 52 V.P.'s to the enemy 32; if we lose by 40 imps, we score 8 V.P.'s to 74; a win by 56 imps or more is a "blitz"—84 to 0.

There is to be a significant difference from the qualifying rounds in computing the IMP result for each individual board. Up to now, there have been eight results on each deal; the top and bottom scores have been discarded, and the remaining six results averaged. Everyone's

IMP score is calculated by comparing his actual result with this average. Now, though, there will be only five results on each deal, so it has been decided to average all the results—without discarding top and bottom. This means that one freak result can have an enormous effect on the average. For example, here is a routine deal from the first final match:

East dealer
North-South vulnerable

```
                        NORTH
                        ♠ Q J 8 7
                        ♡ Q 4 2
                        ◇ A 3
                        ♣ A K 4 2
        WEST                                    EAST
        ♠ A 9 6                                 ♠ 10 5 4 3
        ♡ A 7                                   ♡ K 10 9 6 5
        ◇ K 8 2                                 ◇ 7 6 4
        ♣ Q J 10 9 5                            ♣ 8
                        SOUTH
                        ♠ K 2
                        ♡ J 8 3
                        ◇ Q J 10 9 5
                        ♣ 7 6 3
```

At three of the five tables (ours included), East becomes declarer at two hearts, down two, for 100 to North-South. At one table, there is a slight variation—South buys the contract for two diamonds, and goes down one. Normal so far. But at the fifth table, North is declarer in the undignified contract of three notrump doubled, down 800. Under the old system, throwing out the extreme scores, the average would be plus 30 North-South: The North-South pairs with the normal good result, plus 100, would have gained 2 imps; the pair with the normal poor result, minus 100, would lose 4 imps; and the disastrous result would lose 13 imps. With the new method, the average is minus 120 instead of plus 30. So the normal good result gains 6 imps; the normal poor result gains 1 imp; the disaster loses 12 imps.

Obviously, the new scoring is poor, since one silly result throws the average out of kilter, randomly penalizing and rewarding innocent bystanders at other tables. In response to protests from contestants, the method is changed slightly before play starts: any result so extreme as to be more than 800 points away from the next result will be cut down before being thrown into the average. This will prevent a really ludicrous miscarriage of justice in the event of a 2800 set or similar disaster but will have little effect otherwise.

We all thought that the carryover from the qualifying into the finals would be far too puny, since it is limited to a 42-V.P. (half a match) spread between top and bottom. Actually, though, it has worked out reasonably well. We carry over a little less than half our score, so that 11 imps earned in the early stage are equal to 5 imps in the finals. The figures for each pair are: Feldesman-Freeman 42; Lazard-Rapée 37; Kantar-Miles 31; Lawrence-Stansby 20; Kaplan-Kay 18; Root-Roth 8; Baron-Schleifer 8; Kehela-Murray 6; Hamman-Mathe 1.5; Becker-Hayden 0.

Our first match on Monday is against Kehela-Murray. We are hoping that the Canadians do well in the Trials, for we would like to have them on the team; but we are rooting for ourselves even harder. Norman and I have always lost our first Trials match, and it is about time for this to stop.

We begin with a series of dull boards, 1-imp swings going back and forth. Then, the first big break goes to us:

Wit and Wisdom

In an international event, a player opened two spades holding:

♠ J 8 5 4 3 2   ♡ J 5 3   ◇ 5   ♣ 7 5 2

"He is playing weak two's," Edgar told the Vu-Graph audience, "and certainly he is weak."

South dealer; East-West vulnerable

NORTH
♠ 5
♡ 8 6 4
◇ A 9 6 4 3
♣ 9 8 3 2

WEST	EAST
♠ K 10 8 6 4	♠ Q 9 7 3 2
♡ K 7 5	♡ J 10
◇ K 7	◇ 10 5 2
♣ A 7 4	♣ Q J 10

SOUTH
♠ A J
♡ A Q 9 3 2
◇ Q J 8
♣ K 6 5

SOUTH	WEST	NORTH	EAST
Kay	*Murray*	*Kaplan*	*Kehela*
1 ♡	1 ♠	2 ♡	3 ♠
4 ♡	Pass	Pass	Pass

The Canadians use preemptive jump-raises of overcalls, which explains their auction; Norman and I believe in bidding whenever it is our turn, which explains ours. (My two-heart response is somewhat light, but I can see no virtue in passing just because the opponents are in the auction. Admittedly, I cannot feel secure when Norman is pushed to four hearts, but look at the alternative: If I pass at my first turn, the opponents buy the contract for three spades and make it easily. Here, as usual, it is more dangerous to pass than to bid.)

Norman wins the spade opening, ruffs a spade, and takes the heart finesse. Murray returns a heart, and Norman draws trumps. Now he leads the diamond queen and lets Murray hold the king when he covers. So Norman makes four diamond tricks and his contract. Actually, four hearts can never be defeated, even with an early shift to clubs. Declarer can either concede two clubs and make the thirteenth club in dummy, or guess the diamond ten for his contract.

We are the only pair in this skinny game. Two pairs open the South hand one notrump and play right there (making two, when West does not guess to play declarer for ace-jack-alone in spades); one pair stops in three hearts; one pair allows East-West to play in three spades.

Kehela-Murray get this back with imps to spare on a wild deal:

North dealer; neither side vulnerable

```
                        NORTH
                        ♠ 10 9 8 4 2
                        ♡ 9 3
                        ◇ 8 6
                        ♣ 9 4 3 2
        WEST                            EAST
        ♠ A 6                           ♠ —
        ♡ K 8                           ♡ A Q 10 7 6 4 2
        ◇ A 7 3 2                       ◇ 10 5
        ♣ K J 10 8 7                    ♣ A Q 6 5
                        SOUTH
                        ♠ K Q J 7 5 3
                        ♡ J 5
                        ◇ K Q J 9 4
                        ♣ —
```

SOUTH	WEST	NORTH	EAST
Kehela	*Kay*	*Murray*	*Kaplan*
—	—	Pass	1 ♡
2 ♠	3 ♣	4 ♠	4 NT
5 ◇	5 NT	Pass	6 ♣
6 ♠	Pass	Pass	7 ♣
Pass	Pass	7 ♠	Double
Pass	Pass	Pass	

My odd-looking Blackwood bid is made in the hope that the opponents will assume that I do not have a void, and so will be likely (a) to let us buy the contract, and (b) to lead spades. My scheme does not work very well; I let myself get pushed to seven, but Murray saves. Perhaps we should bid seven notrump, but Norman is worried about the queens of our suits, and I am worried about the kings. Actually, the fault is mine. Norman's five-notrump bid shows three aces as we play; I can hardly be expected to believe this, but I should realize that he has invented a master bid to show me all the missing key controls.

We take the obvious four tricks and score 700, a huge loss since three

East-West pairs are allowed to play in club or heart grand slams.

There is little action on the remaining boards, and we lose the match by 5 imps. No one has been hurt, but here we are off to a poor start again. The standings remain much the same, as three of the five matches are close. Feldesman-Freeman nearly blitz Hamman-Mathe, pushing them deep into the cellar; Lazard-Rapée win big from Baron-Schleifer, so the two leaders are off and running.

On Monday night, we play Baron-Schleifer on Vu-Graph. It is not a lively set of boards, and there is only one big swing in the whole match:

North dealer
East-West vulnerable

```
                      NORTH
                      ♠ Q 9 8 6
                      ♡ K J 10 8 5
                      ◇ 7 5
                      ♣ Q 10
        WEST                          EAST
        ♠ J 7 5 2                     ♠ 3
        ♡ A 9 7 4                     ♡ Q 6 2
        ◇ Q                           ◇ J 9 8 4 3 2
        ♣ K 4 3 2                     ♣ A J 5
                      SOUTH
                      ♠ A K 10 4
                      ♡ 3
                      ◇ A K 10 6
                      ♣ 9 8 7 6
```

SOUTH	WEST	NORTH	EAST
Kay	*Schleifer*	*Kaplan*	*Baron*
—	—	Pass	Pass
1 ◇	Pass	1 ♡	Pass
1 ♠	Pass	2 ♠	Pass
3 ♠	Pass	4 ♠	(All Pass)

Four spades is a reasonable contract, but it seems doomed by the unlucky distribution in spades and diamonds. However, Norman confounds the Vu-Graph commentators, who are busily speculating how many he will go down, by making his contract. The club two is led, won by Mrs. Baron's jack. She cashes the club ace and shifts to a diamond (it would be better to shift before taking the high club). Norman wins and leads his heart; Schleifer ducks, hoping to get partner in to give him his diamond ruff, and Norman goes up with the king. He ruffs a heart back to his hand, sneaks through the club eight to discard dummy's diamond, and gallops home with 10 tricks on a crossruff.

This is worth 9 imps, since no one else makes the game, and we win the match by 11 imps—53 V.P.'s to 31. All the other matches are close too, so the standings are not much changed. We have inched up to fourth, replacing Kantar-Miles who have dropped out of the first five after losing two matches in a row. Feldesman-Freeman lead, closely followed by Lazard-Rapée. Forty-five V.P.'s behind in third place are Lawrence-Stansby, and we are a mere four V.P.'s behind them. However, there are two pairs hot on our heels.

We can expect a lively third-round match, for we play Kantar-Miles, The action starts right out with our first board, when I hold as dealer (South), none vulnerable:

♠ 7   ♡ A Q J 10 9 8 3   ◊ 5   ♣ A 9 7 5

SOUTH	WEST	NORTH	EAST
Kaplan	*Miles*	*Kay*	*Kantar*
1 ♡	Pass	2 ◊	2 ♠
3 ♡	4 ♠	5 ♡	Pass
?			

Should I bid six hearts? Norman's five-heart bid shows extra values, for we play a pass in his position as forcing after a two-over-one response in a minor. I visualize his hand as containing the heart king and good diamonds, like ace-king-queen-fifth or -sixth; even ace-king-jack of diamonds gives me a play, and he may, after all, have the club king or a singleton. So I bid the slam. Wrong! Norman holds:

♠ 9 8 2   ♡ K 4 2   ◊ A K 7 3 2   ♣ Q 4

I cannot quarrel with his bidding, for all his cards look good to him.

But with the spade-ace lead from Miles, I have no play at all; 10 imps go down the drain. Ah well, the boys made it very tough for us. Perhaps I should make it harder for them and open with four hearts (three Souths did select this bid). But then Norman no doubt would hold the diamond queen or club king instead of his club queen, and my preempt with two first-round and two second-round controls would cost us a slam.

On the next deal, I pick up:

♠ K 8   ♡ A K 3   ◊ Q 4   ♣ A Q 10 9 6 2

I am in fourth seat, vulnerable vs. nonvulnerable, and there are three passes to me. Are the boys going quietly? No, I open one club, Miles doubles, Norman bids one spade, and Kantar announces a skip bid: four diamonds. Infuriating! I have no sensible action—everything is an out-and-out gamble. I bid five clubs, Miles bids five diamonds, and Norman raises to six clubs, ending the auction. His hand:

♠ Q J 7 6 5 4 2   ♡ 9 2   ◊ —   ♣ J 7 5 3

Miles leads the diamond king, and the club king is right, so I make the slam. The ace-of-spades lead would beat me, since Kantar has a singleton, but we didn't have the chance to disclose our big spade fit to each other, much less to the opponents. They would be down only two in six diamonds, but who would save against us after our performance on the first board? We gain 14 imps and are in the lead.

Not every board is as wild as the first two, but somehow or other we produce swingy results on even the flattest-looking deals. For example: [*See next page.*]

You would expect every North-South pair to make about 110 in a diamond partial, and so it proves at each table except ours.

SOUTH	WEST	NORTH	EAST
Miles	*Kay*	*Kantar*	*Kaplan*
—	Pass	Pass	Pass
1 ◊	Double	Redouble	3 ♡
4 ♣	Pass	4 ◊	(All Pass)

West dealer
North-South vulnerable

NORTH
♠ K J 9 7 4
♡ J 8 3
◊ K 9 6
♣ Q 5

WEST
♠ A Q 5 2
♡ A 10 4
◊ Q 3
♣ 9 8 7 3

EAST
♠ 10 6 3
♡ K 9 7 6 2
◊ J 5 4
♣ 6 4

SOUTH
♠ 8
♡ Q 5
◊ A 10 8 7 2
♣ A K J 10 2

We cash out our three major-suit winners and wait for our trump trick, achieving the only East-West plus score. Personally, I disapprove of the redouble on this vulnerability: it is an open invitation to me to pay our opponents back for the hard times they have been giving us when the vulnerability favored them.

When the match is over, our imp totals look like a basketball score. We have the better of it, winning 55 V.P.'s to 29. We are still fourth, although we have passed Lawrence-Stansby; Roth-Root have drubbed Hamman-Mathe (who have yet to win a match) and leap-frogged over us into third place. Lazard-Rapée lead; Feldesman-Freeman have slipped to second.

At night, we meet Lawrence-Stansby (this is Young California day for us). This pair has been a factor in the Trials, occasionally seizing a high ranking but then dropping back. They led the field by a fair amount going into the last day of the qualifying rounds, but scored zero V.P.'s in their last two matches. When I got back to the hotel that night after dinner, I saw Mike Lawrence in the lobby, ruefully studying the lead headline in a Pittsburgh paper: "Lawrence Sinking Fast" (it referred to the Pennsylvania ex-governor, who was dying). Lawrence-Stansby combine an aggressive bidding style with a keen awareness of what is going on at the table, and with excellent technique. Their in-and-out performance may be due to temperament problems as well as to a somewhat slap-dash attitude toward their offensive bidding.

We have a low-scoring match with small swings going back and forth. On one of the most interesting deals, no imps at all change hands:

West dealer
Neither side vulnerable

NORTH
♠ K 9 5
♡ 8 6 5
◇ Q 6
♣ A K 7 6 5

WEST
♠ 8 7 6 4 3
♡ —
◇ 10 9 8 4
♣ J 8 4 3

EAST
♠ 2
♡ Q J 10 4
◇ K 5 3 2
♣ Q 10 9 2

SOUTH
♠ A Q J 10
♡ A K 9 7 3 2
◇ A J 7
♣ —

Stansby, South, becomes declarer at six hearts after Lawrence opens the bidding. The diamond ten is led, covered by the queen, king and ace. Then declarer lays down the heart ace and goes down one. Obviously, it is a most unlucky split; and it is only just, in a sense, that every pair goes down and no one loses imps. But should not the contract be made against a diamond lead? Jack of diamonds, ruff a diamond, and a heart from dummy to the nine (unless East splits) insures against the five percent chance that all four trumps are with East. This line loses only if diamonds are six-two (with the short diamond hand holding a singleton trump honor) or worse—less than a one-percent chance. It seems clearly right to me to take the safety play, but whether it would have occurred to me at the table is a different question.

The big swing in this match comes when our opponents badly misjudge a competitive auction at the six level and go down 800 instead of setting us two. This is 11 imps, which is exactly our margin of victory. We score 53 V.P.'s and retain fourth place. Virtually no rankings are changed, as all five matches are close.

On Wednesday, we meet Hamman-Mathe in the afternoon. The spectacular collapse of this highly-regarded pair—they won only two of their last 10 qualifying matches and have lost four straight in the finals—is the talk of the tournament. They have been unlucky but have contributed heavily to their own misfortunes with a rash of uncharacteristic bidding disasters. It is a tribute to their competitive qualities that they are still fighting hard.

This set of deals turns out to be the wildest of the Trials; out of 28 boards, 10 involve slam decisions. We lose a large swing when Norman doubles a slam for a lead that does not beat it; we get it back when Mathe-Hamman miss a laydown slam bid by everyone else; we lose heavily on an unlucky deal in which we get to four notrump after a slam-try and go down with everything offside. The match is finally decided by two touch-and-go slams.

Wit and Wisdom

"I doubt that today's best players are the equal of the best of the past. Today's partnerships are clearly better than those in the old days. However, the energies of today's youth are invested in the bidding, not the card play. The best card players of old were usually a trick or two too high, and they had to learn how to retrieve contracts. The best then were more creative than today. Perhaps the difference is caused by the systemic signaling on defense. The old-timers, less rigid, tried to create illusions in declarer's mind. This required cooperation; the partner of the swindler had to behave as though he had an appropriate hand. Today, declarers also think only of their perspective, not how things may be made to appear to the opponents."

West dealer; neither side vulnerable

NORTH
♠ A J 8
♡ A K 10 4 3 2
◇ J 10
♣ 9 6

WEST
♠ 7 4 2
♡ 7
◇ K 9 7 5 2
♣ Q J 8 5

EAST
♠ 10 6 3
♡ Q J 9 8 5
◇ 8 6
♣ 10 4 2

SOUTH
♠ K Q 9 5
♡ 6
◇ A Q 4 3
♣ A K 7 3

SOUTH	WEST	NORTH	EAST
Kay	Mathe	Kaplan	Hamman
—	Pass	1 ♡	Pass
1 ♠	Pass	2 ♠	Pass
3 ♣	Pass	3 ♡	Pass
4 ◇	Double	4 ♡	Pass
4 NT	Pass	5 ♡	Pass
6 ♠	Pass	Pass	Pass

The contract is a very good one, and our auction is sensible. (Norman knows that I have three strong spades, for it becomes obvious that I could have rebid hearts at my second turn but chose the raise instead.) However, with the diamond king wrong and the hearts foul, it is easy to go down.

Mathe leads a trump, which is not as friendly as it looks. Norman wins in hand, capturing the ten, and plays a low diamond, hoping to catch Mathe napping. But Mathe puts up his king and returns a diamond. Now Norman cashes his club honors, ruffs a club with the ace, overtakes the spade jack to draw trumps, and makes the balance. A second trump lead would have set him (he could not get out of dummy after ruffing a club loser), but this is difficult to diagnose at the table. In my opinion, Mathe's mistake was doubling four diamonds. Even Norman, who plays contracts as if he can see the opponents' cards, would probably have gone down if he hadn't been warned. The other slam:

South dealer; East-West vulnerable

NORTH
♠ Q J
♡ K 10 8 7 6 2
♢ A J 5
♣ 8 2

WEST
♠ 9 2
♡ Q J 5 4 3
♢ 8 4
♣ A J 5 3

EAST
♠ K 10 8 7 6 5 3
♡ 9
♢ 7 6 2
♣ 9 7

SOUTH
♠ A 4
♡ A
♢ K Q 10 9 3
♣ K Q 10 6 4

SOUTH	WEST	NORTH	EAST
Kay	Mathe	Kaplan	Hamman
1 ♢	1 ♡	Pass	1 ♠
2 ♣	Pass	2 ♡	Pass
2 ♠	Pass	3 NT	Pass
5 ♣	Pass	6 ♢	(All Pass)

I cannot double Mathe's brave vulnerable overcall, for this would promise spades as we play. However, my subsequent auction reveals the trap pass, and Norman's delicate spade cue-bid (which, combined with Hamman's spade bid, increases the value of my queen-jack holding) plus his later jump enable me to leap confidently to six. Again, we have reached a good slam that is endangered by bad breaks.

Mathe leads the spade nine; dummy's jack is allowed to win. A club to the king loses to the ace, and the second spade lead is won by declarer. Norman cashes his queen of clubs and then makes the key play—the heart ace. (If he does not cash the heart, Hamman will discard his singleton heart when the third club is ruffed high in dummy and will eventually get a heart ruff.) Now the slam is made without further difficulty by ruffing two clubs with dummy's trump honors.

These two slams let us win by 9 imps, and we move at last into the crucial third position, replacing Feldesman-Freeman, who have been mauled by Baron-Schleifer and fall to fifth. Lazard-Rapée still lead, Roth-Root are second. Becker-Hayden have climbed into fourth by beating Kehela-Murray decisively. (The Canadians were the only other pair to bid either of the above slams. But Kehela was down in both, receiving no help in the auction on the first deal and getting the killing trump lead on the second.)

At night we have a key match, for we play against Becker-Hayden, who are snapping at our heels. From start to finish, everything goes our way. They go down in three touchy game contracts when we guess right on all three and they guess wrong. Dorothy Hayden has troubles with four-spade opening bids. She bids four spades with:

♠ A K Q J 10 9 7 4   ♡ 5 3   ◇ K 8 5   ♣ —

and misses a good slam. Two deals later, she opens one spade with:

♠ K Q J 9 8 4 2   ♡ A 5   ◇ 10   ♣ Q 7 3

This time she is pushed to four spades on a competitive auction, is doubled and set 500.

To cap it all, I pick up:

♠ —   ♡ A K Q 10 9 8 7 5 4   ◇ 5   ♣ A K 2

I am in fourth seat, vulnerable vs. nonvulnerable, and the bidding goes one spade, pass, two spades to me. Bravely, I jump to four hearts. It goes pass, pass, four spades. Undaunted, I gamble out five hearts, and everyone passes. I expect a yarborough in dummy, but Norman showers down with:

♠ K Q 10 7   ♡ 6 3   ◇ K 9 6 3   ♣ 10 8 6

Becker and Hayden, of all people, have been bidding all around me with two aces and no kings between them. Trumps divide (giving dummy an

212

entry), but the diamond ace is wrong, so five hearts is our limit—and every other pair has bid six.

Well, I don't mind getting lucky. We win 75 V.P.'s to 9 and smash into first place, for the previous leaders, Lazard-Rapée and Roth-Root, have played each other to a draw. What is more important, we are 64 V.P.'s ahead of Kehela-Murray in fourth place. With the finals two-thirds over, the first three pairs are in commanding position; a big gap has opened up. We have all seen startling reversals of form in the late stages of previous Trials, but we are starting to sniff Miami's ocean breezes nevertheless.

All day Thursday we will be playing our prospective teammates—Roth-Root in the afternoon and Lazard-Rapée at night. Against Roth-Root, we get off to a bad start, as first Roth and then Root becomes declarer in a tricky vulnerable game and plays it superbly to make. That is 19 imps down. But things get worse instead of better. We bid these cards to six clubs:

WEST	EAST
♠ A J 10 6	♠ Q 9 7
♡ —	♡ J 9 7 5 3
◇ A Q 9 4	◇ K 2
♣ K 8 7 6 2	♣ A Q 9

Roth doubles for a heart lead through the jack-fifth. The spade king is wrong, the trumps split four-one, and we go down 300. It's a bad day.

Two deals later, I pick up as dealer, with both vulnerable:

Wit and Wisdom

Asked whether he had any regrets over using his intellect to advance a recreation, Edgar said no, and added: "Everyone is playing a competitive game. Nobel-quality chemists are competing for prizes; financial advisors are ever mindful of the bottom line. Mistakes by such people have far greater consequences than mistakes by bridge players. Bridge has by far the greater social utility."

♠ A K 4 3   ♡ K Q J 9 5 4 3   ◇ —   ♣ K 8

I open two clubs; Root, on my left, jumps to three diamonds; Norman passes, and Roth, of course, skips to five diamonds. Regretting my skimpy two-club opening, I bid five hearts. Pass to my left, six clubs from Norman, pass. Since Norman did not bid over three diamonds, this is obviously a control-bid, so I sign off at six hearts. Seven clubs from Norman. Oops! The club bid was genuine after all, and here we are in a grand slam almost certainly off the ace of hearts. Pass on my right, pass by me, and—sure enough—double by Root on my left; all pass. A trump is led, and I await the dummy (for I am declarer) hoping against hope for a heart void to come down. It is:

♠ 10 9 6 2   ♡ —   ◇ 6   ♣ A Q J 10 9 5 4 2

Hallelujah! I nearly make some exultant remark to Bill Root about his nerve in doubling me, but he is too nice a guy to needle. So I play briskly and confidently, winning the club in my hand, ruffing a heart, drawing trumps, ruffing a second heart, then back to the king of spades for the kill—pushing the heart king through for the marked ruffing finesse. Disaster—it loses! The whole deal:

South dealer; both sides vulnerable

NORTH
♠ 10 9 6 2
♡ —
◇ 6
♣ A Q J 10 9 5 4 2

WEST
♠ —
♡ 10 7 2
◇ K 10 9 8 7 5 4 2
♣ 7 6

EAST
♠ Q J 8 7 5
♡ A 8 6
◇ A Q J 3
♣ 3

SOUTH
♠ A K 4 3
♡ K Q J 9 5 4 3
◇ —
♣ K 8

Root's double of seven clubs was the "undouble," showing no defensive tricks and asking Roth to save. If I had the brains I was born with, I would have realized this and made the grand slam, for I can ruff hearts three times, dropping the ace. Instead of losing 11 imps, I should gain 14 imps; my idiocy has cost us 25 imps!

We lose the match 11 V.P.'s to 73, and, although we drop to only second place, we are in trouble. The whole complexion of the tournament has changed. Roth-Root, of course, are way ahead in first place, seemingly sure of a berth on the team. Lazard-Rapée have been butchered by Lawrence-Stansby and fall to fourth place. Kehela-Murray cream Kantar-Miles and move into third. Only 16 V.P.'s separate us from Lawrence-Stansby in fifth place. Becker-Hayden and Feldesman-Freeman, sixth and seventh respectively, are in striking range.

At night, our match against Lazard-Rapée gets off to a poor start for us. They pick up a number of tiny swings by accurate bidding and play, and gain heavily when they make four spades with these cards:

WEST	EAST
♠ A Q 6 4 3	♠ K 7 2
♡ A 6	♡ 8 4
◇ 4	◇ A Q 10 8 7 6
♣ J 10 6 5 2	♣ A 9

Lazard, West, ducks the opening heart lead and wins the continuation. Now he leads a low club to dummy's nine. Since the doubleton king of clubs is in front of the ace, he makes 10 tricks easily, even though trumps split four-one. This doesn't feel like a disaster at the time, but we lose 10 imps on the board. One pair is in six spades down one, and two declarers find ways to go down in four spades.

Shortly afterwards, I open a first-seat weak notrump, nonvulnerable vs. vulnerable. Lazard doubles, and Norman holds:

♠ A Q 9 7 6 2   ♡ 9 5   ◇ K 9 4   ♣ 10 3

He bids only two spades, hoping that he can trap Lazard, an active competitor, into further action. Sure enough, after two passes Lazard doubles again. Rapée has nowhere to go and passes the double, so

Norman's imaginative underbid has paid off. Paid off for the opponents, that is, for they win the first six tricks (Rapée has a key singleton and gets three ruffs), and we are down one in two spades doubled although cold for three notrump!

The crusher comes on the very next board, when I hold:

♠ A 7 6 5 4   ♡ Q J 10 3 2   ◇ A 2   ♣ K

I am in fourth seat, vulnerable vs. nonvulnerable. After two passes, Rapée on my right opens three diamonds. I double for takeout, and Norman duly takes out to four clubs. If I pass, we will go down 400 undoubled and lose 9 imps. Instead, I leap out of the frying pan and bid four diamonds, asking for a choice of the majors. Norman obliges with four hearts. Lazard makes a sporting double with six trumps to the king plus other goodies, and we go down 1100. Our foolish opponents could have beaten us 1400 with keener defense, but they win 14 imps anyway. Miami seems farther and farther away.

However, we recover nicely in the second half of the match, gaining on one deal after another. Here is one of our pickups:

North dealer
East-West vulnerable

```
                    NORTH
                    ♠ A K Q 8
                    ♡ K 8
                    ◇ 10 7 2
                    ♣ A 10 8 7
    WEST                            EAST
    ♠ 9 2                           ♠ 7 6 4
    ♡ Q 7 6 5                       ♡ A 10 3 2
    ◇ J 8 6 4 3                     ◇ Q 5
    ♣ 3 2                           ♣ Q J 9 5
                    SOUTH
                    ♠ J 10 5 3
                    ♡ J 9 4
                    ◇ A K 9
                    ♣ K 6 4
```

SOUTH	WEST	NORTH	EAST
Kaplan	*Lazard*	*Kay*	*Rapée*
—	—	1 ♣	Pass
1 ♠	Pass	2 ♠	Pass
2 NT	Pass	4 ♠	(All Pass)

Lazard, West, leads the club three to dummy's seven, East's nine and my king. I draw three rounds of trumps ending in my hand, as Lazard discards the diamond three. If West is short in clubs, this diamond discard is likely from five, in which case an endplay should develop; and if he is long in clubs, a third club trick is sure. So I play a club to dummy's eight; East wins and returns the five of diamonds. I take my diamond ace, cash the king (the drop of the queen is a welcome sight) and lead my last club to dummy's ace. Now I play the fourth club and discard my losing diamond, leaving Rapée on lead to give me a heart trick and the contract.

We have picked back most of our early losses and get 36 V.P.'s to their 48. Meanwhile, Roth-Root have been beaten decisively by Baron-Schleifer; they are still leading, but are back with the pack. Kehela-Murray have won a small match and taken over second place, 13 V.P.'s behind. Rapée-Lazard are third, 12 V.P.'s behind second and 1 V.P. ahead of us in fourth place.

However, our chances are rather better than they seem. For one thing, Lawrence-Stansby have been mauled by Hamman-Mathe (who win their first match of the finals), and a big gap has opened between fourth and fifth. Either Becker-Hayden or Lawrence-Stansby might still make the team, but they need a miracle; it looks like a four-horse race. For another thing, Roth-Root play Kehela-Murray in the last match, so one of them must lose, and we will get in if we have a good match. If we win 69 V.P.'s, nothing can keep us out of the finals.

On that fateful Friday afternoon, we face Feldesman-Freeman, the early leaders, who have slithered steadily downhill and now lie eighth. From first to last, the match is a pleasure for us, as everything goes our way. Our close games make, theirs go down. We make a slam, they miss a slam. We judge right on two wild deals, and they judge wrong. Towards the end, we pick up these cards (East-West vulnerable):

NORTH
♠ A Q 9 7 4
♡ Q 8 2
♢ J 6 2
♣ Q 6

WEST
♠ 10 8
♡ A J 7 5 4
♢ A 10
♣ 10 8 5 3

EAST
♠ J 6 5 2
♡ K 9 6 3
♢ 9 7
♣ A J 4

SOUTH
♠ K 3
♡ 10
♢ K Q 8 5 4 3
♣ K 9 7 2

SOUTH	WEST	NORTH	EAST
Kaplan	*Feldesman*	*Kay*	*Freeman*
—	—	Pass	Pass
2 ♢	Pass	Pass	Double
Pass	2 ♡	3 ♢	Pass
Pass	3 ♡	Pass	Pass
4 ♢	Double	(All Pass)	

There is no way to beat the contract, and we gain heavily. (Weak two-bids have proven consistently successful throughout the Trials.) Norman and I shake hands, for we feel that we are safe. And so it proves—we win by 71 V.P.'s to 13 and are sure to make the team.

Roth-Root are in trouble, for they have lost 73 V.P.'s to 11. But Lazard-Rapée lose to Hamman-Mathe, who have found their teeth as the Trials end, and are out (a heart-breaking result, for this pair has played magnificently, staying at or close to the top throughout the ten days). Becker-Hayden can take third place if they beat Lawrence-Stansby 75 V.P.'s to 9, but they win by 71 V.P.'s to 13, failing by 4 V.P.'s.

So the team is Kehela-Murray, Kaplan-Kay, Roth-Root. I couldn't ask for a better one. I am optimistic, and not only because of three close partnerships and a capable captain. We have a factor conspicuously absent from many previous U.S. teams: We like one another.

Don't sell us short.

HOW THE GAME IS PLAYED

Bridge is unique among popular sports in that a pair's agreed strategy must be announced to the opponents in advance. Furthermore, there are severe constraints on the ways in which players may communicate with partner during play. In the absence of a strong educational effort (which has rarely been present), these aspects are not well understood. The result is much confusion over what constitutes correct behavior and occasional lapses that may impinge unfairly on the opponents.

How to influence participants to honor the spirit of the game (and the letter of its Laws), and how to adjudicate situations in which improper actions have occurred, have long been thorny problems for legislators and tournament administrators. Edgar's was a leading voice in changing attitudes and constructing helpful procedures.

New Science

For several years now, *The Bridge World* has been conducting a campaign against what it calls the "new scientists." Its position is that old-fashioned standard bidding is still better than anything else around, and that any change should be in the direction of the free-wheeling British style, not toward a more precise system. I don't agree—I think U.S. standard bidding is too loose now, and that it's about time this magazine published a defense of "new science."

The epithet "new scientist," as it comes smoking from the pungent pen of Editor Moyse, conjures up the image of studious players trying for impossible accuracy on every hand, using a dozen delicate bids to reach some silly contract, while old-fashioned pairs arrive at the top spot in two bids. We visualize the scientists making life easy for opponents by painting pictures of their hands, instead of leaping boldly and putting on the pressure.

Well, this is nonsense. No school of bidding advocates complicated auctions, so full of inferences and cue-bids that no one knows what's a suit and what isn't. But players of all persuasions can be guilty of this—look at Mr. Moyse's paladins, Reese and Schapiro, in action in the '54 World Championship:

NORTH
♠ A x x x
♡ A Q x x
◇ A 10 x x
♣ K

SOUTH
♠ x x
♡ K x x x
◇ K Q x
♣ A Q x x

Reese was South, Schapiro was North, and the bidding went:

SOUTH	WEST	NORTH	EAST
1 ♣	Pass	2 ◇	Pass
3 ◇	Pass	3 ♡	Pass
4 ♡	Pass	4 ♠	Pass
5 ◇	Pass	6 ◇	Pass
Pass	Pass		

At the other table six hearts was bid with less anguish, fewer calls, and more success.

Now, I am not trying to prove that Reese and Schapiro are "new scientists"; I just want to show that all partnerships, even the greatest, occasionally get enmeshed in their own intricacies. To overcomplicate an auction is an error, and no one is in favor of errors. The "new scientists" don't believe in using as many rounds of bidding as possible. In point of fact, they preempt in twice as many ways, and three times as often, as anyone else.

In *The Bridge World,* the term "new scientist" is one of opprobrium, but there is nothing shameful about a scientific approach to bidding. By scientific bidding I don't mean painstaking accuracy in every auction; I do mean workably narrow limits to the meaning of every bid. Of course, you can't always have exactly the right hand for the bid you make, but if you know exactly what your bid means, you will never be caught very far off base. The "new scientists" object to the many, many sequences in today's standard bidding which have impossibly broad meanings. For example, what does this auction mean in standard bidding?

NORTH	SOUTH
1 ♣	1 ♠
2 ♠	

North could have anything from:

    ♠ A x x   ♡ x x   ◇ J x x   ♣ A K 10 x x

up to

    ♠ A Q x x   ♡ x x   ◇ Q J x   ♣ A K x x

Now, what in the world is responder supposed to do with some hand like:

    ♠ K x x x   ♡ Q x x   ◇ K x x   ♣ Q x x?

Facing the first North hand, he is already in jeopardy at two spades, and he may run into a disastrous penalty if he bids again. Yet, can he pass and miss the back-to-back game if partner holds the second hand? He had better be a good guesser. And, mind you, I have seen top-ranking players use this auction with such a North holding as:

    ♠ J 10 x   ♡ J x x   ◇ x x   ♣ A K Q x x

and also with

    ♠ A K x   ♡ x x x   ◇ A x x   ♣ A K x x

Another sequence that tries to cover much too wide a range is:

WEST	EAST
1 ♣	1 ◇
1 ♠	1 NT

South's bidding goes from bad hands with no fit, such as:

♠ x x   ♡ K 10 x x   ◇ Q J x x x   ♣ x x

up to hands like:

♠ x x   ♡ Q J x   ◇ A Q J x x   ♣ J x x

[because a two-notrump rebid would be forcing—*Editor*] which needs only a little more than a minimum opening to produce game. What is the opening bidder supposed to do with:

♠ A Q x x   ♡ x x   ◇ K x   ♣ A Q x x x?

Facing the first hand, he's no favorite to make even one notrump; facing the second hand he's odds-on to make three notrump.

Don't think that these are isolated cases of auctions with nebulous, unworkable ranges—standard bidding abounds in them. What does South's bidding mean in each of the three following sequences—the first hand given directly below each one, or the second hand?

NORTH	SOUTH
1 ♣	1 ♡
1 ♠	2 ♣

♠ x x   ♡ K Q 10 x x   ◇ J x x   ♣ K J x

♠ x   ♡ K x x x x   ◇ x x x   ♣ J x x x

NORTH	SOUTH
1 ◇	1 ♡
1 ♠	2 ♠

♠ J x x x   ♡ K x x x   ◇ x x   ♣ Q x x

♠ Q J x x   ♡ K Q J x   ◇ x x   ♣ Q x x

NORTH	SOUTH
1 ♠	2 ♠

♠ K Q x x   ♡ J x x   ◇ x x   ♣ K J x x

♠ Q x x   ♡ x x   ◇ x x x   ♣ K x x x x

To all these questions, the answer is "both hands."

Clearly, this cannot be good bidding. It is wrong because with the extreme hands shown above, you will either miss games or take expensive sets when partner misguesses which hand you hold; and it is wrong because with the more normal in-between hands, you won't know whether or not to accept a game-try from partner. To know if you have a minimum or a maximum for your bid, you must have a clear, not a hazy, conception of what your bid means. Look at this deal from the 1956 World Championship in Paris:

Wit and Wisdom

The New Yorker, often considered to be one of America's leading sources of literate humor, sometimes fills small spaces at the bottoms of its columns by citing chuckle-producing linguistic errors that have appeared in print.

Edgar was quoted in this area when he playfully wrote that two participants in a **Bridge World** bidding match "began their bridge careers in the United States but ended up in Los Angeles." Of course, that ostensible nonsense was intentional.

NORTH
♠ J 10 x x
♡ x
♢ K Q x x
♣ 10 9 x x

WEST
♠ 9 x x
♡ A 9 x x x
♢ 10 x
♣ Q x x

EAST
♠ K x x
♡ K Q J x x
♢ J x x x
♣ x

SOUTH
♠ A Q x
♡ 10 x
♢ A 9 x
♣ A K J x x

SOUTH	WEST	NORTH	EAST
1 ♣	Pass	2 ♣	2 ♡
3 ♣	3 ♡	Pass	Pass
Pass			

Charles Solomon was South; Lee Hazen was North.

Obviously, an easy game was missed, but why? It was missed because the partnership did not know exactly what the two-club bid meant. If Hazen had minimum values for the raise, Solomon should have forced to game, not invited it. If Hazen had maximum values, he should have accepted the invitation.

Actually, the bidding system, not either player, was at fault. The range of the two-club bid in standard bidding is so wide that Hazen was not close to either a maximum or a minimum—he was in limbo in between. Such wide limits are really unplayable.

Unplayable? Then how do so many players get such good results with standard bidding? Part of the answer is that good players will do well with any system, and would do better still with more precise bidding. Another part of the answer is that systems with poorly defined bids have a built-in, concealed advantage which, since it is the opposite of "New Science," I shall call "That Old Black Magic." By Old Black Magic, I mean all the bidding without bids that is never heard from Master Solvers [participants in *The Bridge World*'s long-running monthly contest—*Editor*], but is painfully audible at too many bridge tables. I have given many examples to show that standard bidding is too vague, but nothing can be more precise than to respond with a *pianissimo* two spades to one spade on:

♠ Q x x   ♡ x x   ◇ x x x   ♣ K x x x x

and *fortissimo* on:

♠ K Q x x   ♡ J x x   ◇ x x   ♣ K J x x

Black Magic is more accurate than science. The auction:

NORTH	SOUTH
1 ♣	1 ♡
1 ♠	1 NT

in which the one-notrump bid can be either a sign-off or a progressive bid, is ideal when the sign-off is in a flat, listless tone, and the progressive bid is in ringing, pear-shaped tones.

I don't mean to suggest that all standard bidders practice Black Magic or that all scientists wear halos, but it's the simple truth that you don't need inflections to define your bids if they have narrow limits to start with. And it is one of the most compelling arguments for "New Science" that some of the highest-ranking standard bidders are sorcerers.

Ethics, Huddles and Protests

On a recent Sunday, the bridge article in *The New York Times* was devoted largely to a discussion of proprieties and ethics in tournament play. I found that I had a point of view diametrically opposed to A. H. Morehead's—strange, since we would have no disagreement on standards of ethics.

Often, a player feels that he has been damaged by an opponent who took advantage of his own partner's mannerisms—an aggressive bid by one opponent following a slow pass from the other, for example. Increasingly, in recent years, tournament players are speaking up about these common incidents. Much has been written, and dozens of protests are made in every event. The disputed question is what to do about these situations. What should the aggrieved party do at the table? How should the directors and committees rule?

No one, surely, is in any doubt as to the proprieties themselves. It is all in black and white in the rule book. A player may, at his own risk, draw inferences from the mannerisms of his opponents. But "one should not allow partner's hesitation, remark or manner to influence one's call, lead or play."

Simple enough in theory, but of course in practice these cases are prickly, with hairline decisions and outraged feelings. I am chairman of the sub-committee that decides protests at New York tournaments, and it is rare for me to get to dinner before hearing two or three cases involving slow passes or hesitant doubles. (Was there, in fact, a pronounced hesitation? Could this affect partner's action? Was the action then taken outlandish, reasonable or automatic? How was the result affected?)

Morehead's article was based on one such protest from a recent tournament. I remember it very well, because it ruffled sensibilities all around and induced me to drink an extra martini at my belated dinner—which martini, in turn, caused me to utter some gentle reproof to my wife early in the Mixed Pairs that night and so forfeit all chance to win that event.

This was the deal that inspired the protest:

WEST	EAST
♠ A 10 6 2	♠ K J 9 5 3
♡ K Q 7	♡ —
◇ A K 2	◇ Q 7 6
♣ K J 6	♣ Q 10 9 8 7

2 NT	3 ♣
3 ♠	4 ♠
4 NT	5 ♣
5 ◇	6 ♠
Pass	

The opponents claimed that East had huddled before bidding four spades and that this huddle may have led West to try for slam [ostensibly a violation of captaincy—*Editor*]. (The contract was, of course, fulfilled, for there would have been no protest otherwise.) At the hearing, East denied that he had hesitated very long; West denied that his action had been affected by partner's huddle; both were seething with indignation at the protest, feeling that they were being accused of cheating.

Morehead's thesis was that this sort of protest is reprehensible: it is equivalent to an accusation of cheating, since a player is not allowed to rely on partner's hesitation; such a protest creates an "atmosphere of ruthlessness and suspicion that discourages new players in tournaments." Morehead feels that West may have needed no hesitation to prompt his Blackwood bid, and is pleased that the protest was rejected; he appears to regret only that the protesting pair was not reprimanded.

Now, I disagree totally with Morehead's attitude. I did vote to reject the protest, but on different grounds; primarily, because the protest was made only after the slam was fulfilled; secondly, because East-West were a somewhat inexperienced pair. However, had the protest been made against a seasoned pair, and had the director been called when West bid four notrump, then I would have voted to award an adjusted score (and, I would guess from past experience, so would have a majority of the committee).

It is easy to sympathize with Morehead's point about discouraging new players by an atmosphere of suspicion. But "suspicion," in my opinion, is the wrong word for the right attitude. Let me use the analogy that Larry Weiss of Boston suggested in a letter to *The Bridge World.*

Suppose that my opponent drops the ace of hearts face-up on the table. I do not smile sweetly at his partner and suggest that he ignore it; neither do I poison the atmosphere with my suspicion that he will take advantage. Not at all. I call the director, and the rules protect my rights.

Well, the rules also provide that my opponents should not take advantage of each others' mannerisms. Suppose that my opponent "drops" 11 points on the table by a tortured, hesitant pass over my opening bid. If I call the director to protect my rights, why should this create an atmosphere of suspicion any more than if an ace had been dropped? My view is that I should be censured if I do not call the director (and I must admit that I am usually remiss in these situations—from laziness, or fuzzy notions of amenities, or, if you will, from cowardice—and I just sit tight and hope for the best). After all, if my opponent dropped an ace and I were to say, "Just pick it up and forget about it," I would be violating the spirit of tournament play. Why am I entitled to ignore the huddle?

Let me quote from the standard instructions regularly printed on the backs of private scores in France:

"It is your duty to call the director whenever you feel that your opponents have committed an irregularity, and not only those irregularities for which the laws provide penalties, but also others not specifically covered (hesitations, intonations, mannerisms, etc.).

"If your protest is disallowed, you will not be blamed or considered a bad sport. You are doing a service to the community."

Actually, the crucial point on which I disagree with Morehead is his notion that to protest action taken after a huddle is to accuse the opponents of cheating. I do not think it is. I am not just playing with words: I really do not regard a player who allows his partner's mannerisms to influence him in some specific instance as a cheat. Many of my friends in the bridge world have occasionally been guilty of this—in fact, with the possible exception of you and me, every bridge player has fallen from grace once or twice—and I would not have cheats for friends. In the Summer Nationals, I had a word or two to say to an opponent who took out a slow double made by his partner, but I did not think of him as a cheat—he is, in fact, my candidate for the most savagely ethical player in the bridge world. Yet, on this one deal I felt that he had been influenced, subconsciously if you will, by his partner's manner. None of us thinks of violations of this sort as being in the same class with private signals or peeking at boards before playing them. And so long as minor violations of the proprieties are talked of as "cheating," committees cannot properly redress damage unwittingly done.

For example, a few years ago one of my friends was clearly damaged by an opponent's huddle at a national tournament. He opened with three spades. His left-hand opponent, playing "Fishbein," [under which a double suggests trumps—*Editor*] hesitated for nearly a full minute and then doubled for penalties; and his right-hand opponent took the double out to four hearts, holding:

♠ x x x   ♡ A Q x x   ◇ x x x   ♣ K x x

As soon as the hesitant double was taken out, my friend called the director, and the matter came to committee. Why, the committee asked, had the double been taken out? The offender explained his line of reasoning: the three-bidder had to have a long suit, so he could not expect his partner to have a lot of spades when he himself held three of them. He swore on his mother's grave that he had not been influenced by the huddle. So, of course, the committee rejected the protest; the player was a pillar of the community with a wife and three children, and they would not label him a liar and a cheat. Yet, every member of the committee knew in his heart that a prompt double would have been left in, that my friend had been damaged by the huddle, far more than he would have been damaged by an exposed card or a bid out of turn, for which he would have received redress.

My suggestion to all tournament committees is to free yourself to deal with these situations, as we have in New York. Publicize the conception that to request protection from the director after an opponent huddles is not to accuse the opponents of cheating; that it is not only a player's right but his duty to do so. And establish (and publish, as we have) a simple rule for deciding protests: A player who has received unauthorized information from his partner may not take any doubtful or unusual action even if he feels that he would have done so, regardless. Then you will not have to psychoanalyze or judge the offenders; you can simply redress damage.

Here is a typical case—if you have sat on committees, you have heard hundreds like it—that we decided a few months ago. The auction went:

SOUTH	WEST	NORTH	EAST
—	—	1 ♣	1 NT
Pass	Pass	Double	(All Pass)

South had huddled noticeably before passing the first time, and when North doubled the director was called. He allowed the auction and play to proceed; the contract went down two; and the matter came to our committee. North's hand:

♠ K 8 4   ♡ 10 2   ◇ A Q 7   ♣ A J 7 6 4

At the meeting, South, a lady of absolutely irreproachable character, told us that she had hesitated slightly, but only because she had a slight problem, certainly not to give partner information. We believed her. North, a gentleman whom we all knew to be of blameless reputation, told us that he had not allowed partner's hesitation, which he hardly noticed, to influence him. We believed him. And we awarded an adjusted score, for one notrump, *undoubled*, down two.

We did not have to weigh North-South's morals or delve into their minds. North, no matter why, had taken doubtful action after partner huddled; and, under our rule, he was not entitled to do so. We certainly did not think that East-West had been *cheated* (if we had thought so, we would have referred the matter to the Conduct and Ethics Committee). But we did think that they might have been *damaged* (not *were* damaged, but *might have been* damaged, observe), so entitled to redress.

This interpretation of the Proprieties is similar to the new rule for defender's exposed cards. In the old days, a card was exposed if partner saw it; now, it is exposed if held so that partner could see it. Likewise, a player is entitled to redress not only if an opponent did take advantage of his partner's manner, but if he could have done so.

In conclusion, let me return to Morehead's example. There, you will recall, a player opened with two notrump on:

♠ A 10 6 2   ♡ K Q 7   ◇ A K 2   ♣ K J 6

He bid three spades in response to Stayman, and, when partner huddled and went to four spades, tried Blackwood. Here are my reactions:

(1) It is the *duty* of the opponents to call the director (but to call him when four notrump is bid, not after waiting to see the result). (2) This is not an accusation, but simply an attempt to protect themselves from damage through an opponent's irregularity, just as in the case of a revoke. (3) The committee should award redress without regard to whether four notrump is a possible bid, merely considering whether it is an unusual or doubtful action. Thus, whether the player might have bid four notrump anyway becomes irrelevant unless he is so inexperienced that he can be expected to try for slam whenever he has shown a strong hand and his partner bids game.

Notice that I am in favor of giving new tournament players a little extra consideration, but merely because it is difficult to determine what is an "unusual or doubtful" action for them. Tournaments now are twice as large as they were five years ago, and they will probably be twice again as large five years from now. I am not afraid of discouraging new players by an "atmosphere of ruthlessness and suspicion." I am interested in discouraging new players from carrying over into tournaments the loose standards of home games, where shameless advantage is taken of partner's mannerisms. The sooner they learn that tournament bridge is not a "no-holds-barred" game, the better off they will be.

And tournaments will become more enjoyable when there are fewer violations of the Proprieties. Such violations will be less common when directors and committees can deal with them just as with violations of the Laws; when an opponent can say "I have been damaged" without implying "I have been cheated"; when it becomes as much of a disadvantage to a player to expose his points with a huddle as to expose a card.

Bridge is played by fallible human beings, and accidents will happen. But I have a feeling that when it is clearly established that violations of the Proprieties will, if anything, hurt the offender, they will become rare indeed.

Opinion: An Interview with Edgar Kaplan

*O*pinion presents an interview with Edgar Kaplan, chairman of the Greater New York Bridge Association's protest committee, and an active party in attempting to correct some of the glaring deficiencies in present methods of handling protests of violations.

Journalist: In your article, "Ethics, Huddles and Protests" (*The Bridge World*, January 1964), you indicated that you felt there was a clear distinction between certain common violations of the proprieties, such as taking action owing (perhaps subconsciously) to partner's hesitation, and cheating, via such methods as private signals or prior knowledge of hands. Accepting this distinction, let us first discuss these huddle situations. You have indicated that you think that "dropping 11 points" on the table via a slow pass should be treated similarly to dropping a card face up on the table. Granting the greater difficulty in establishing the facts in the former case, what specific rules would you promulgate to handle it?

Kaplan: It is not necessary to promulgate any new rules. The section of the Laws devoted to Proprieties states, in part, "One should not allow partner's hesitation, remark or manner to influence one's call, lead or play." What the Protest Committee has been doing in New York tournaments is to enforce this Propriety very strictly, giving redress to players who are damaged by violations of it.

In deciding protests, we guide ourselves by this interpretation of the rules: no player who has received unauthorized information from his partner will be allowed to profit by any doubtful action that he takes subsequently. The key question is not whether a player actually did take advantage. (No one has ever admitted to a committee that he was influenced by partner's huddle; invariably, the offender states that he would have taken the action anyway, had not noticed the huddle, etc.) The deciding factor is whether a player *could have* taken advantage. If his action was not clear-cut, and if it could have been based, subconsciously perhaps, on illegal information, we award an adjusted score.

Obviously, this results in an occasional injustice to the offending side. A player might well have been about to take the winning action regardless of partner's huddle; we cannot read his mind. Thus, it becomes a disadvantage to tip your hand to partner; it can hurt your side instead of the enemy. In consequence, we expect fewer huddles, softer doubles, and fewer antics all around.

Journalist: Can you give us some examples of typical rulings?

Kaplan: Here are three recent cases. . . . [details omitted]

*

Journalist: How can it be ascertained that a bid was based in any way on partner's action? Consider this situation:

Matchpoints
North-South vulnerable

East holds:

♠ x ♡ Q x ◇ Q x x x ♣ A K Q J 10 x

The bidding:

SOUTH	WEST	NORTH	EAST
1 ♡	Pass	2 ♠	?

West took considerable time before passing over one heart, and South is known to be a straightforward player, not given to psychics (particularly with unfavorable vulnerability). East can be quite sure, looking at his own cards, that West does not have a strong hand. Why the huddle? Obviously, West has a desperately weak hand, perhaps with a long diamond suit, and was contemplating some sort of obstructive action. It is a sure-thing bet that West does not have a balanced 8-count, the sort of hand that would defeat a slam. Without the huddle, East would probably bid five clubs. With the extra information given by the huddle East can bid seven clubs with perfect confidence that he is not buying a phantom. This call will certainly fix North-South, and it would be very difficult to pin anything on East, "After all," he could argue, "South opened and North jump-shifted, so I knew my partner had nothing. The huddle did not influence me at all." How would you rule in this case?

Kaplan: I would not be interested in East's reasoning. He took a most unusual action after receiving help from his partner and is not entitled to benefit from it. I would award average-plus to North-South, average-minus to East-West.

*

Journalist: It has been our experience, and the experience of others, that when we call a director to protect us in such a huddle situation we are always at a disadvantage. The director, first of all, acts as though we are making an accusation of cheating, and the burden of proof of damage falls on us. Secondly, if the director rules that we have not been injured, we must, if we disagree, protest to a committee, under the threat of disciplinary action if the protest is ruled "frivolous." Thirdly, if the director feels there is merit to our argument, he does not take any action (perhaps because he does not have a set of specific penalties to apply). Instead, he tells us to refer it to the committee. We must convince the committee of the situation as we have already convinced the director. Players let the matter die rather than go through this process. What can be done about this?

Kaplan: We are trying very hard to sell the idea that it is not an accusation of cheating to call the director to protect your rights after a huddle. In New York, the directors are sold on this already—half the protests we act on are made by the offending side protesting the director's ruling. And the director is always present when the protest is heard.

*

Journalist: Leaving the question of the opponents' ethics for a while, let us consider some ethical problems we have had. How should one behave when an opponent shows cards? How often should one tell someone to hold his hand back? Is it ethical to take advantage of information obtained this way?

Kaplan: This is a simple one. You are not entitled to peek, but you are entitled to see—and act on what you have seen. Tell your opponents to hold their cards back as often and emphatically as possible; after all, you have already seen, and the opponents will be working for you when they leave your table.

Journalist: Some partnerships have many more agreements than could possibly be listed on a convention card. Is this a violation of the proprieties? We are not thinking of specific "conventions" with names but things that have broad meanings in "standard" methods. What approach should we take to this problem?

Kaplan: My own feeling is that matters of partnership style do not have to be announced in advance. The opponents must be made aware of (1) bids that sound strong but are weak (or vice versa); (2) bids that indicate length in suits other than the one named. All agreements in these categories should go on the card. Anything else may properly be the subject of a question by the opponents. If they do not care to know, that is their headache.

Journalist: Now for the question of *very* unethical conduct, even outright cheating. How can you, the committee, or any player distinguish between a result obtained by dumb luck and one due to prior knowledge of a deal? We have made it a practice to go to the director after a round on which opponents played as though they had seen all the cards and to inform him of our observations, in the (apparently vain) hope that he can get a "book" on this pair, if they persist in getting these "lucky" results. This, however, doesn't help our score on the deal. Protesting to the committee seems fruitless, . . .

Kaplan: No committee will ever award redress because your opponent made a bad bid and got a good result. However, you are quite right to report any particularly suspicious occurrence to the director. We keep these incidents on file, and a series of "lucky" bids lands a suspect before the Conduct and Ethics Committee. You will not improve your score when you report these cases, but you are doing a service to the game.

Journalist: This leads directly to our view of the best way to get the goods on those whose actions rob the majority of players of much of the enjoyment of the game. We feel that every player should consider it his *obligation* to report to the committee any untoward actions by his opponents, particularly when he obtains a good board. This puts you in a much better position, since you are now acting as a public-spirited person, and not in your own self-interest. For example:

Matchpoints; both sides vulnerable

```
                        NORTH
                        ♠ Q 10 x
                        ♡ J 10 9 x
                        ◇ J 10 9 x
                        ♣ A K
        WEST                              EAST
        ♠ K x x x x                       ♠ x
        ♡ A 8 x                           ♡ K Q x x
        ◇ x x x                           ◇ A Q x
        ♣ x x                             ♣ Q 10 x x x
                        SOUTH
                        ♠ A J 9 x
                        ♡ x x
                        ◇ K 8 x
                        ♣ J 9 x x
```

SOUTH	WEST	NORTH	EAST
—	—	1 NT	Pass
Pass	2 ♠	Pass	Pass
Double	Pass	Pass	Pass

North-South plus 1100.

In this constructed deal, North opened with a weak notrump, and East made it clear that he had a terrible problem. He grabbed for the card, studied it, and asked, "Is that a weak notrump?" West had an "automatic" balance, of course, and he bid two spades. South applied the axe, and they carted West out in a wicker basket.

A North-South pair that sat back and enjoyed their top, and took no further action, would, in our opinion, be guilty of dereliction of duty. They should definitely report this East-West pair to the Ethics Committee (not the tournament Protest Committee, since they do not seek redress). Do you think this is the right thing to do?

Kaplan: No, I disagree with you here. My view is that there is a clear distinction, not of degree but of kind, between this sort of improper conduct and cheating—clipping boards or having private signals. If I think I have been cheated, I will report the matter regardless of the result. However, I do not regard a player who draws inferences from partner's mannerisms as a cheat. Most of the time, this type of violation is not fully deliberate; every player I know, even the most scrupulously ethical, has offended against the Proprieties once or twice. So I report these cases only when I feel that I have been damaged and am entitled to redress.

Note the distinction. If you feel that you have been damaged by, say, a private understanding between your opponents, a violation of the "honor code" of bridge, you should report it. But do not expect redress—the committee is not likely to decide that your opponents are crooks on the evidence of one or even two deals. What you are doing is building up a dossier for future action if your suspicions are verified. In contrast, if you are damaged by, say, an inference drawn from a huddle, which we treat as a technical violation of the rules similar to an exposed card, you will be protected against damage. If you have not been hurt, do not call the director—just as you do not when you are a defender and declarer exposes a card.

We hope to discourage the invitational pass, the tentative penalty double, and hesitation Blackwood not by stigmatization or suspending the violators but by making it a disadvantage to break the rules. Once it becomes evident that there is a penalty attached to these violations, they may become as rare as revokes.

Journalist: By the way, what is the right time to call the director in a situation like that one? Should you call as soon as East huddles and passes? Suppose East huddles and then bids something. Should you call then? Should you call for protection when West bids two spades, or should you wait until you have seen West's hand? When is it too late to attempt to get redress?

Kaplan: The time to call the director is right at the moment that an opponent takes what may be unusual action after receiving illegal information. In your example, call the director when West bids two spades. If he has a seven-card suit, or six-five shape, do not be embarrassed. You have not accused him of cheating; you have merely protected your rights. In the example, the director is likely (at least in New York) to disallow the overcall, let you play in one notrump, and bar a spade lead. But you cannot have it both ways, waiting to see how you do against two spades before protesting. Of course, if the director allows the action, you may appeal his ruling when you see the deal later. But you must, to protect your rights, call the director when you suspect that a violation has taken place.

AT THE TABLE

The prerequisites for becoming a top player include expertise in both bidding and play. However, in the publication of bridge feats in the popular press (and, although to a lesser extent, even in specialty magazines), coups by declarer or defender take priority. This is a matter of practicality: Appreciating (or even understanding) the bidding of experts sometimes requires detailed knowledge of the system in use. Restricting one's audience to fans of a particular pair or method is not a recipe for success. In contrast, card-play technique is accessible to everyone. Accordingly, only rarely will a columnist bring forth a deal that does not have a point in the play.

Edgar was fascinated with all aspects of bridge, but his research, experimentation and creativity centered largely on bidding. In "The Great Debate," he was a strong supporter of the viewpoint that the bidding was more important than the play in determining the outcomes of tournaments. But it would be a gross error to believe that Edgar did not successfully cross swords with the best card players. Indeed, as illustrated in this collection of table experiences from his early tournament years, his at-the-table talents extended into realms where other expert players rarely venture.

Edgar Kaplan may be the only leading expert first to break into print by virtue of an opening lead. In the 1952 National Men's Pairs, he held:

♠ 10 9 6 5   ♡ 6 3   ◇ K 2   ♣ A J 10 7 4

His left-hand opponent opened one club, and partner inserted a preemptive jump-overcall of two diamonds. This was especially noteworthy, because Edgar's side was vulnerable against nonvulnerable opponents—the term "unfavorable vulnerability" was not in vogue in those days. The intervenor needed considerable playing strength to justify this intervention; on Edgar's holding of the king of diamonds, he suspected (correctly, as it happened) an eight-card suit.

Right-hand opponent bid two hearts; Edgar interfered with three diamonds—all he could afford under the circumstances—and opener's raise to four hearts ended the auction.

It seemed impossible that the defense could take two diamond tricks, and if the overcaller had the weak defensive hand that his bid advertised, there was only one chance to defeat the contract: Edgar led the ace of clubs. When dummy showed 4=4=1=4 and everyone followed low to the first trick, there was no way to determine the club distribution, but he continued hopefully with a second club, choosing the four-spot as a suit-preference signal for a diamond return if things went well. Partner ruffed and responded to the signal by underleading the ace of diamonds to get a second ruff, defeating the contract.

* * *

Edgar's first major victory was in the 1953 Vanderbilt. This deal from the semifinals served notice that he was an imaginative competitor, a force to be reckoned with:

South dealer; East-West vulnerable

NORTH
♠ Q 8 5
♡ 10 8 7 4
◇ K 10 6 3
♣ K 5

WEST
♠ K 10 7 2
♡ 9 2
◇ A Q 8 7 5 4
♣ Q

EAST
♠ A 9 4 3
♡ 6 3
◇ J 2
♣ A J 9 3 2

SOUTH
♠ J 6
♡ A K Q J 5
◇ 9
♣ 10 8 7 6 4

SOUTH	WEST	NORTH	EAST
Kaplan	*Rosen*	*Sherman*	*Agruss*
1 ♡	Pass	2 ♡	Pass
4 ♡	Pass	Pass	Pass

Nowadays, a weak two-bid or a light one-bid with the South cards would be found attractive to certain classes of tournament enthusiast. Edgar's strategy of a lead-directing light opening bid and deliberate overbidding with a weak defensive hand was at that time an avant-garde approach. North had considerable defense, so "stealing" the deal in four hearts, conceding 100 points for down two undoubled, was no great triumph: the opponents could make three spades, for a near-equivalent score, but might have overreached to four spades and "gone minus."

The potential unsettling of the opponents by the bold tactics was more important than the result. As it happened, there was plenty of overreaching at the other table:

SOUTH	WEST	NORTH	EAST
Evans	*Lipton*	*Cohen*	*Kahn*
Pass	1 ◇	Pass	1 ♠
2 ♡	2 ♠	4 ♡	Double
Pass	4 ♠	Pass	Pass
5 ♡	Double	(All Pass)	

North, Barry Cohen, who later changed his name to Crane and became one of the most successful players ever, bounced his opponents into an uninformed decision—and they went wrong. However, he also gave his partner a false impression of his hand, leading to a superficially attractive but in fact disastrous sacrifice, down three doubled, a penalty of 500. Being on the same page counts for a lot.

This was the critical deal from the final:

Wit and Wisdom

"Bridge teaches one to endure misery. And one usually loses. Winners bring a huge desire to win, and they seem to summon total concentration; losers permit distractions, which are omnipresent. Individuals who pursue purity, or principle, at the expense of practicality, are eventual losers; so are players who prefer being 'right' or fear appearing stupid."

East dealer; East-West vulnerable

NORTH
♠ Q 8 4
♡ 10 5
◇ K 7 6
♣ K J 10 8 6

WEST
♠ J 9 3
♡ A Q J 6 2
◇ 8 2
♣ A 5 4

EAST
♠ A K 10 7 5
♡ K 9 8 4 3
◇ —
♣ Q 9 3

SOUTH
♠ 6 2
♡ 7
◇ A Q J 10 9 5 4 3
♣ 7 2

In one room, a massive preempt did its dirty work:

SOUTH	WEST	NORTH	EAST
Kahn	Silodor	Lipton	Roth
—	—	—	1 ♠
5 ◇	5 ♠	(All Pass)	

Declarer took 12 tricks, for a score of 680.
In the other room, milder interference led to eventual fireworks:

SOUTH	WEST	NORTH	EAST
Field	Sherman	Sobel	Kaplan
—	—	—	1 ♠
4 ◇	4 ♠	5 ♣	Pass
5 ◇	5 ♡	Pass	6 ♡
Pass	Pass	7 ♣	Double
Pass	Pass	7 ◇	Pass
Pass	7 ♡	(All Pass)	

Absolute standards can but rarely be applied to wild auctions, but all of the East-West decisions—to compete at the five level, to bid slam in the newly-discovered monster fit, to take a chance on an uncertain grand slam rather than accept a small penalty (at total-point scoring)—stand up well on either a theoretical or practical basis. With the lucky spade position, declarer scored 2210 at seven hearts.

* * *

On this deal from the 1955 Life Masters Individual, Edgar functioned as both participant and after-the-fact bidding theorist:

West dealer
Both sides vulnerable

NORTH
♠ 8 7
♡ 6 4
♢ Q 10 8 7 4 3
♣ Q 9 5

WEST
♠ J 6 5 3
♡ J 10 5
♢ A 6
♣ A 10 7 4

EAST
♠ Q 10 4
♡ Q 9 8 3
♢ J 2
♣ K 8 6 2

SOUTH
♠ A K 9 2
♡ A K 7 2
♢ K 9 5
♣ J 3

As in real estate, location is often critical. Many Souths opened with one notrump in fourth position, and their partners produced a weakness response of two diamonds—during that era, two of any suit other than clubs was a signoff; transfers had only recently been born, and neither two-way Stayman nor any other fancy devices had yet made a significant impact.

During the inevitable post-mortem, the question arose as to how opener, with a maximum and a strong fit in responder's long suit, could express game-interest. (Three notrump, though it makes as the cards lie, is against the odds with this North-South combination; however, it would be a desirable contract if one of South's major-suit aces were instead the ace of diamonds.) Edgar expanded earlier techniques by

(Repeated for convenience)

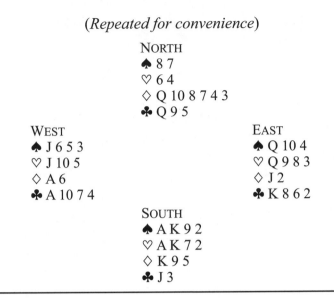

NORTH
♠ 8 7
♡ 6 4
◇ Q 10 8 7 4 3
♣ Q 9 5

WEST
♠ J 6 5 3
♡ J 10 5
◇ A 6
♣ A 10 7 4

EAST
♠ Q 10 4
♡ Q 9 8 3
◇ J 2
♣ K 8 6 2

SOUTH
♠ A K 9 2
♡ A K 7 2
◇ K 9 5
♣ J 3

suggesting that where a two-notrump rebid, instead of the expected pass, showed a suitable maximum with two of the top three honors in responder's suit (e.g., ace-queen-low); a direct raise to three indicated a fit of ace- or king-fourth (in the hope of hitting a six-card suit including the other top honor). These agreements were adopted by scientific pairs prior to the invasion of more complex artificiality in responding to notrump.

When Edgar held the North cards, he opened with a psychic one diamond in second position. East, also stirring the pot, doubled; South, waiting to get more information, passed. West innocently (if a bit aggressively) jumped to two notrump; then, joining the others inserting their personalities into the auction, redoubled when South doubled.

Now it was Edgar's turn to take the heat. As he explained afterwards, there were two possibilities: (1) South had enough strength to expect to beat two notrump opposite partner's opening but not enough to redouble earlier (which would have required at least 10 points). (2) South had so much strength that North's psychic had been clear on the first round of bidding. In Case (1), North-South were in for a probable matchpoint zero whatever North did. So Edgar assumed Case (2); he passed two notrump redoubled, and the penalty was 2200.

* * *

On this big-swing deal from the 1955 Vanderbilt Cup final, Edgar is not listed among the players. Nonetheless, he had an important role in the supporting cast.

West dealer
Both sides vulnerable

NORTH
♠ J 10 5 3 2
♡ K 9 7 5 2
♢ 5 3
♣ 4

WEST
♠ A Q 9
♡ A J 8
♢ K 9 6
♣ K Q 9 5

EAST
♠ K 4
♡ Q 6 3
♢ A Q J 8 7 2
♣ 8 2

SOUTH
♠ 8 7 6
♡ 10 4
♢ 10 4
♣ A J 10 7 6 3

CLOSED ROOM

SOUTH	WEST	NORTH	EAST
Leventritt	Crawford	Sobel	Becker
—	1 ♢	Pass	3 ♢
Pass	4 ♣	Pass	4 ♢
Pass	4 NT	Pass	5 ♢
Pass	6 ♢	(All Pass)	

Crawford, West, anticipating rebidding two notrump after a major-suit response, started with a lead-inhibiting one diamond. Serendipitously, this steered his side into the optimum contract: six diamonds *by West*, where there could be no damage done by an opening heart lead through the ace. Assuming no freakish distribution, even if declarer did not profit from a heart into his tenace, he could expect to be able to win the opening lead, draw trumps ending in dummy, and play a club. If that trick was won in the closed hand, West could discard a club from dummy on a spade and at worst lose one heart trick. If a club honor lost

(Repeated for convenience)

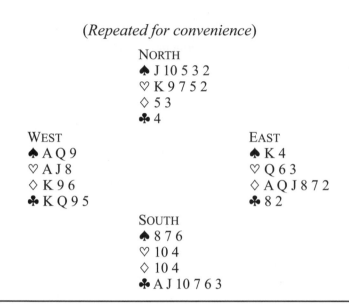

NORTH
♠ J 10 5 3 2
♡ K 9 7 5 2
◇ 5 3
♣ 4

WEST
♠ A Q 9
♡ A J 8
◇ K 9 6
♣ K Q 9 5

EAST
♠ K 4
♡ Q 6 3
◇ A Q J 8 7 2
♣ 8 2

SOUTH
♠ 8 7 6
♡ 10 4
◇ 10 4
♣ A J 10 7 6 3

to the ace, declarer could try to ruff out the jack-ten of clubs, then if necessary rely on the heart finesse. All in all, a sound contract.

But Serendipity was wearing two hats on this deal. North led a club to South's ace and received a ruff in return, immediately setting the contract.

Those proceedings were recorded and eventually reported in *The Bridge World* by Alfred Sheinwold. (It would be a long time before any official records were kept at Nationals, even in major national team championships. If no scribe took the trouble to retain a description of the bidding and play, they were lost to history.)

Of course, in order to have the complete story of the match, Sheinwold needed someone recording in the other room. This task fell to Edgar Kaplan, usually a willing conspirator in such projects. He deposed as follows:

OPEN ROOM

SOUTH	WEST	NORTH	EAST
Ogust	*Rapée*	*Koytchou*	*Schenken*
1 ♣	Pass	1 ◇	Pass
2 NT	Pass	3 ◇	Pass
3 NT	Pass	5 NT	Pass
6 NT	Pass	Pass	Pass

Here, after a more natural opening bid, Ogust and Koytchou faced a delicate choice between playing the right strain (diamonds) from the wrong side or the wrong strain (notrump) from the right side. These are the decisions that try men's souls. Six notrump has the disadvantage that after a (likely) neutral lead, declarer has no surety if he wins the first trick in clubs with a closed-hand honor—North might be withholding the ace, and West would need to guess whether to play South for the ace of clubs or the king of hearts.

Declarer took the opening spade lead in dummy, led a club to the king, crossed back to dummy in diamonds, and led another club, soon claiming 12 tricks. Here is how Sheinwold told the rest of the story:

"You're a fine reporter," I pointed out smugly to Kaplan. "Didn't it ever occur to you that North might be holding off with the ace of clubs? Switch the ace of clubs and the king of hearts, and North *must* refuse the first club trick to lure declarer into repeating the club play. If North takes the first club, he forces declarer to try the winning heart finesse."

"That thought didn't occur to me," Kaplan pointed out, equally smugly, "because I was sitting behind Rapée and could *see* that he didn't have the ace of clubs. And it didn't occur to *Ogust*, because he played the king of clubs with a do-or-die air, like a man who had the king but not the queen. Rapée followed suit without a problem, and that gave *Ogust* no problem."

And this, my children, goes to show that there's more to bridge than you'll find in most textbooks.

*   *   *

After mastering technique and building partnerships, experts aspire to being a tough opponent. This is a difficult skill to achieve, for it requires both alertness to the possibility of using already-discovered devices and the imagination to visualize new ones. Edgar sat East on this deal from the 1955 National Men's Pairs:

North dealer; neither side vulnerable

```
                      NORTH
                      ♠ 9 3
                      ♡ A Q
                      ◇ A Q 10 7 6 4
                      ♣ 10 9 8
WEST                                      EAST
♠ 10 4 2                                  ♠ A K 8 6 5
♡ J 10 8 5 3 2                            ♡ 7 4
◇ 9 5                                     ◇ J 3
♣ A 5                                     ♣ K J 7 4
                      SOUTH
                      ♠ Q J 7
                      ♡ K 9 6
                      ◇ K 8 2
                      ♣ Q 6 3 2
```

SOUTH	WEST	NORTH	EAST
—	—	1 ◇	1 ♠
1 NT	2 ♡	3 ◇	Pass
3 NT	Pass	Pass	Pass

West led the deuce of spades. As the bidding marked declarer with a spade stopper and a diamond fit, it was immediately clear that East's only chance to defeat the contract was to find West with the ace of clubs. Realizing this, Edgar conceived a double-deception—and he did so instantly, for it was an essential element of the plot that he play smoothly to the first two tricks, concealing the possibility of any alternatives. He won the first trick with the spade *ace* and shifted to the *king* of clubs.

When a low club was continued at trick three, what could declarer possibly think but that East's spades were headed by the ace (leaving West the king of spades to justify his entering the auction) and his clubs by the ace-king (and that he had continued clubs hoping to find his partner with an original holding of three to the queen).

When declarer put up the queen of clubs at trick three, West won and crossed back to the East hand in spades for the setting tricks in clubs. This is one of the most brilliant spontaneous compound deceptions on record.

* * *

Being "at the table" sometimes means recognizing special occurrences—those that have technical or systemic significance, or points of general interest. The last of those is of great importance to a writer, because bridge deals are generally reported for one (or both) of two reasons: they played a role in the outcome of an event, or they enhance one's knowledge or enjoyment of the game. In the latter category, Edgar was unsurpassed as an unearther of offbeat highlights. Here is a report he wrote about deals with unique characteristics:

Here are two deals from the [1956] Summer Nationals.

```
                        NORTH
                        ♠ 6 5
                        ♡ 9 6 4 3
                        ◇ K 9 7 4
                        ♣ 10 6 2
        WEST                            EAST
        ♠ K Q 9 7 4 2                    ♠ 8 3
        ♡ Q 5                            ♡ 10 8 7 2
        ◇ 10 8 2                         ◇ Q 5 3
        ♣ Q 4                            ♣ A J 9 3
                        SOUTH
                        ♠ A J 10
                        ♡ A K J
                        ◇ A J 6
                        ♣ K 8 7 5
```

Both Souths, Ogust and Kay, opened two notrump (21-22 points). Koytchou raised Ogust to three notrump, while Hirschberg passed two notrump. At total-point scoring, vulnerable, it's a very close decision.

At both tables, the king of spades was led and won by declarer, who then passed the diamond jack to the queen. Two more rounds of spades cleared the suit. Kay, in *two* notrump, cashed one high heart and three diamonds. Now, with six spades and three diamonds marked at his left, he took the heart finesse for his eighth trick and went down 200.

Ogust, in *three* notrump, couldn't sensibly adopt this line of play, as he needed nine tricks, not eight. With only one entry to dummy, he was forced to play the queen of hearts to drop doubleton and the club ace to be onside. Everything worked like a charm.

What is the moral of this sad little tale? I can hear some players growl, "Don't be so scientific—bid your games." But should you lose 800 points for missing a game where you need a six-two spade split, a diamond split, a doubleton queen of hearts with six out, and the ace of clubs right?

Second case:

```
                         NORTH
                         ♠ Q 10 8 7 3
                         ♡ 3
                         ◇ A 6 5
                         ♣ K Q 10 4

        WEST                               EAST
        ♠ K J 9 6 4                        ♠ —
        ♡ K 6 2                            ♡ Q J 7 5 4
        ◇ J 9 7 2                          ◇ 10 3
        ♣ 6                                ♣ A J 9 7 5 2

                         SOUTH
                         ♠ A 5 2
                         ♡ A 10 9 8
                         ◇ K Q 8 4
                         ♣ 8 3
```

SOUTH	WEST	NORTH	EAST
1 ◇	Pass	1 ♠	Double
Pass	Pass	Redouble	1 NT
Pass	2 ♡	3 ♣	Pass
3 NT	Pass	Pass	Pass

Sheinwold was East; I was West. I led a low heart, won by declarer's ace. South played the ace and a low spade, which I ducked. Declarer came back to his king of diamonds and led a third spade. I won, and the position now was:

NORTH
♠ Q 10
♡ —
◇ A 6
♣ K Q 10 4

WEST
♠ J 9
♡ K 6
◇ J 9 7
♣ 6

EAST
♠ —
♡ Q 7 5 4
◇ 10
♣ A J 9

SOUTH
♠ —
♡ 10 9 8
◇ Q 8 4
♣ 8 3

Superficially, it appears that if I play the king of hearts and a heart to East's queen, and Sheinwold leads a third heart, declarer is down, as East has the club ace in-card for his fifth heart. However, the fourth round of hearts would squeeze me—I can't pitch either a spade or a diamond without giving declarer a ninth trick. If I throw my club, South leads ace, queen and a low diamond, to endplay me.

Can you guess what Sheinwold did?

When I played the king of hearts and a low heart, he didn't take the trick but ducked! Now declarer was dead; no squeeze or endplay would operate.

* * *

It is a simultaneous fascination and frustration of bridge that even the most thoughtful calls and plays do not always (to put it mildly) achieve the best results. On this deal from the 1958 National Masters Teams (nowadays contested for the Spingold trophy), Edgar held the South cards:

South dealer
Both sides vulnerable

NORTH
♠ 8 3
♡ 7 5 4
♢ A J 5 3 2
♣ K Q 3

SOUTH
♠ K 9
♡ A 6
♢ Q 9 8 7
♣ A 7 6 5 2

SOUTH	WEST	NORTH	EAST
Kaplan	*Roth*	*Sheinwold*	*Stone*
1 NT	3 ♡	3 NT	(All Pass)

The jump-overcall goaded North-South into a game they would not have attempted unjostled.

Roth led the king of hearts, which held, then the queen of hearts, on which Stone discarded a low spade. From declarer's perspective, West was marked with seven hearts, apparently at least two spades (East would not likely have kept quiet with eight or nine spades), and, by necessary assumption, the king of diamonds; unless West had at least one additional diamond, there would be no problem.

In summary, when it mattered there was little chance that clubs would break three-two—in the critical cases, South would need *five* diamond tricks, and therefore he needed to retain a club entry to dummy, because *diamonds would be blocked if West held king-doubleton.* Having worked all this out, after winning with the ace of hearts, Edgar led a diamond to dummy's jack.

The finesse lost, and now declarer needed to find the ace of spades with East to avoid disaster. But that ace of spades was West's side card. The defense ran both majors, putting declarer down eight—known in the trade as "800 the hard way."

* * *

One of the hazards of achieving expert status is being continually bombarded with questions. Thus, one faces problems both at the table and away from it. Edgar was a favorite target of inquisitors, partly for the respect in which his views were held and partly because there was a good chance that one would receive a cleverly worded response.

When a freak hand was dealt at the 1961 Summer Nationals, an indefatigable supplicant submitted it to 18 acknowledged masters who had not seen it. The question was what action to take as dealer with this holding:

♠ —   ♡ A K Q J 10 9 8 4 2   ◊ —   ♣ 8 7 5 3

Of the first 17 to be surveyed, 11 passed, four bid four hearts, one bid five hearts, and one bid six hearts. When asked for his view, Edgar replied that he wasn't sure what he would have done at the table, but as an academic exercise he would open seven hearts, because he always answers such problems correctly. It is not clear what, if anything, the questioner learned from this, but this was the full deal:

NORTH
♠ A K Q 6 5 4
♡ 3
◊ 9 7 5 4 3 2
♣ —

WEST
♠ J 9 7 3
♡ —
◊ K Q J 10
♣ K J 9 6 2

EAST
♠ 10 8 2
♡ 7 6 5
◊ A 8 6
♣ A Q 10 4

SOUTH
♠ —
♡ A K Q J 10 9 8 4 2
◊ —
♣ 8 7 5 3

*   *   *

One of the great delights of the game is the post-mortem. Being right or wrong in the actual deal (or in the secondary analysis) is often inconsequential. The insights gleaned from the investigation are so often valuable that players at all skill levels freely enter such conversations. Indeed, hearing opinions and becoming aware of previously-unseen possibilities is one of the best ways to improve.

On this deal from the 1959 Life Masters Pairs, Edgar was successful both as declarer and as discussion leader. The situation came to the attention of the cognoscenti, because the location of an eight-spot determined the "final truth" of the matter.

NORTH
♠ 8
♡ J 8 6 2
♢ 10 5 3
♣ K 7 6 3 2

WEST
♠ A J 3
♡ K Q 10 9 7
♢ K 8 4
♣ 5 4

EAST
♠ Q 9 7 6 4 2
♡ 5 4 3
♢ J 9 2
♣ Q

SOUTH
♠ K 10 5
♡ A
♢ A Q 7 6
♣ A J 10 9 8

SOUTH	WEST	NORTH	EAST
1 ♣	Double	3 ♣	3 ♠
5 ♣	Double	(All Pass)	

West led the king of hearts. Edgar, South, won with the ace, drew trumps in two rounds ending in dummy, and led the eight of spades. East put on the nine, and the finesse of the ten went to the jack. This put West in a tough spot; he had to guess an exit. He selected a diamond, and the rest was easy for declarer.

Understandably, West later asked whether he could have defeated the contract had he adopted an alternative defense. Edgar gave this convoluted answer: "Possibly if you returned the queen of hearts, but not," as he took a look at West's cards, "if you had the eight of diamonds."

Let's untangle this. After West wins a trick with the spade jack, a spade continuation will set up a discard for a diamond from dummy. Only a heart continuation leaves the defense a chance. Suppose West leads the queen of hearts (a lower heart leads to the same ending). Declarer ruffs, trumps a spade in dummy, discards a diamond on the jack of hearts, ruffs a heart, and trumps his last spade in dummy, leaving:

```
                    NORTH
                    ♠ —
                    ♡ —
                    ◇ 10 5 3
                    ♣ 7
    WEST                            EAST
    ♠ —                            ♠ Q
    ♡ 10                           ♡ —
    ◇ K 8 4                        ◇ J 9 2
    ♣ —                            ♣ —
                    SOUTH
                    ♠ —
                    ♡ —
                    ◇ A Q 7
                    ♣ J
```

When a diamond is led from dummy, East must play the nine to prevent declarer from ducking the trick to West. After low—nine—queen—king, West is endplayed, forced to lead a diamond; if declarer handles diamonds correctly, he can avoid any further loser (and, the bidding ignored, West is twice as likely to have started with king-nine or king-eight than king-jack, a restricted-choice situation).

But if East had started with jack-nine-eight of diamonds, the endplay would not come off.

* * *

Edgar's explanation of his successful handling of a freak hand in the 1965 Spingold sheds light on his bidding philosophy.

South dealer; North-South vulnerable
NORTH
♠ —
♡ J 10 4 2
◊ A Q J 7 3
♣ Q 10 5 2

SOUTH
♠ A K Q J 9 8 6 3 2
♡ —
◊ —
♣ A K J 4

SOUTH	WEST	NORTH	EAST
Kaplan		Kay	
2 ♣	Pass	2 ◊	Double
2 ♠	2 NT	Double	3 ◊
Pass	Pass	Double	Pass
4 ♣	Pass	4 ◊	Pass
5 ◊	Pass	6 ♣	Pass
7 ♠	Pass	Pass	Pass

Edgar's forcing pass to elicit information at a convenient level demonstrates a standard expert tactic. It is his explanation of the decision to drive to seven that illustrates the form of judgment-based quantitative bidding on which many of his best results were based: "If Norman had, say, four low clubs, he would have bid five clubs directly over my four-club bid instead of electing to show the diamond ace. In other words, he liked my club bid and was now ready to go along with me to a slam. He would not have liked a slam unless he had the club queen, for surely, on the bidding, his diamond ace figured to be worthless to me."

Edgar's style of using judgment-based rather than artificially-fixed meanings carried over to his treatment of defensive card-play signals. In his partnerships, the meaning of a signal (if any) was determined by the information that judgment dictated partner would most likely want to receive. Indeed, throughout his approach to bridge, Edgar favored the use of brain power over rigid rules, a formula he applied successfully in every aspect of his life.